LIFESPAN TRANSITIONS AND DISABILITY

This book brings a refreshing perspective to preparing students with disabilities and their families for all aspects of independent life. Many of the transitions experienced by younger children set the stage for future changes, yet do not receive the attention they deserve in the literature. This publication offers a strengths-based approach that includes philosophical perspectives and evidence-based practices to assist this vulnerable population with lifespan changes and challenges.

Each chapter addresses transitional needs and their assessment, and relevant interventions from the perspectives of an application to schools, families and communities. Multicultural perspectives are integral to all these chapters. The book covers transition:

- from home to early childhood education
- from early childhood education to primary school
- from primary school to secondary school
- from and to special settings
- from juvenile justice settings back into the community
- from school to work
- from school to further education or training
- from post-school settings to retirement.

Lifespan Transitions and Disability: A holistic perspective is a necessary companion for postgraduate education students and researchers who have an interest in exploring the nature and context of special and inclusive education today.

Iva Strnadová is Associate Professor at the School of Education, University of New South Wales, Australia. She also holds an honorary position in the Faculty of Education and Social Work at the University of Sydney.

Therese M. Cumming is Senior Lecturer at the School of Education, University of New South Wales, Australia.

Foundations and Futures of Education

Peter Aggleton, *UNSW, Australia*
Sally Power, *Cardiff University, UK*
Michael Reiss, *Institute of Education, University of London, UK*

Foundations and Futures of Education focuses on key emerging issues in education as well as continuing debates within the field. The series is interdisciplinary, and includes historical, philosophical, sociological, psychological and comparative perspectives on three major themes: the purposes and nature of education; increasing interdisciplinarity within the subject; and the theory–practice divide.

Lifespan Transitions and Disability
A holistic perspective
Iva Strnadová and Therese M. Cumming

Religion in the Primary School
Ethos, diversity, citizenship
Peter J. Hemming

Discerning Critical Hope in Educational Practices
Edited by Vivienne Bozalek, Brenda Leibowitz, Ronelle Carolissen and Megan Boler

Education and Masculinities
Social, cultural and global transformations
Chris Haywood and Mairtin Mac an Ghaill

Bullying
Experiences and discourses of sexuality and gender
Ian Rivers and Neil Duncan

Language, Learning, Context
Talking the talk
Wolff-Michael Roth

Postfeminist Education?
Girls and the sexual politics of schooling
Jessica Ringrose

The Right to Higher Education
Beyond widening participation
Penny Jane Burke

The Struggle for the History of Education
Gary McCulloch

Radical Education and the Common School
A democratic alternative
Michael Fielding and Peter Moss

The Irregular School
Exclusion, schooling and inclusive education
Roger Slee

School Trouble
Identity, power and politics in education
Deborah Youdell

Schools and Schooling in the Digital Age
A critical analysis
Neil Selwyn

Being a University
Ron Barnett

Education – An 'Impossible Profession'?
Tamara Bibby

Re-designing Learning Contexts
Technology-rich, learner-centred ecologies
Rosemary Luckin

Education and the Family
Passing success across the generations
Leon Feinstein, Kathryn Duckworth and Ricardo Sabates

Learners, Learning and Educational Activity
Judith Ireson

Gender, Schooling and Global Social Justice
Elaine Unterhalter

Education, Philosophy and the Ethical Environment
Graham Haydon

Schooling, Society and Curriculum
Edited by Alex Moore

LIFESPAN TRANSITIONS AND DISABILITY

A holistic perspective

Iva Strnadová and
Therese M. Cumming

LONDON AND NEW YORK

First published 2016
by Routledge
2 Park Square, Milton Park, Abingdon, Oxon OX14 4RN

and by Routledge
711 Third Avenue, New York, NY 10017

Routledge is an imprint of the Taylor & Francis Group, an informa business

© 2016 Iva Strnadová and Therese M. Cumming

The right of Iva Strnadová and Therese M. Cumming to be identified as authors of this work has been asserted by them in accordance with sections 77 and 78 of the Copyright, Designs and Patents Act 1988.

All rights reserved. No part of this book may be reprinted or reproduced or utilised in any form or by any electronic, mechanical, or other means, now known or hereafter invented, including photocopying and recording, or in any information storage or retrieval system, without permission in writing from the publishers.

Trademark notice: Product or corporate names may be trademarks or registered trademarks, and are used only for identification and explanation without intent to infringe.

British Library Cataloguing in Publication Data
A catalogue record for this book is available from the British Library

Library of Congress Cataloging in Publication Data
A catalog record for this book has been requested

ISBN: 978-0-415-73885-9 (hbk)
ISBN: 978-0-415-73887-3 (pbk)
ISBN: 978-1-315-81710-1 (ebk)

Typeset in Bembo
by Swales & Willis Ltd, Exeter, Devon, UK

We dedicate this book to our families, who have supported and nurtured us:
IS: James Michael Stanbury, Sláva Strnad, Iva Strnadová and Tomáš Strnad
TC: James Cumming and Emily Smedley

CONTENTS

List of illustrations   *x*
About the authors   *xi*
Preface   *xii*
Acknowledgements   *xiii*

1 Introduction   1

2 Transitions: historical perspectives and current practices   7

3 Transitions in the early childhood years   23

4 Transitions to primary school   34

5 Transition from primary school to secondary school   45

6 Transitions to and from special settings   58

7 Transitions from juvenile justice settings back into the community   74

8 Transitions from school to work   88

9 Transitions from school to further education or training   103

10 Transition to retirement   118

11 Wraparound services to support lifespan transitions   129

12 Conclusion   141

References   *145*
Index   *162*

ILLUSTRATIONS

Figures

1.1	Bronfenbrenner's ecological theory of human development applied to lifespan transitions	5
2.1	The five categories of the Taxonomy of Transition Services Framework	15
4.1	The six-sequential-step intervention	41
7.1	Response to Intervention (RtI)/positive behavioural interventions and support (PBIS) pyramid	83

Tables

4.1	Changes experienced by children and their families during transition to primary school	38
4.2	Strategies for families of young children to develop self-determination skills	42
6.1	Obstacles facing adolescents with chronic illnesses and potential solutions	62
8.1	Evidence-based practices organised by Kohler's taxonomy, and the skill taught	94
9.1	Potential barriers to post-secondary education experienced by individuals with disabilities	105
9.2	Questions about the teaching approaches used by a preferred post-secondary educational setting	116

ABOUT THE AUTHORS

Iva Strnadová is Associate Professor in the School of Education at the University of New South Wales (UNSW), Australia. She also holds an honorary position in the Faculty of Education and Social Work at the University of Sydney. Since 2005, Iva has conducted more than 20 different research projects at national and international levels. She has published two professional studies books in the field of special education, co-authored eight other books and co-edited two books. Prior to her academic career, Iva worked for 7 years with adults with intellectual disabilities and with autism. Her ongoing research interests include transitions in the lives of people with disabilities, the lifespan experiences of families caring for a child with a disability and the well-being of people with intellectual disabilities and autism. Her interests also include inclusive education and women with intellectual disabilities.

Therese M. Cumming is Senior Lecturer in the School of Education at UNSW, Australia. She has conducted special education research projects in both the USA and Australia. She has authored and co-authored numerous journal articles and book chapters in the areas of behavioural support, mobile technology, social skills instruction and inclusive research. Prior to her university and research work, Therese had 18 years' teaching experience in mainstream, special and mental health settings. Her ongoing research interests come under the umbrella of transition and include the use of technology to support students and families, positive behavioural interventions and supports and inclusive education across the lifespan.

A note on authorship

This book was a collaborative effort, and was therefore written with equal contribution from both authors.

PREFACE

Lifespan Transitions and Disability: A holistic perspective offers an integrated overview of the transitions experienced by people with disabilities across various environments, including schools, families, community and employment. We label the book's perspective 'holistic' because it embraces a variety of approaches, strategies and interventions which are rooted in evidence-based theory and practice, and these are examined in relation to the whole individual and all of the people and environments he or she would routinely interact with at that stage of life.

To facilitate understanding, the chapters that follow are organised into sections that include a focus on transitional needs characteristic for the transition type discussed, an assessment of these needs and evidence-based interventions that can be applied. We discuss different types of transitions across relevant environments, e.g. school, employment, family and community, and the importance of coordination across all of the spheres of the person's life before, during and after these transitions.

As schools are called upon to provide services to an increasingly diverse population of students, education professionals are seeking ways to provide for the needs of all students in an effective, person-centred and evidence-based manner. This involves both the upskilling of staff and greater collaboration with families, experts and agencies in the areas of health, welfare and justice. It is crucial that all stakeholders have access to current research-based information on the key issues and effective practices relevant to lifespan transitions for students with disabilities. We hope this book provides readers with this information, as well as a more holistic view of the transitions experienced by people with different disabilities across the lifespan.

ACKNOWLEDGEMENTS

There are a number of people without whom this publication would not be possible. First of all, we would like to thank our husbands James and Jim, and our families, for their ongoing untiring support and encouragement.

We would also like to thank all the people with disabilities and their families, teachers and support staff members that we worked with, and those who have participated in our research studies throughout the years. Their life experiences, often including exclusion, neglect or even abuse, inspired us to continue our efforts in raising awareness and improving the quality of their education and their lives.

We would also like to thank our mentors, Marie Černá and Kyle Higgins, for role modelling for us the devoted, hard-working and self-reflecting academics that we aspire to be.

The School of Education at the University of New South Wales, Australia has provided us with support, encouragement and the means to continue our work in the field of special education. We are grateful that we are able to pursue our passions at such a prestigious and successful educational institution.

1
INTRODUCTION

The importance of transition support in the lives of students with disabilities and their families has long been recognised both in the academic literature and in practice over recent decades. Historically, from the perspective of education and schooling, the phrase 'transition services' applied to students with disabilities from their mid to late teenage years, and referred to individually designed educational and vocational supports to prepare individuals for life after school (Crawford, 2012). These services generally consisted of an educational action plan that detailed the activities that were to be focused on to facilitate the movement of a student with disabilities from school to post-school life. Traditionally, these plans were individualised and strengths-based and aimed to foster the student's self-determination skills by taking into account his or her interests. Transition plans and their corresponding activities involve not only the student, but the family, the school, the community and relevant outside agencies.

Across the English-speaking world, transition planning has been an important component of educational planning for students with disabilities for the last two decades; however the earlier and the later transitions in the lives of the members of this population were frequently ignored. These oversights can be seriously detrimental to individuals with disabilities, as these transitions have great impact (Gagnon & Richards, 2008; Hanewald, 2013; McIntyre et al., 2006). The first transition, from home to early childhood education, sets the tone for the child's later school career and has in the past focused on chronological age rather than readiness. The literature emphasises several readiness variables, including cognitive, social emotional, physical and family factors (McIntyre et al., 2006). The second major transition that is largely ignored in the literature is the transition from primary to secondary school. This omission, both by researchers and practitioners, can have a serious impact on the lives of students with disabilities, as an ill-handled transition from primary to secondary school may mean the student's abandonment of the educational system as such, or lost chances for education in mainstream schools (Forlin, 2013). Another important transition that is largely ignored but can be prepared for, even at the school level, is the transition to later life and retirement. If the purpose of schooling is to prepare students to lead quality lives, it is crucial that this area too not be ignored (Leinonen et al., 2012).

Attention should also be given to other important transitions within these traditional chronological and developmental transitions. The first of these, the transition between mainstream schooling and special schooling, is important because some students make the transition between these two environments several times during their school careers, and their success in either setting is dependent on their adjustment to, and the support provided in, that environment (Strnadová & Cumming, 2014). Schools themselves need policies and frameworks in place to allow teachers and other personnel within them to support effectively students and their families in coping with the changes that take place upon their entry into that specific setting (Standing Committee on Social Issues, 2012). The second important transition – for some individuals, anyway – is the transition of students from the juvenile justice system back into their previous home, community and school settings. It is especially important that all involved schools and agencies collaborate to make this a smooth and successful transition, and to coordinate continued support, in order to support the student and prevent recidivism (Gagnon & Richards, 2008).

Importance of quality transition planning and support

One cannot overestimate the value of quality transition planning and support. Times of transition are frequently challenging for all people, but these challenges may be greatly exacerbated for those with disabilities. There are several examples in the current literature of poor outcomes for people with disabilities, including: (1) poor post-school outcomes; (2) high rates of suspension and dropping out; (3) low or lack of participation in secondary education; and (4) high rates of unemployment (Crawford, 2012). Many of these outcomes can be traced back to disengagement from school early on, such as during the transition to secondary school (Hanewald, 2013). At the very least, these poor results indicate that a closer examination of current transition processes, as well as transition support practices that have proved to be effective, is warranted.

Research has shown that the most successful transition supports are those where there is a strong collaboration among the student, the school, families and other stakeholders (Sitlington et al., 2010). In practice, this is not always the case, especially when it comes to fostering a person's self-determination skills by encouraging full involvement in the transition process. Crawford (2012) points out that, although the encouragement of student self-determination and involvement is typical in the USA, at least in contexts where policy requires it, in many systems the student is left out of many of the processes, including planning and important decision making. When implementing a team approach to transition assessment and planning, it seems only logical to include the student as the most important member of the team. In order for the student to participate fully in future planning, he or she must have the self-determination skills to voice his or her opinions and preferences, and the social skills to do so in an appropriate manner.

Good-quality transition practices include effective communication among all stakeholders. This should be fostered from the very first transition, when students are leaving home to enter school for the first time. Parents are often apprehensive about trusting others with the care and education of their children with disabilities, and the effective communication of information may go a long way in empowering them and allaying their fears (Hirst et al., 2011). This first transition is also of paramount importance to both students and parents, as it is their first experience with the education system and will impact heavily on their opinions and attitudes (Hirst et al., 2011).

When the transition takes place from one school to another, it is imperative that teachers from both schools communicate with one another as well as with the student, family and any other relevant service provider(s). Students should be introduced to and allowed to experience the new environment in advance. This will provide a sense of familiarity to students and assist staff in assessing both the student and the new environment to determine the supports that the student will require in order to be successful (Strnadová & Cumming, 2014).

Some of the most important, yet overlooked, transitions are the transitions from one setting to another. These include moving from a mainstream setting to a more restrictive, specialised setting and vice versa. The more restrictive setting could be a special education classroom or school, or a hospital or juvenile justice setting. These transitions can be fraught with challenges, many of which are connected to the increased amount of stakeholders and systems (education, health, justice) involved (Gagnon & Richards, 2008). The transition from the specialised setting back into the mainstream setting is particularly worth noting, as returning students to their original environments after incarceration or time in a mental health or drug treatment centre requires careful planning and support to ensure successful reintegration (Gagnon & Richards, 2008).

Despite being the most researched transition, the transition from school to post-school settings brings its own set of challenges. First of all, it is more than likely that there will be a variety of stakeholders involved, such as employers, universities, community colleges, vocational schools, social and medical services (Test et al., 2009). Coordinating communication and planning at this level is often left to the school, and undertaken by special education teachers or transition specialists. Coordination of the important transition to post-school life can be difficult due to a fragmentation of services and a lack of information about what is actually available to students in regard to supports, and this can be detrimental because, without the appropriate planning and support, students are at risk of a range of poor outcomes (Test et al., 2009).

Bronfenbrenner's Ecological Model

The wide variety of lifetime transitions experienced by individuals with disabilities therefore requires a holistic perspective, one that considers all of the people, environments and institutions that are involved. Urie Bronfenbrenner (1994) developed the ecological systems theory, which was designed to explain how the quality and context of a child's environment and interactions with others affect his or her development and quality of life. The resulting model offers a helpful guide when examining the importance of the environment as a whole to transition assessment and planning. Bronfenbrenner's model consists of five nested systems, with the individual in the centre, radiating out to the chronosystem, or the larger culture's attitudes and ideologies. In between these two extremes are the microsystem, which consists of the groups that impact the child the most, such as family and school, the mesosystem, the exosystem and the macrosystem.

If one views the student as being the core of, existing in and influenced by, these five systems, then each must be taken into account when assessing transitional needs (Figure 1.1). The individual lies in the centre of all of the systems, and is referred to as the 'child' (although the model also applies to adults, as the theory covers the lifespan and how people, systems, environments and life events influence the individual's development). Characteristics of the child that will be considered in regard to transition include academic and social abilities, self-determination, attitudes, goals, needs and desires. The microsystem involves those people closest to the child, and when looked at through the lens of transitions, involves family and their hopes, expectations and plans for the child. The influence of family friends also figures in this system, as do the tenets of family culture and religious beliefs. For the purposes of lifespan transitions, this system also includes teachers, school peers, coursework, friends, employers, workplaces, co-workers, neighbours and people the individual encounters regularly in community settings.

Interactions between the various microsystems form the mesosystem. School–home communication and collaboration are good examples of a mesosystem process, as are the collaborative team efforts that go into designing individualised education plans (IEPs), individualised transition plans (ITPs), behaviour plans and adult community, employment and group home support plans. Transition planning not only results in an increase in the student's microsystems, it also increases the number of environments that must communicate with one another in the mesosystem.

The child is influenced, as are the systems above, by the larger exosystem. This system includes entities that the child does not have direct contact with, albeit she or he is still influenced by them. These may include state and federal economic systems, the monies and resources available to schools for transition support, government and educational philosophies and support for transition processes, and laws regarding students and adults with disabilities. Taking this a step further outward is the macrosystem, which consists of the overarching values and beliefs about transition and quality of life for individuals with disabilities. These include society's views, theories, research and existing evidenced-based transition processes in general.

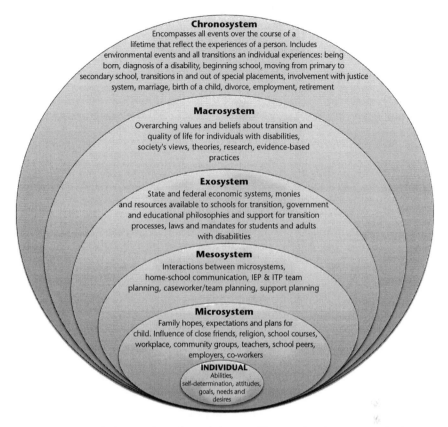

FIGURE 1.1 Bronfenbrenner's ecological theory of human development applied to lifespan transitions

The chronosystem is the overarching system of the ecological theory that affects the child's development through transitional periods. This system encompasses all events over the course of a lifetime that reflect and influence the experiences of the individual. These environmental events and transition experiences include, but are not limited to, birth, diagnosis of a disability, entering school, moving from primary to secondary school, transitioning in and/or out of special placements, involvement with the police and justice system, employment, marriage, birth of a child, illness, death in the family, divorce and retirement.

Overall, Bronfenbrenner's Ecological Model provides a holistic lens by which to view the different environmental factors that drive an individual's development through his or her lifetime, particularly through the different transitions that he or she experiences. It offers teachers and other education professionals the impetus to view lifespan transitions from an ecological perspective and is an appropriate model to frame the various transitions covered in this book. Using the model, this book aims to offer an integrated overview of transitions experienced by people with disabilities across various environments, including schools, families, leisure time, community, vocational education and university.

Educational focus

Any discussion of lifespan transitions for students with disabilities must have education at its centre. Children spend much of their time during their developmental years in school, which is a primary part of the mesosystem during the ages 3–18 years. The principal focus of formal education is to prepare children to live independent, productive and quality lives. In order for this to take place, there is a set of knowledge and skill domains that individuals must develop. According to Sitlington et al.'s (2010) revised comprehensive transition model, these skills include: (1) communication; (2) academic; (3) social; (4) self-determination; (5) community participation; (6) health and fitness; (7) technology; (8) leisure and recreation; (9) mobility; (10) independent living; (11) work-readiness; and/or (12) university or college readiness. The purpose of any IEP and transition assessment and planning processes is to ensure that students receive instruction and support to provide them with the relevant skills to be successful in both present and future environments.

Thus, alignment between the IEP and the ITP is a crucial aspect of effective transition planning (Sitlington et al., 2010). In order to be successful in achieving transition goals, students must be able to access the curricula that will provide them with the knowledge and skills required for the settings they are transitioning to, whether this be another school, independent living, further schooling, employment or a combination of these. An examination of the student's goals, along with an assessment of the student's strengths and needs, is required, as is an ecological assessment of the requirements of the proposed setting(s). The results of these assessments can drive the educational planning process, resulting in an IEP designed to facilitate transitions by supporting students in acquiring the necessary knowledge and skills to be successful in the next setting (Sitlington et al., 2010).

A student's IEP therefore, drives his or her education. Schools have traditionally responded to this with a continuum of placements and supports, along with a variety of specific educational options. These options range from schooling aimed at preparing students with disabilities for university study to teaching students basic life skills such as health, hygiene, homemaking, and mobility and community living. Cobb and Alwell (2009) conducted a review of transition studies, and found that career education, vocational training (particularly that which included real work experiences) and student-centred planning are the most effective educational processes in regards to preparing students for post-school life. Career planning, family involvement and transition supports were also shown to be crucial to success after school. The current call for educators to employ only practices that have a solid foundation in research stresses the importance of research that identifies effective educational transition practices. It is the importance of these evidence-based practices that provides the basis for this book.

2
TRANSITIONS

Historical perspectives and current practices

The history of transition

The history of transition processes is very much aligned with the history of disability reform globally. The international history of transition can be viewed through the lens of several prominent researchers. Neubert (1997) provides an extensive history of transition in the USA from the 1940s to the late 1990s. Mendelsohn (1979) covers transition support and history in his history of disability reform in Australia and Crawford (2012) describes the legislative framework that underpins the UK's Education Act (Department of Education and Science (DES), 1993). Most of the printed history refers to the transition from secondary school to post-school options for students with intellectual disabilities, while laws and policies tend to support programmes and strategies for students with disabilities in general.

The USA

Prior to 1940, vocational and life skills educational efforts for individuals with disabilities included social skills, practical skills training, handiwork and manual arts (Neubert, 1997). Flexer et al. (2013) describe this as a time when vocational rehabilitation was emerging as a result of the need to rehabilitate wounded World War I veterans. Several policies and laws supporting vocational training, employment services and disability technology were enacted at this time. These included the Smith–Hughes Act (1917), the Smith–Sears Act (1918) and the Smith–Fess Act (1920). Although much of this legislation was limited to veterans and civil servants with disabilities, the population eligible for services was expanded to all civilians with disabilities through the Barden–LaFollette Act in 1943.

8 Historical perspectives and current practices

In the 1940s–1950s, educators debated whether school curricula for students with intellectual disabilities should focus on traditional academics, or living and work skills. Following this, the next decade saw the development of various educational and training programmes that stressed functional and vocational skills. These programmes formed the basis for many curricula still used today. In the 1960s, work-study programmes became popular. Components for successful transition to employment were identified as: (1) vocational activity; (2) a positive social environment (including civic responsibility); and (3) including a focus on self-concept (Mirfin-Veitch, 2003). Many work-study programmes at the time were similar to programmes today, and included in-school and community work experience, a vocationally based curriculum and involvement with a vocational organisation. There were also calls for research on the outcomes of these programmes.

'Career education' became the focus of the 1970s, and a priority for all students, whether they were participating in general or special education. Career education was seen as a solution to the drop-out rate and a way to make education relevant to all students. The intention was that it would be delivered in such a way that it would combine academic and vocational curricula so that all students who completed high school would be prepared either to enter the labour force or attend higher education. The Career Education Act was passed in the USA in 1974 to support states in this endeavour. Many career education curricula and models emerged at this time, and components of these are still used today.

The 1970s were also a time of developing legislation to support the education of students with disabilities, particularly P.L. 94-142, the Education for All Handicapped Children Act. This legislation prompted interagency collaboration between educational and vocational agencies for assessment, training and employment activities for students with disabilities. A continuum of service options was developed: (1) vocational education; (2) adapted vocational education; (3) separate special vocational education; and (4) individual vocational training, at the job site (Neubert, 1997). Many considered these options to be exclusionary, and legislation was introduced to encourage more inclusive vocational education practices. This encouraged special educators and general educators to work together to provide career and vocational education services in mainstream environments.

As more students with severe disabilities began to attend public schools, new curricula were developed to meet their needs. These included a focus on the areas of: (1) social skills for work; (2) domestic skills; (3) leisure skills; and (4) community functioning. They were also structured to include ecological assessment, task analysis and age-appropriate activities. Techniques that had previously been employed in sheltered workshops (segregated employment for people with disabilities) to teach job skills were being used in schools to prepare students with moderate to severe disabilities for post-school employment.

Research in the 1980s identified poor post-secondary outcomes for young people with intellectual disabilities, which again brought into question the purpose of secondary special education (Neubert, 1997). Although transition services were not yet compulsory in the 1980s, most secondary education for students with

Historical perspectives and current practices 9

disabilities included elements such as individual transition planning, job experience and functional skills curricula. The tension between the competing education agendas (academic vs functional) continued throughout this decade, fuelled by competency testing, the inclusion movement and increased requirements for obtaining a high school diploma. Some advocated a shift away from academic subjects in order to improve post-school outcomes for students with disabilities (Neubert, 1997).

The transition movement was prominent throughout the 1990s, with several key elements of legislation enacted. The Individuals with a Disability Education Act of 1990 required that transition services be included in a student's individual education plan (IEP) from age 16 onwards. It also mandated that the transition goals be based on the student's individual needs, preferences and interests (Mirfin-Veitch, 2003). Transition planning and processes continued to evolve into what they are today – services to support individuals with disabilities through several junctures throughout the lifespan, to a variety of settings.

Although US legislation receives the most attention in the transition literature, the evolution of transition planning and processes internationally was also mediated by legislation and policy, albeit mostly related to disability or education. Many nations based their policies on the United Nations (UN) Convention on the Rights of Persons with Disabilities (United Nations, 2007) and the UN Convention on the Rights of the Child (United Nations, 1989), which stress that children are human beings, not the property of their parents, and therefore have rights and needs all their own. The Conventions speak of changing disabling public attitudes towards disabilities, making environments accessible, and the participation of students and families in setting goals, making decisions and shaping services. The Conventions also advocate for support services to be provided within the student's community so that neither the student nor the family has a need to move in order to access them. While great strides are being made, there is still a way to go until the provision for people with disabilities demonstrates a measure of human progress.

The UK

Although UK legislation is mostly focused on individuals with disabilities or young people, with very little emphasis on the combination of young people with disabilities, there have been several general initiatives that are aimed at improving the quality of life of persons with disabilities (Crawford, 2012). Both the Disability Discrimination Act 1996 and the Disability Equality Duty (DRC, 2006) prohibit public bodies, including the education sector, from discriminating against individuals with disabilities. The Education Act 1993 mandated that transition planning be undertaken, particularly in the areas of post-school support services (Barron et al., 2007). This was supported further when the Education Act was amended by the Special Educational Needs and Disability Act 2001 (United Kingdom, DfES, 2001).

Unfortunately, Heslopp et al. (2002) found that there was much variance in the level of compliance with disability and transition services legislation. Specifically,

20 per cent of students with disabilities left school with no transition plan, and almost half of those who had a plan had no involvement in its design or implementation. They also discovered that the plans' components were very different from what families thought was important. They determined that transition is an area that still requires reform. Barron et al. (2007) advocated for an integrated systems approach to transition that includes communication, coordination, choice and continuity. They posit that flexibility is crucial in meeting each individual's transition needs.

Several national transition programmes have been initiated in response to calls for reform. These programmes aimed to standardise transition processes and promote good practice throughout the country (Conlon, 2014). For example, the Transition Support Programme was a 3-year programme initiated in 2008 to improve the condition of service delivery across the education, social care and health sectors. The Preparing for Adulthood Programme commenced in 2011 and supports successful transition into adulthood. It focuses on areas that are critical to successful transition, mainly: (1) paid employment; (2) health; (3) independent living; (4) social relationships; and (5) community inclusion (Conlon, 2014). Preliminary evidence suggests that programmes such as these can be effective in improving post-school outcomes for students with disabilities (Conlon, 2014).

Australia

In Australia, the history of disability, rehabilitation and transition is broadly similar to that of the USA, as it dates back to the introduction of the Invalid Pension in 1908, and continued on with vocational rehabilitation programmes that were designed to meet the needs of the wounded veterans from World Wars I and II. The first major piece of legislation, the Disability Services Act 1986, was introduced in 1986 and the Disability Discrimination Act 1992 followed. While neither of these acts mentioned the transition process specifically, they both focused on self-determination, de-institutionalisation and community living, which are all components of effective transition. The Disability Standards for Education 2005 provide education authorities with a framework for providing students with disabilities support and adjustments in order for them to participate fully in school learning and activities with their non-disabled peers. The Standards do not mention the term 'transition' and are very much open to interpretation by each school or education authority. The lack of specific transition legislation, and therefore no mandate that any transition processes must be in place, has resulted in a wide variety of transition practices and services throughout Australia, differing not only from state to state, but also from school to school.

Canada

In Canada, the history of special education, including transition, is largely similar to that of its southern neighbour, the USA. Canada's education system moved from segregation of students with disabilities in the 1950s, to categorisation in the 1960s, mainstreaming in the 1970s and 1980s, to the inclusion movement, which began in the 1990s and continues today (Andrews & Brown, 2012).

The federal government of Canada has made significant movement forward to identify disability issues as a priority, but, unlike the countries mentioned previously, Canada does not have an overarching federal disability policy (McColl et al., 2010). There have been movements historically to protect the rights of those with disabilities and make schools, workplaces and communities more accessible. The Canadian Charter of Rights and Freedoms (1982) is of specific importance, as it ensures that 'Every individual is equal before and under the law and has the right to the equal protection and equal benefit of the law without discrimination and, in particular, without discrimination based on race, national or ethnic origin, colour, religion, sex, age or mental or physical disability' (p. 15).

Of particular note is also the self-determination and self-advocacy demonstrated by Canadians with disabilities in 1980–1981, when individuals with varied disabilities fought and won the right to be included in the new Canadian constitution (Park, 2008). Despite that victory and a promise by the federal government in 2004 to pass a national Canadians with Disability Act, nothing has been put in motion to make this happen (McColl et al., 2010). Several pieces of legislation that relate to education, training and employment protect the rights of students and workers with disabilities, but no mandated educational transition processes and practices exist. Therefore, like Australia, transition planning and processes are dependent upon the philosophy and means of the educational organisation that the student attends.

Although the countries discussed above have varied histories, laws and policies, their philosophies remain broadly consistent. This is probably best demonstrated by the fact that all have signed the UN Convention on the Rights of the Child, which has also been ratified by 192 countries, excepting the USA (Unicef, 2005). This has prompted the expansion of the definition of the term 'transition' to encompass all educational and life transitions, not just the transition from high school to post-school settings. Despite differences in histories and legislation, researchers globally have investigated transition practices to establish an evidence base of best practices. The following sections explore some of these practices.

The development of models of transition

As the idea of planning for school to post-school transitions for students with disabilities took hold, research was conducted, particularly in the area of post-school outcomes for students with disabilities. These studies raised awareness of the issue, and produced several models to guide practitioners through the transition process (Blalock & Patton, 1996). The US Office of Special Education and Rehabilitative Services (OSERS) Model of Transition was one of the first. The model was developed in 1983 by Madeline Will, and was somewhat limited, as it was developed for students who were 16 and older, and focused only on training and services that were based on the transition from school to work. Halpern (1985) recognised the limited scope of the OSERS model (Wills, 1984), and designed a revision that included the non-vocational areas, such as community adjustment (dimensions of quality living arrangements and social networks). This revision reflected the thinking of other transition professionals who were advocating for a multidimensional comprehensive transition approach (Blalock & Patton, 1996).

Ianacone and Stodden (1987) expanded the model even further, as they broke the transition process into a series of phases: planning, preparation, linkage and exit. These phases were to occur over an individual's lifetime, rather than only in the last 2 years of school. The model places a strong focus on student and family involvement and particularly in the areas of preferences and decision making. It also emphasises community participation and stakeholder inclusion in planning. Ianacone and Stodden's lifetime comprehensive approach forms the basis for many later more modern models, such as that shown in Box 2.1, which offers an example of a current typical timeline of transition activities for students with disabilities.

BOX 2.1 TIMELINE OF TRANSITION ACTIVITIES

Birth to 5 years old

- Access an evaluation for related and/or early childhood services, such as speech therapy, Applied Behaviour Analysis, physiotherapy, etc.
- Connect with organisations in your area that provide services and supports for children with disabilities and special healthcare needs.
- Connect with agencies that provide funding for services and supports in your area for children with disabilities and special healthcare needs.
- Connect with organisations that provide parent training, and support networking opportunities.
- Learn about individual family service plans, individualised education plans (IEPs) and individualised transition plans (ITPs), their processes and what to expect.
- Develop a one-page introduction about your child. This should highlight strengths, preferences, interests and needs.
- Locate online, print and in-person resources that can provide answers to questions parents have about special education and other necessary services.
- Keep a diary of what works/doesn't work with your child, so you can share this information with educators and service providers.
- Keep records of healthcare and school information.
- Begin teaching your child about safety (e.g. strangers, public places, transportation).
- Begin fostering your child's self-determination skills.

Primary years (5–11 years old)

Seek out materials that will help your child attend and participate more fully in IEP/ITP meetings, such as the one available at http://www.parentcenterhub.org/repository/meetings/.

- Begin implementing the phases of career development (awareness, exploration, preparation, career placement/continuing education) with the awareness phase. Taking the child to work will assist in this endeavour.
- Continuously foster the student's self-determination skills and strategies. Students at this stage should understand supports/needs and accommodations.
- Teach financial independence and responsibility by having the child open and maintain a savings account, save for personal purchases, comparison shop.
- Apply for a library card from the public library and read books about different careers.
- Establish chores at home and allow the child to help with adult chores such as cooking and gardening.
- Teach child about his/her medical needs and medications.
- Assess for assistive technology needs.
- Attend parent nights, conferences and IEP meetings.
- Participate in transition fairs/expos.

Early secondary years (12–15 years old)

- Students lead IEP meetings and write present levels of performance.
- Meet with benefits/funding organisation and discuss the impact that employment has on disability benefits.
- High school completion options are discussed among parents, students and school staff.
- Student reads biographies of famous people and their careers and goals.
- Career development exploration phase: students explore their preferences, hobbies and interests.
- Academic preparation for post-secondary education (university or career tech track).
- Students obtain picture identification and work permits.
- Students obtain part-time jobs and/or volunteer in the community.
- Students complete career interest inventories.
- Students request own accommodations.
- Try to narrow down accommodations and modifications to those that are absolutely necessary and beneficial to the students. It is also helpful for students to practise using only the accommodations that are allowable on high school exit exams.
- Home and school focus on decision making, problem solving and accountability.

Later secondary years (14–22 years old)

- Students develop and attain transition-related IEP goals.
- Prepare a post-school transportation plan: teach about public transportation and safety skills; students obtain driver's permit/licence if appropriate.

(continued)

(continued)

- Career development preparation phase: students examine what courses and skills they need to meet their education and career goals.
- Prepare for post-secondary education.
- Complete any required paper work for post-secondary education funding.
- Contact disabilities services at the post-secondary setting you plan to attend.
- Take any post-secondary education admissions tests.
- Tour universities, community colleges and vocational schools.
- Students who are 18 register to vote.
- Implement self-awareness/self-advocacy curriculum: students learn about local, state and federal laws that protect the rights and opportunities of those with disabilities.
- Students open a bank current account and use an ATM card and learn about online banking.
- Students obtain and use a mobile phone.
- Students learn about citizenship, the law and the justice system, particularly in the area of rights.
- Students complete independent living assessments.
- Access information and technical assistance from independent living centres.
- Explore guardianship options.
- Plan for assistive technology to transition from school to post-secondary setting with the student.
- Career placement/continuing education phase: courses necessary, independent living arrangements/supports.
- Post-secondary education/training, employment and independent living.
- Discovery of support services available to adults with disabilities.

Early adulthood

- Support necessary to access housing, vocational, employment, recreational, medical and mental health services.
- Day centres.
- Dating, marriage, family: resources for information, support and assistance if necessary.
- Parenting classes.

Transition to retirement

- Retirement options
- Financial planning
- Recreational planning
- Social circle
- Further education

Adapted from the Oklahoma Transition Council (https://www.ou.edu/education/centers-and-partnerships/zarrow/timeline-of-transition-activities.html).

The Taxonomy of Transition Services Framework (Kohler, 1996) was designed to improve secondary students' post-school outcomes. This conceptual model includes educational and transition practices, organised into five categories of strategies and practices to guide educators in providing transition-focused education. The five categories and their descriptions can be found in Figure 2.1.

Kohler and Field (2003) stress the need for schools to reflect on how well they are doing in providing transition-focused education to their students. They recommend that programmes be evaluated in regard to implementation, needs and overall transition-focused education. The Taxonomy has withstood the test of time, and continues to be widely used in the design of current transition-focused education internationally.

Current practices

Neubert (1997) identified a number of evidence-based practices that are still considered best practice today (Stewart et al., 2010). These include vocational assessment, individual transition plans (ITPs), student and parent involvement, academic skills and vocational training, paid work experience in integrated settings, and career education and community curricula and experiences.

The following subsections describe these practices and how they can be included in the overall transition process for students with disabilities. It should be noted that

---

Student-focused planning: This category focuses on using assessment as a tool to help foster student self-determination, goal setting and planning. Once goals are decided upon, an individual education plan is written to assist the student in reaching his or her goals.

Student development: The focus here is on using assessment to design and provide students with accommodations and education that will enhance their interpersonal, life and occupational skills. This is accomplished through the use of both school-based and work-based experiences.

Collaboration: Collaboration with outside employment and community agencies and organisations throughout all phases of the transition process. Agreements are designed that articulate each stakeholder's role and responsibilities.

Family involvement: Family is involved from the start, and continues through the planning and delivery of transition services. Families may require training and support in order to collaborate capably with teachers and community service providers.

Programme structure: The structure of the school and educational system can greatly influence the effectiveness and culture of transition-focused education. Schools must operate from a transition viewpoint, and build a culture that values the outcomes of all students, regardless of ability.

FIGURE 2.1   The five categories of the Taxonomy of Transition Services Framework (adapted from Kohler, 1996)

the majority of transition literature and research is focused on the transition from secondary school to post-school settings, so although they are applicable to other educational and life transitions, the practices discussed here need to be contextualised to the other transitions.

Assessment

Sound assessment is the foundation of successful transition planning and processes. Kohler (1996) views assessment as an important tool to practise 'student-focused planning' during the transition process, as it allows for setting relevant goals for a student. As students move through different educational and vocational settings, they will have different assessment needs. The Division on Career Development and Transition (DCDT) of the US Council for Exceptional Children defines transition assessment as an

> ongoing process of collecting data on the individual's needs, preferences, and interests as they relate to the demands of current and future working, educational, living, and personal and social environments. Assessment data serve as the common thread in the transition process and form the basis for defining goals and services to be included in the Individualized Education Plan (IEP).
>
> *(Sitlington et al., 1997: pp. 70–71)*

This definition identifies four major domains to be assessed: (1) current and future educational environments; (2) current and future career and vocational environments; (3) current and future living environments; and (4) personal and social skills and relationships. The US National Secondary Transition Technological Assistance Center (NSTTAC) (2013) recommends that, within these domains, assessment be gathered about a student's academic abilities, level of self-determination, vocational and career interests and preferences and adaptive behaviour/independent living skills.

The assessment of current and future educational environments is important throughout a student's school career and beyond, as there are a number of educational transitions typically experienced: home to preschool, preschool to primary school, primary school to secondary school, secondary school to university or vocational/trade school, and finally, many individuals access adult/extension education later in their lives. The individual's preferences, present level of functioning and accommodation needs are assessed, and then they are compared to an ecological assessment of the new educational setting, including performance and skill requirements as well as the available accommodation resources (Flexer et al., 2013).

The assessment of current and future career and vocational environments also involves a comparison of the student's preferences, skill level and accommodation needs, but in relation to career and vocation. Some examples include a career interest inventory, a vocational aptitude test or work-related characteristics. Flexer et al. (2013) point out career assessments should also consider the individual's career maturity, personal skills, social skills, values and attitudes.

The assessment of current and future living environments has the potential to be a wide-ranging exercise, as it is dependent on the student's self-determination, preferences and independent living skills. The decision of supported vs independent living is not one that should be taken lightly, so assessment of the following skills is imperative: health and hygiene, home care, safety, community survival skills and self-advocacy (Flexer et al., 2013). Family participation is crucial to all assessment, but particularly in this one. Links to representatives of various disability agencies, organisations, support providers and housing authorities are to provide information on all available housing options.

The importance of personal/social skills and relationships cannot be overstated, particularly since they have a large effect on the student's quality of life (Schalock et al., 2008). Assessment in this area is desirable throughout the variety of lifespan transitions experienced by the student. This area is largely dependent upon the student's preferences, which will most likely change over time. For example, as a student enters adolescence, peer acceptance and relationships become a very important life priority. All students should be provided with opportunities throughout their educational careers to establish friendships with their peers.

Hobbies, sports and other forms of community participation should also be explored under this category. Student preferences and plans for the future should be considered here, as well as issues of relevance to sexuality, dating, marriage and child raising. Outcomes in all of these categories are largely dependent on the student's social skills, so these should also be assessed and represented in the student's IEP and transition plan.

Transition assessment can be either formal or informal (NSTTAC, 2013). Formal assessments are usually standardised, norm-referenced, with evidence of reliability and validity. Examples of these include adaptive behaviour assessments, general and specific aptitude tests, interest inventories, intelligence tests, achievement tests, temperament instruments, employability tests, self-determination assessments and transition-planning inventories (DCDT, 2011). Informal assessments usually lack evidence of standardisation and reliability. Examples of informal assessments include: (1) interviews and questionnaires; (2) direct observation; (3) curriculum-based assessments; and (4) environmental analysis (DCDT, 2011). Both formal and informal assessments are increasingly available in electronic form; some are Internet-based. One such example is the Northeast Indiana Cadre of Transition Leaders Transition Assessment Matrix (http://www.iidc.indiana.edu/styles/iidc/defiles/cclc/transition_matrix/transition_matrix.html), which allows users to select the domain, grade level and disability area of their student, and a list of appropriate transition assessments for those parameters is generated. The list includes links to the information on how to locate and purchase the assessments, or, in the case of free assessments, links to the assessments themselves.

Transition plans

The purpose of transition assessment is to develop an ITP, which includes realistic and meaningful IEP goals and objectives (DCDT, 2011). This plan is then used to make instructional programming decisions based on the student's strengths, interests, preferences and needs. Students should be actively involved in the planning process, as this will help them to make the connection between school and their post-school goals (DCDT, 2011). The plan contains provisions for education and support in the areas that were assessed, in order to provide a full picture of the student and his/her goals, and steps that can be taken to assist the student in reaching those goals.

Effective transition planning is person-centred, that is, it involves the development of services and supports that are responsive to each individual's needs and preferences, and focuses on the student's strengths and abilities, rather than disabilities. The first step in transition planning is to build a planning team. A person-centred team includes the student and family, and also consists of teachers, related service providers and other important stakeholders (which will vary depending upon the student, and which educational or life transition is being planned (Stewart et al., 2010).

Once the team is in place, its job is to gather information about the student and the environment that s/he is transitioning to. This may be accomplished through a series of formal and informal assessments (see the previous section on assessment). The team uses the assessment results to design the transition plan. The team considers where the student is presently functioning, his or her goals for the future, the student's and family's preferences, current services and supports, and resources available in the next environment and designs a plan that encompasses all of these factors. The plan should address the domains of employment, education, housing/living arrangements and social/community life (Stewart et al., 2010). It should be noted here that if the individual is of school age during this transition planning, the transition plan should align with and be a part of the student's IEP.

The team sees to it that the plan is implemented and is evaluated for effectiveness and goodness of its fit on a regular basis. If changes need to be made, the team meets to discuss this, and puts a plan in place to implement the changes. An exit meeting is held when the plan is no longer necessary, i.e. the student is making the transition. The team finalises the plan, identifies all goals and objectives that have been accomplished and addresses any that have not. It is important that transition planning begins early, well ahead of any anticipated transition, as it is a process, and accomplishing the goals in the plan may take some time (Stewart et al., 2010).

Student and family involvement

As transition planning is a person-centred approach, the individual and his or her family should be at the centre of the planning process, which is consistent with the Taxonomy of Transition Services Framework (Kohler, 1996). This requires effective communication and collaboration among the student, family, transition team members, school personnel and service providers. Both students and parents should be supported to participate fully in transition planning. Students' self-determination and self-advocacy skills are part of effective transition preparation from the beginning, and parents are encouraged to foster these skills at home as part of their involvement in the transition process (Kohler, 1996). There is a chance that the parents may have disabilities themselves and the team needs to acknowledge these and other needs that parents may have, and support them in any way possible.

To support the involvement of the student and the family, educational agencies need to ensure that parents understand the transition processes, are given all documents well ahead of meetings and have support in participation. Families should be afforded the opportunity to communicate in their native language, as Kim and Morningstar (2007) found that otherwise parents from culturally and linguistically diverse backgrounds have low levels of contributions during school meetings.

The team should acknowledge and draw on parents' knowledge and expertise about their child, be aware of their emotional investment in their child and be respectful of their opinions and feelings (Sitlington et al., 2010). Parents often have a 'one-day-at-a-time' coping philosophy in regard to their children, and education authorities may have to be patient when including parents and encouraging them to participate in the transition process. Family resources need to be taken into account when planning meetings and supports. Some families find it impossible to attend meetings during the school day due to employment commitments, and others may have difficulty getting to the school to attend meetings due to transportation issues. Additionally, family members may have had disappointing and/or traumatic educational experiences of their own, which may make them uncomfortable in the school environment. To counter this, meetings can be held at other locations in the community, such as the public library. Supports should be located within the community and include existing resources that are local, culturally appropriate and easy to access (Flexer et al., 2013).

Academic skills training

An increasing number of students with disabilities access post-secondary education (Sitlington et al., 2010). For students who have goals relating to attendance at a university or technical school, high-level academic skills are imperative. Students who wish to attend university will most likely need to take entrance exams, and technical colleges and vocational schools often require evidence of minimum competency levels. The involvement of representatives of the educational institution that the student is considering will ensure that the transition-planning team is addressing the key requirements necessary for admission into and sustained participation in that environment (Flexer et al., 2013).

General education teachers should be represented on the transition team and at transition-planning meetings. This will allow them to share their insights into the student's abilities in their content areas, as well as assist in the planning and implementation of any educational modifications or adaptations. Such teachers may also be able to assist students with preparation for high school proficiency exams, university entrance exams and admissions applications. While academic matters are important to students who have post-secondary education as a goal, this learning must be balanced with the teaching of other skills required for such environments, such as study skills, organisational skills, time management and social skills. Both general and special educators are instrumental in supporting students in attaining skills in these areas.

Sitlington et al. (2010) suggest ways that teachers can incorporate transition goals, skills and strategies into their classroom instructions. In the primary grades, students can explore who they are and what they want to be when they grow up by reading books, listening to guest speakers and participating in field trips. Teachers should afford students the opportunity to discuss and explore their interests, talents and preferences and speak about careers in a non-gender-specific manner. In secondary school, students can get involved in the community to learn about roles and relationships. This can include service-oriented community projects, job site visits and job shadowing. The Internet is a good source for research on jobs and careers, and information on vocational schools, community colleges and universities. Sitlington et al. (2010) also recommend that self-determination development be a part of transition planning and the curriculum from the very beginning for all students and continued at all levels. It is also important for the family to support and reinforce the development of self-determination skills at home.

Career education and vocational training

Vocational training can be accomplished in several ways. Optimally, career education and vocational training should be incorporated into the curriculum for all students, regardless of ability, to facilitate the transition process from school to work (Neubert, 1997). Matching academic skills to occupational skills is one way to achieve this. Special schools and special education units in comprehensive schools often also incorporate community-based instruction into their curricula. This type of instruction may include field trips to the supermarket, restaurants, recreational facilities and job sites. Accessing public transportation is often another facet of community-based instruction. All of these activities help prepare students for the transition to independent living. This is consistent with the notion of 'programme structure', one of Kohler's categories of strategies and practices guiding educators in providing transition-focused education (Kohler, 1996).

Employability skills, including social skills, can be taught both within and separate from the general curriculum. Social skills training typically is more of a focus in the early years of school, but is also an evidence-based practice included in the Positive Behaviour Interventions and Support model, so is also used as a target intervention for students who demonstrate a need for it. Other employability skills, such as communication, teamwork, problem solving and organisation, can be embedded within general education, but if a student's transition assessment results call for it, intensive instruction in those areas can also be provided to prepare him or her to achieve employment transition goals.

Paid work experience

Transition teams may assist the student to find paid employment while still in school. This allows the student to explore options and receive on-the-job training. The team can arrange to have support in the areas of training and monitoring to ease the student's transition to employment and provide training and advice throughout the experience. Schools sometimes offer students paid work experience on site in order to provide them with vocational experience in an environment that is familiar and comfortable, and with individuals who can support and guide them through the process.

Several models have been developed internationally that incorporate some or all of the practices listed above. Rather than attempt to provide a list of models with their details, we encourage readers to discover what models are available and being used in their context. The models should be examined for efficacy through the search for a research base or a thorough investigation of the model's components to discover whether they are evidence-based practices.

Supports and barriers

Stewart et al. (2010) have examined supports and barriers for youth with disabilities experiencing transitions. They found that personal factors such as self-awareness, coping strategies, resilience and perseverance had positive effects on the success of students with disabilities in regard to their transition to adulthood. Other positive traits, such as high levels of literacy and adaptive behaviour, have also been identified as characteristics that increase success. And, perhaps most importantly, self-determination and self-advocacy are strong supports that assist individuals with disabilities throughout their lives. These personal attributes represent the individual level of the ecological theory (Bronfenbrenner, 1994), and demonstrate how the student's attributes affect his or her experiences, and therefore success during transitions.

When environmental factors, including the abilities, attitudes and opinions of others, are viewed through the lens of Bronfenbrenner's ecological theory (Bronfenbrenner, 1994), it is apparent that they can be both positive and negative influences on a student's ability to transition to the next environment successfully. Stewart et al. (2010) conducted a literature review and identified a range of different environmental supports. They are examined here in relation to ecological theory.

People's attitudes towards the student with disabilities influence all aspects of communication, which in turn influence the transition process. This is evident in the microsystem, where people close to the student, such as parents, other family members and teachers, can easily support and encourage or discourage the student through their communication and interactions with them. The opportunities, experiences and choices that those close to the student provide are also factors in the microsystem that can positively or negatively influence transition outcomes.

The transition team itself belongs to the mesosytem, and it is here that the knowledge of other individuals can improve or adversely affect the student's transitions. The team should have a wide knowledge of the student's abilities and needs, as well as available options to suit the student's abilities, interests, preferences and needs. At the systems level, or exosystem, factors such as continuity of services, access to services and funding can help or hinder student success.

It is easy to envision how all of these factors can positively or negatively influence the student's transitions from one setting to another. These experiences are what shapes the youth's chronosystem, or overarching lifetime events. It is important that those in the student's microsystem and mesosystem recognise that their actions and interactions can positively or negatively affect an individual's success during and after educational and life transitions, and take appropriate actions to ensure that their contributions are positive.

Conclusion

There remains a need for empirically based evidence to support specific transition practices, particularly those that show longitudinal benefits for individuals with moderate and severe disabilities. One of the main issues currently is the need to balance the academic curriculum with its high-stakes testing with the vocational, functional and life skills education needs of students with disabilities. The gap between research and practice is still a concern, particularly in regard to the transition processes and practices for the less traditionally researched transitions, such as transitions in and out of specialised settings or the transition to retirement.

The importance of person-centred planning, student and family participation in transition processes, and a knowledgeable, dedicated transition team is evident from the research findings currently available. Another common theme is that of timing – transition planning should begin well ahead of the transition, regardless of its type. This will give the team involved ample time to plan supports and training to allow the student to reach his or her goals during the transition process and in the next environment or life stage. The chapters that follow detail a variety of transitions and how the practices and policies described here are contextualised for each.

3
TRANSITIONS IN THE EARLY CHILDHOOD YEARS

Zeki

Çiğdem is a 24-year-old mother of Turkish heritage, who lives with her parents and her 2½ year-old son Zeki in a small house in New York, USA. Çiğdem and her husband separated shortly after Zeki was diagnosed with a spastic quadriplegic cerebral palsy and profound hearing loss. Çiğdem is unemployed and relies on her parents for financial support. Both grandparents are heavily involved in caring for Zeki. Since Zeki has been diagnosed, Çiğdem has been in contact with a number of professionals, including a paediatrician, a psychologist and a social worker. Zeki has been receiving therapy focused on his developmental delays (e.g. sitting, reaching and walking) since he was 13 months old.

As Zeki and his family were found eligible for early intervention services, the first Individualised Family Service Plan (IFSP) meeting was scheduled at Çiğdem's home. Çiğdem felt nervous about the meeting, so Sara – the family's service coordinator – suggested meeting in advance, to explain to Çiğdem the process of establishing and working within the team. Çiğdem welcomed this opportunity and also invited her parents to be present at the initial meeting. Sara led the first IFSP meeting. Beside Çiğdem, her parents and Zeki, an early childhood special education teacher, an audiologist, an occupational therapist, a physical therapist, a speech-language pathologist and a social worker also attended. Çiğdem expected that all the professionals attending the meeting would tell her what to do. She was surprised when instead she was asked

(continued)

(continued)

about her own thoughts, opinions and priorities for Zeki. Sara explained to her that the IFSP team functions as a team of experts, with parents being experts, given their extensive knowledge of their child.

Introduction

Early childhood usually refers to the period from birth to 8 years of age (Kemp, 2014). There is a great variation in the transitions children with disabilities and their families experience in these early years. In some settings, the services available for children in this age group may include early intervention and early childhood education (Brandes et al., 2007; Rous et al., 2007). Early childhood intervention refers to the specialised individualised programmes available to infants/toddlers with disabilities (age 0–3 years) and their families. These services are often family-centred and home-based in nature, although only a small percentage of children and their families may receive these services in a child centre setting (Brandes et al., 2007; Podvey et al., 2013). A range of professionals, such as early childhood special education teachers, occupational therapists, speech-language pathologists and social workers, can offer early childhood intervention services.

Early childhood education includes childcare and preschool. Due to work commitments, many parents in countries such as Australia, the UK, Canada and the USA place their children in childcare, either full-time or part-time, when they are a few months old (Kemp, 2014), and the practices that are used by childcare providers may influence a child's development and well-being (Cryer et al., 2005). One of the important factors associated with good-quality childcare is the continuity of the caregiver; accordingly, infants or toddlers should spend most of their time with the same teacher. However a number of childcare service providers adhere to 'the lock-step elementary school practice of moving children to a different class/teacher at the end of the year', with some childcare service providers moving children even more often than that (Cryer et al., 2005: p. 39).

There are a number of changes that children may experience during transition to a preschool setting, such as change in class size, and more formal teaching practices (Daley et al., 2011). For children with disabilities, this transition may mean their first mainstream education experience, or even their first time being educated with children without disabilities (Daley et al., 2011). Parents of children with disabilities may experience serious anxiety during this transition, as they and their child often move from service providers that they have been collaborating with for a number of years to a form of preschool service provision, which differs in structure and types of services provided (Daley et al., 2011).

In alignment with the Ecological Model, both early intervention services and preschool settings constitute microsystems for a child (Bronfenbrenner, 1994). As pointed out by Podvey et al. (2013), when a child transfers from an early intervention service to a preschool setting, a new mesosystem needs to be developed – one that is collaborative and supportive in its nature. This can be a challenging task for all parties involved. Families participating in a research study conducted in the USA that investigated families' experiences with their child transitioning from early intervention to preschool special education reported that they felt like they went from an 'insider' role to an 'outsider' role during this transition (Podvey et al., 2013). One of the reasons for this was related to their changing role in early intervention and in preschool, i.e. while they had had a key role in developing and following an IFSP, their role in developing an individualised education plan (IEP) was much more peripheral. In addition, the level of involvement with personnel providing support and educational services to their children changed dramatically – from regular communication with educators and therapists to receiving short messages about their child's activities and progress in a communication book. While this shift could be expected due to the changing nature in service provision, it needed to be handled carefully by all stakeholders. Service providers need to be aware that each transition experienced by children with disabilities and their families during early childhood puts a lot of pressure on the child's parents, who need to learn how to negotiate with different service providers, while also advocating for their child (Myers, 2008). Multiple studies have highlighted the importance of parents' involvement in IEP teams (Rous et al., 2007); therefore parents should not feel peripheral to the IEP development and implementation. When viewed through the lens of the Ecological Model (Bronfenbrenner, 1994), it can be said that limiting parents' active involvement may lead to weakening of the mesosystem, with potentially 'compromising positive outcomes for the child' (Podvey et al., 2013: p. 218).

Assessment

Given the number of IFSP/IEP team members who are usually involved in transition planning, such as a child's family, early childhood educators, psychologists, social workers, occupational therapists, speech-language pathologists, physiotherapists, nurses and other health professionals, a transdisciplinary approach to assessment is particularly important during early childhood transitions (Stepans et al., 2002). When applying such an approach, a child's parents and other family members are asked to provide their subjective assessment of the child's needs, as well as their priorities for their child's development. Then the team plans for and conducts assessment, applying methods from all of the disciplines involved (Stepans et al., 2002).

Among the professionals who play important roles in the assessment of a child's needs in this process are occupational therapists. Occupational therapists are instrumental in an evaluation of skills that a child with disabilities will need in an environment she is transitioning to, and how possible issues in skills development can be addressed prior to the transition. Given their knowledge of task demands in diverse environments, occupational therapists are well placed to teach children with disabilities how to develop their skills needed in the next environment, such as developing their fine and gross motor skills (Myers, 2008). Their expertise in conducting environmental assessment and activity analysis, and in suggesting modifications and accommodations to an environment or to a task, is an important contribution to transition planning (Myers, 2008). Myers (2007) investigated how occupational therapists, physiotherapists and speech-language pathologists participate in early childhood transition processes. Most of the participants across these three professions stated that they participated in transition planning by collaborating with families in different ways, such as discussing with families the types of assessment used, and explaining to families some of the skills important for transition meetings. Nurses are also important members of the IFSP/IEP team and its assessment activities. Their primary domain is often a child's health history, as well as preliminary assessment in the area of sensory (visual and auditory) and developmental screening, which can be further used by other professionals in the team (Stepans et al., 2002).

Early childhood educators can use peer play as an opportunity both to assess and to develop the skills of children with disabilities. As discussed by Eggum-Wilkens et al. (2014), peer play is important for children to learn how to receive feedback and negotiate conflict situations, and to practise and further develop communication and social skills. Another effective play-based assessment is transdisciplinary play-based assessment, which uses an arena format team approach. Here, one or two members of the team play with a child, while the others (including the child's parents) observe and document the child's behaviours and demonstrated skills (Kelly-Vance & Ryalls, 2008).

Besides play-based assessments, other methods of assessment can be used, such as interviews, checklists, rating scales and portfolios (Jiban, 2013). The IFSP/IEP teams need to develop an assessment plan with a clear purpose, so that all team members have a clear vision of what decisions will be informed by the assessment results. When making decisions about appropriate assessment tools, a variety of issues needs to be considered: (1) what assessment tool to use; (2) for what purpose; (3) in what setting and how; (4) what information will it provide about a child with disabilities; and (5) the tool's authenticity (Jiban, 2013). The ultimate aim of assessment in the context of early childhood transitions is to determine a child's needs and abilities, which need to be a focus of the IFSP/IEP team's attention and efforts in order to make the child's transition to the next environment as smooth as possible.

Zeki

The first step of Zeki's and Çiğdem's IFSP team was to collect information relevant to Zeki's strengths, abilities and needs, and to conduct relevant assessments. Zeki's arms and legs at that time were spastic and stiff. He could not crawl, but when assisted with remaining upright, he could take a few steps using a walker. When Zeki was secured in a chair, he had full head movement control and adequate trunk control.

Sara met Çiğdem a couple of times to learn more about Zeki and his family. Initially she asked Çiğdem about her concerns, but this question was too broad and overwhelming for Çiğdem to respond to. Therefore Sara decided to use a routine-based interview approach, and asked Çiğdem questions about her family's typical daily routine. Çiğdem felt better about this approach, and when discussing her family's typical daily routine, both Çiğdem and Sara got a clearer idea about Çiğdem's priorities for Zeki. Sara also observed Zeki at home, in a playground setting and when accompanying Çiğdem to a shopping centre. She also talked to Zeki's grandparents. Christine, the occupational therapist, explained to Çiğdem that her role was to help Zeki to develop the skills necessary to take care of himself, such as eating and getting dressed, as well as the skills that will be necessary to participate in his next environment. Jane, Zeki's audiologist, conducted all relevant hearing assessments. The IFSP team also conducted an arena format of assessment, which provided in-depth information about Zeki's skills and developmental needs, which was then discussed from multiple perspectives.

The assessment results showed that the IFSP team needed to focus on the further development of Zeki's fine and gross motor skills, especially in the areas important for his transition to a preschool setting. These skills include the ability to eat, dress and perform basic hygiene-related skills as independently as possible. Based on assessments, the IFSP team developed a tailored programme for Zeki, consisting of play-based activities to improve his fine and gross motor skills.

Typical student needs during transitions in early childhood

Transition from home to a preschool setting can be challenging for a child with disabilities and his/her family. This can be due to many factors, such as shifting from receiving services and interventions at home and/or in a community-based setting to receiving these interventions in a classroom (Myers, 2007). The shift becomes even bigger when a child transitions from a preschool setting to kindergarten. The child's IEP team usually plans for this transition during the team's meetings (Myers, 2008). Eggum-Wilkens et al. (2014) described a number of changes impacting children during this transition, such as children in kindergarten spending more time in larger peer groups, experiencing a more formal learning environment and the teacher's engagement with children becoming more instrumental.

There are new expectations for the child in a number of areas, such as in academic matters, learning social skills (sharing, turn taking, etc.), classroom conduct, communication and self-care skills (Myers, 2007, 2008; Rous et al., 2007). Different types of disabilities can impact on children's performance and development in each of these areas. For example, autism spectrum disorder may cause qualitative impairments in social interaction and participation. Students with intellectual disabilities on the other hand may struggle in an academic area, and also possibly with self-care skills. Support in each of these areas can be of crucial importance. Professionals who are commonly involved and collaborate with a child's family within the IFSP or IEP teams commonly include speech therapists, occupational therapists, healthcare professionals and physiotherapists (Myers, 2007; Villeneuve et al., 2013), therefore these teams are transdisciplinary in their nature. In order for such teams to be effective, their members need to be able to prioritise the team's overall decisions, rather than promote their discipline-specific views. Extensive communication with families by experts is equally important (Myers, 2007).

Evidence-based interventions

A number of evidence-based practices can be used to provide support during the diverse transitions experienced by a child with disabilities and by his/her family during early childhood. Among these are: developing IFSPs, transition planning, developing IEPs and family involvement.

Development of Individualised Family Service Plans (IFSPs)

The needs, priorities and concerns of families are often documented in IFSPs. An IFSP is a key document developed by relevant professionals and a child's family for children between 0 and 3 years of age, and serves as a guide for support needs for infants and toddlers and their families (Jung, 2007). It includes a description of strengths and areas of need of a child with a disability, a description of the family and their desired outcomes, and the types of services which would allow these outcomes to be achieved (Podvey et al., 2013). A child's family is a key partner with an equal role in developing the IFSP (Kemp, 2014). The IFSP process typically involves three key stages: (1) gathering information; (2) summarising assessment information and determining key priorities; and (3) selecting and writing the IFSP outcomes (Jung & Grisham-Brown, 2006).

The first stage of the IFSP development involves gathering appropriate assessment information. While conducting an 'ongoing developmentally appropriate assessment' is of critical importance as far as children with disabilities are concerned, traditional assessment methods can be used only in some cases (Jarrett et al., 2006: p. 23). An alternative to traditional assessment is portfolio assessment. This approach allows for gathering data about children with disabilities from multiple sources, and over an extended period of time, which facilitates tracking the child's development (Jarrett et al., 2006). Early education intervention professionals and the child's family collaborate in determining the assessment methods, which may include interviews with family members, observations of a child within his/her daily activities, analysis of video recordings, conversations, and use of developmental scales. These assessment methods should ideally be carried out in a child's natural environment, such as the home, a grocery shop and the park (Jarrett et al., 2006; Jung & Grisham-Brown, 2006).

The second stage of the IFSP process is determining key priorities for a child and his/her family, based on the gathered and evaluated assessment information. The gathered information provides the IFSP's members with insights of a child's strengths and areas that need further development.

The last stage of the IFSP process is determining the outcomes for a child and his/her family. Jung and Grisham-Brown (2006) suggest four main questions to guide the selection of the IFSP outcomes: (1) what to teach the child and why? (2) how to teach the child the skills selected by the IFSP team? (3) where should the intervention be provided? and (4) by whom (e.g. speech therapist, parents, babysitter)? The outcomes determined by the IFSP team need to be 'specific, measurable, achievable, routines-based, and tied to a priority or concern' (Jung & Grisham-Brown, 2006: p. 5). Another important part of the IFSP is information about how the progress of the IFSP and its implementation will be monitored (Wu et al., 2007). The IFSP should be reviewed regularly, and at least once every 6 months.

One of the key transitions facing children with disabilities and their families in these early years is the transition from the IFSP to IEP, which is tailored for children aged 3–5 years. This shift is huge, as by its nature the IFSP is developed with a focus on a family and a child's natural environment, and coordinates multiple services supporting a child with disabilities and his/her family (Byington & Whitby, 2011). The process of transitioning from IFSP to IEP needs to be based on family-centred practices, with reference to a family's overall well-being (Byington & Whitby, 2011). When developing both IFSP and IEP, professionals are encouraged to collaborate with families on creating an agenda for each meeting, as well as to provide families with examples of these documents, so that they become familiar with these (Byington & Whitby, 2011).

Zeki

Zeki's IFSP team repeatedly met to discuss the collected assessment information about Zeki and his family, and to develop the priority outcomes and goals. Çiğdem's priority for Zeki was that he should be able to sit up by himself, as she wished for his increased participation in daily activities. Christine, the occupational therapist, agreed and added that Zeki's ability to maintain balance when sitting also deserves the team's attention. The team agreed that this was a priority for Zeki's IFSP, and phrased the outcome in the following way: Zeki 'will sit up without support so that he can participate in bath time, shopping, playtime, and meals' (Jung & Grisham-Brown, 2006: p. 8). The team

(continued)

(continued)

also identified places and ways in which to target and achieve the identified goals. Particular places and events where Zeki's sitting up could be practised included sitting in a bathtub during bath time, sitting in a trolley when shopping, sitting on the floor during playtime and sitting during meals. These goals would be achieved using a supportive pillow when Zeki sits on a floor, and a ring sitter for bathtub. The IFSP team was mindful that outcomes needed to be achievable within 4–6 months.

Transition planning

Transition planning is a well-established evidence-based practice across all transitions within an individual's lifespan. As highlighted by Forest et al. (2004), one of the goals of transition planning is to eliminate parents' anxiety and to preclude potential barriers to successful inclusion. There are a number of different environments that need to be considered during early childhood when it comes to transition planning. These include childcare, the preschool setting and kindergarten.

Planning for transition to a preschool setting and/or a kindergarten should include a number of steps, which need to be undertaken at least 1 year prior to this transition. Based on previous studies, Forest et al. (2004) distinguish four phases of transition to a preschool setting. The first phase takes place 1 year prior to transition to a preschool setting. Transition steps in this phase include: (1) identifying the type of preschool setting/kindergarten that would be most suitable for the child's needs (i.e. mainstream preschool setting/kindergarten, special preschool setting/kindergarten); (2) identifying services that the child with disabilities will require, in addition to the preschool setting/kindergarten (speech therapist, occupational therapist, etc.); (3) identifying the child's skills relevant to this transition and planning for the development of these skills; (4) creating a transitional timeline, including transition milestones for the child and his/her family and roles and responsibilities of everybody involved in this process; and (5) identifying a transition contact person in the preschool setting/kindergarten, who will be in contact with the family (Forest et al., 2004).

The second phase happens 6–12 months prior to a transition, and includes visiting classrooms in a preschool or kindergarten setting that was previously identified as possibly suitable for the child with disabilities, selecting the most suitable placement and formalising the transition plan, including steps that need to be undertaken in order to make this transition successful (Forest et al., 2004).

The third phase typically takes place within 6 months prior to the transition. The focus here is on the child's early intervention teacher visiting a preschool setting/kindergarten classroom where the teachers from previous and current settings can exchange their experiences, thoughts and observations. The child with disabilities may also visit his/her future preschool/kindergarten setting. The child's parents and teachers from previous and current settings may also meet to discuss the curriculum focus, child's strengths and needs, and any accommodations and modifications of curriculum that needs to take place, along with creating the child's daily schedule. A meeting between professionals from related services identified in the first and/or second phase and parents and teachers will facilitate the coordination of the service provision (Forest et al., 2004). The last phase includes a review of the transition process after 3 and 12 months, when all parties involved evaluate the transition process and make any relevant changes in service provision (Forest et al., 2004).

Zeki

After the establishment of Zeki's IFSP team, the transition to a preschool setting was discussed repeatedly. Sara and the other IFSP team members explained to Çiğdem what was involved in the transition to a preschool setting, and the whole team created a list of transition milestones. Çiğdem was adamant for Zeki to enrol in a mainstream preschool setting. After an extensive search and numerous meetings with preschool directors, Çiğdem selected a local preschool which had very good references from parents. She visited the setting a couple of times with Zeki, and her satisfaction with these visits further confirmed her decisions. The IFSP team identified additional services that Zeki would require in his new preschool setting, which included an audiologist and an occupational therapist. A key part of the transition was moving on from the current IFSP team to developing a new IEP team. This change caused a lot of anxiety for Çiğdem, as she had been very satisfied with Zeki's IFSP team. Sara assured her that continuity would be maintained for Zeki and Çiğdem.

Zeki's IEP team was established, consisting of Zeki, Çiğdem, Zeki's preschool teacher, Sara (who joined for the first 6 months to allow for continuity and a transfer of information from the IFSP team), an occupational therapist, an audiologist, a social worker and a nurse. The IEP considered and implemented a preschool staff's professional development course on cerebral palsy, with Çiğdem being a special guest speaker, sharing Zeki's strengths and needs. She also highlighted the importance of appropriate positioning for Zeki, as well as the need to change his activity/position at least every 20 minutes.

Family involvement

Rous et al. (2007) have identified the importance of preparing families of children with disabilities for transition from home as an important transition practice. Some local authorities, states or districts have guidelines, aligned to national legislation, that include suggestions on how to smooth these transitions for families. These suggestions include inviting families to visit relevant service providers (such as preschool settings), offering home visits so teachers can meet families in their comfort zone and providing opportunities for parents to observe their child in early intervention centres or preschool settings (Podvey et al., 2013). Myers (2008) also suggests that parents need to become acquainted with the preschool curriculum, and to have early discussions with professionals about the differences between the early childhood and preschool programmes. As highlighted by several authors (Malone & Gallagher, 2009; Rous et al., 2007), the families of children with disabilities need to perceive and experience their child's transition as a process rather than a one-off event. Having continuity between the sending and receiving of programmes is very important for families, as well as opportunities to make choices and decisions about the transition (Myers, 2008). A key strategy in empowering families during early childhood transitions may be to encourage parents to bring an advocate to meetings. The presence of an advocate is important as he/she can provide social and emotional support and help parents' feel less isolated in their meetings with professionals (Byington & Whitby, 2011).

Developing foundations for self-determination skills

Self-determination can be defined as 'volitional actions, where "volition" refers to making conscious *choices* or the power or will to make conscious choices' (Wehmeyer, 2007: p. 5). The importance of self-determination to student outcomes and quality of life is reflected in the fact that self-determination has become a crucial component of lifespan transition processes and practices. Halloran (1993) goes so far as to refer to self-determination as the ultimate goal of education. While the importance of developing self-determination in individuals with disabilities across their lifespans will be explored more fully in the following chapters, we want to highlight here that early childhood is an ideal time for laying the foundations for self-determination. It cannot be expected developmentally that children with disabilities will be acting in self-determined ways (i.e. making choices and problem solving) at this age; however, families and professionals can together prepare these children for later self-determination (Palmer et al., 2013). Palmer et al. (2013) suggest that: (1) child's choice and problem solving; (2) child's self-regulation; and (3) child's engagement are three crucial elements for developing future self-determination. For example, while most very young children can make simple choices (e.g. about food, toys or activities), some children with disabilities may need prompting or approaching in a specific mode (e.g. verbally, using picture representations) to make such a choice. Palmer et al. (2013) further suggest that a child's choice, self-regulation and engagement can be developed in early childhood by both intentional strategies (such as providing children with options to choose clothes they prefer to wear, or a game they wish to play) and environmental accommodations (such as placing toys within reach). When considering ways in which the foundations for a child's self-determination can be put in place, professionals need to consider family culture and values. This is very important, as within some cultures children may not be permitted to make decisions on their own (Erwin et al., 2009).

Conclusion

As demonstrated in this chapter, transitions in the early childhood years are complex and often involve change across multiple environments (such as between a child's home, childcare, a preschool setting and a kindergarten) and multiple professionals across various disciplines. Therefore a transdisciplinary approach to the assessment of a child's needs and planning for the next environment is of crucial importance.

There are a number of evidence-based practices that can be used to support children with disabilities and their families in the transition process during the early childhood period. These include transition planning, the development of an IFSP and IEP, family involvement and interagency collaboration. Early childhood is also a time when the foundation for some of the essential skills for the child's future can be laid, with respect to the areas of self-determination and the development of academic and social skills, self-help skills and other competencies.

4
TRANSITIONS TO PRIMARY SCHOOL

> **Grace[1]**
>
> Grace is a 6-year-old girl living with her parents in a family house in Auckland, New Zealand. Her parents, Holly and Rachel, are a lesbian couple who adopted Grace when she was 4 years old. Grace was born with a condition called spina bifida, which required her to be pushed around in a pram for some time. After undergoing a number of operations, Grace can walk, although for longer walks she still needs her pram. Additionally her most recent surgery left her doubly incontinent, and thus she needs to have her nappies changed regularly. She is supported by a number of professionals from both the education and health sectors.
>
> Holly and Rachel met numerous times with Ms Campbell, a special educator from an early childhood intervention centre, who has been working with Grace and her parents for the last 2 years. They are concerned about choosing the most suitable primary school for their daughter. Ms Campbell encourages them to consider a number of factors, such as the size of a school they think would be most suitable for Grace, classroom layouts, physical accessibility, proximity of a school from home and type of school. Holly and Rachel both prefer a local mainstream school. They conducted an Internet search for local schools in their neighbourhood and arranged meetings with the head teachers. They visited four primary schools where they met senior staff. They also went with Grace to the orientation days run by these schools. Following this they decided to have their daughter enrolled in the Kings Place primary school, a small state school, which is already attended by a couple of students

with physical disabilities who use a wheelchair. The school principal, Mr Harris, reassured Holly and Rachel that his school embraces all children, and that the school personnel will make sure that Grace's and her parents' needs are met.

Introduction

Transition to primary school can be both an exciting and stressful time for children and their parents. There are many changes that children need to get used to, such as new rules and routines, a more structured educational environment and new learning expectations (Hirst et al., 2011). A successful transition to primary school can contribute to a child's social, academic and emotional outcomes (Hirst et al., 2011; Larson, 2010), and experiences with this transition can impact on future transitions of a child with disabilities and his/her family (Larson, 2010; Rous et al., 2007), as well as a child's well-being and educational achievements (Sanagavarapu, 2010).

Researchers report that most families of children with disabilities perceive transition to primary school as a stressful time (Janus et al., 2008; Rous et al., 2007). For some children, this is the beginning of the development of their mesosystem (Bronfenbrenner, 1994). Throughout this transition, a child's family is likely to interact with a variety of professionals, such as school personnel, individualised educational plan (IEP) team members, special educators, case managers, therapists (e.g. occupational therapists and speech-language pathologists) and sometimes medical staff. Typical sources of frustration for families at this time may include a lack of communication between early childhood settings/services and the child's primary school, and the delayed implementation of resources by the school, despite the promises perhaps made at the school entry (Janus et al., 2008). Some of these may be due to issues in the exosystem (Bronfenbrenner, 1994), such as a lack of funding for students with disabilities, as well as laws and policies regarding the education of young children with disabilities. Some of these stressors may be easily resolved by clear communication during enrolment at the school, including providing a timeline for when promised resources will be available for the child and his/her family. Furthermore, collaboration among families of students with disabilities, education providers, administrators and other relevant stakeholders, and their involvement in the transition process are critical for successful transitions (Rous et al., 2007).

To keep the student's mesosystem (Bronfenbrenner, 1994) strong, close and purposeful, collaboration among stakeholders in the two settings the child is transitioning between is of crucial importance, in order to allow for continuity (LoCasale-Crouch et al., 2008). While it is recommended in the general transitions literature that transition-related activities need to start well ahead of an individual physically moving to a new setting, this is often omitted in practice. As highlighted by LoCasale-Crouch et al. (2008) in their study conducted in the USA, if a child's family is contacted prior to a child's school entry, it is often in an impersonal manner, such as through the use of school flyers and brochures.

Assessment

One of the key factors that need to be taken into account at school entry is school 'readiness' (Rous & Hallam, 2012). Traditionally, the concept of school readiness meant that a child's eligibility for school entry was predicated upon his or her possessing a certain skill set (Dockett & Perry, 2009; LoCasale-Crouch et al., 2008), with social skills being perceived to be more important than academic skills for successful inclusion (Rous & Hallam, 2012). Typically, primary school personnel and/or other professionals assess children to determine whether they are ready to enter school or whether a delay is needed (Dockett & Perry, 2009). Snow (2006: p. 12) reviewed the literature on the impact (and academic outcomes) of delaying school entry, concluding, 'that being close to the age cutoff . . . may be a risk factor for later academic success'. She further critiqued the fact that the skills deemed to be crucial for school success are often measured in isolation, without taking other relevant factors such as whether the child can generalise skills and use them in the appropriate situations, into consideration. Moreover, the concept of a child's school readiness as well as the consequences of readiness assessment have been heavily criticised, from the perspective that it is the school that must be ready for the children (Ahtola et al., 2011).

An ecological approach to school readiness highlights the importance of a 'ready schools' framework, within which a child's skills are viewed within a broader context and all relevant factors (i.e. child's family, peers, school, educational programme and curriculum, as well as a community) are considered (LoCasale-Crouch et al., 2008). Sayers et al. (2012) highlight that school readiness is best conceptualised within the Ecological Model's framework as being the result of four components: (1) family readiness (i.e. family situation, home learning environment); (2) community readiness (i.e. available community supports for families and children, such as parental support groups, play groups and respite care); (3) the readiness of services (i.e. programmes and services that teach children skills needed in school, such as early childhood education or early intervention); and (4) the readiness of schools (i.e. inclusive schools that are prepared to educate all children and embrace diversity, and are ready to adapt their learning environment). Equilibrium between these four components results in ready children. In other words, an ecological approach to school readiness (and to transitions in general) allows for 'a more contextualized approach to transition' (Rous & Hallam, 2012: p. 234).

Grace

Mr Harris, the school principal, Mr White, Grace's primary school classroom teacher, Ms Campbell, a special educator from an early childhood intervention centre, Grace's parents and Grace attended one of the transition planning meetings at the Kings Place Primary School. Mr White asked Holly and Rachel about their vision for Grace's future. Holly and Rachel said that they hope for Grace to be as independent as possible, to live a good-quality life and to have supportive and meaningful relationships. Holly and Rachel also spoke about their daughter's strengths, preferences and learning needs. Grace likes to play with other children, listen to stories, draw and sing. She gets tired easily, and needs assistance with going to the toilet due to her condition. Holly and Rachel were worried that Grace might be teased or even bullied by her classmates because of this. Both Mr Harris and Mr White assured Grace's parents that their school embraces the Positive Behaviour Intervention Support model and has strong antibullying policies in place.

Mr White also introduced the practice of establishing an IEP team. He explained that the priority for this team lies in working together towards ensuring that Grace reaches her potential, while receiving a quality education. He highlighted that the expertise Holly and Rachel have, as parents who know Grace best, is of the utmost importance for developing and implementing her IEP successfully. He also said that Grace would be an integral part of the IEP team. This surprised Holly and Rachel, as they felt Grace was too young to make any decisions. In the discussion that followed, Mr White and Mr Harris explained to Grace's parents how the development of their daughter's independence and self-determination skills needed to begin in early childhood. Mr White provided both parents with some strategies and activities they could use at home.

Mr White also asked about the community supports available to Holly and Rachel. Holly and Rachel talked about their engagement in a parent group run under the umbrella of the Spina Bifida Association New Zealand. However they admitted that they were exhausted from the constant care that Grace required, and had concerns about the lack of respite services available for parents like them.

Typical student needs for the transition to primary school

Transition to primary school can be a considerable change for any child, yet alone for a child with disabilities. There will be many changes facing children with disabilities when entering primary school, such as getting used to a new environment, different modes of learning and engaging in different social experiences (Danby et al., 2012; Mirkhil, 2010). These changes are complex (Table 4.1), and may be demanding on the children's cognitive, motor, social and emotional development, and therefore, behaviour.

Compared to their counterparts without disabilities, children with disabilities are more likely to experience difficulties when transitioning to formal schooling

TABLE 4.1 Changes experienced by children and their families during transition to primary school

	Pre-school setting	*Primary school setting*
Approach to teaching and learning	Socially oriented	Cognitively oriented
Environment	Smaller, home-like spaces	Larger spaces
	Lower ratio of students to adults	Higher ratio of students to adults
	Relatively low level of structure	High level of structure
Family–educational setting relationship	More informal interaction	More formalised interaction

Based on Hirst et al. (2011).

(Hirst et al., 2011). Therefore it is imperative that relevant supports are in place and different stakeholders collaborate in the transition process. The transition-planning process should start at least 1 year prior to a child with disabilities entering primary school (Healthy Child Manitoba, 2002). The process is usually, but not exclusively, led by early childhood education providers, working in collaboration with a child with disabilities and his or her parents, representatives from a primary school and other relevant professional staff (e.g. occupational therapists, speech therapists). A useful tool that can be used to establish what are the child's transition needs is the Early Years Transition Planning Inventory, which covers the child's healthcare needs, sensory areas (i.e. hearing and vision), mobility, motor skills, psychological, emotional and cognitive skills (such as attention and concentration skills and communication), independence and adaptive skills (e.g. toileting, eating, dressing) and social skills (Healthy Child Manitoba, 2002). Essential skills for children with disabilities entering primary school include working independently, following directions and using diverse materials (Daley et al., 2011). Social skills in developing peer relationships and gaining confidence in these relationships are critical for a successful transition (Walker et al., 2012). As evidenced by Danby et al. (2012), students who have high levels of acceptance by peers also adjust better to new educational settings.

Grace

Holly and Rachel arranged a meeting with Mr White to discuss their concerns regarding Grace's needs. Based on this meeting and taking into consideration a medical report from Grace's doctor, a number of accommodations were developed. Grace can only sit on a school chair for 20 minutes, which needs to be considered by her class teacher when planning individual lesson sequence and activities. Grace's consulting occupational therapist joined this meeting and made suggestions regarding changes for her seat. He suggested a specifically adapted chair and a writing slope, which would improve Grace's physical well-being at school. The occupational therapist also pointed out that Grace had sore legs, her right foot turned in and at times she had difficulties with moving, all of which contributed to her mobility problems. Mr White discussed the need for accommodations for Grace at the staff meeting. The consensus was that teachers need to learn about spina bifida and how this and similar conditions affect students in the school environment. Subsequently, a staff professional development session on spina bifida was scheduled. Furthermore, any excessive furniture in Grace's classroom was removed, to prevent her from tripping over it.

Evidence-based interventions

A number of evidence-based practices can be used to support students with disabilities and their families when students enter formal schooling. These include reciprocal visits from early childhood services representatives and primary school teachers in a child's early education setting and primary school; joint professional development events attended by early childhood professionals and primary school teachers; parent groups; and family involvement (Sayers et al., 2012). Schools can support families in the transition planning process, supporting their confidence by providing them with information. It is also very important that positive relationships are developed between school personnel and parents, as this will help parents to feel more connected to their child's schooling and to feel involved (Hirst et al., 2011).

Interagency collaboration

Collaboration between a child's previous and current educational environments is vital (Skouteris et al., 2012). Hirst et al. (2011), for example, highlight how intensive collaboration between early childhood professionals and primary school personnel allows for consistency and continuity in provision, as well as for building on a child's existing skills, knowledge and experiences. Ideally, besides the involvement of the child, his/her family, a primary school and an early childhood provider, the involvement of the wider community will also be considered. With the growth of multiculturalism, there is a possibility that the child and his/her family may come from a minority ethnic, linguistic or religious community. Involving this wider community in the transition process can often make the family more comfortable, and more willing to be involved (Hirst et al., 2011). According to the Bangladeshi parents living in Sydney, Australia in Sanagavarapu's (2010) study, peers from the same language or cultural background were instrumental in facilitating their child's adjustment to primary school.

Development of self-determination skills

Another evidence-based practice that needs to be included in the planning of the child's transition to formal schooling is the development of self-determination. Wehmeyer (2007) identifies the following essential skills of self-determination: choice making, decision making, problem solving, goal setting and attainment, independence, risk taking and safety, self-observation, evaluation and reinforcement, self-instruction and self-advocacy and leadership (i.e. self-awareness and self-knowledge).

Although research evidence stresses the importance of developing students' self-determination skills to improve school and post-school outcomes, many teachers do not focus on self-determination skills development. The most commonly cited reason for this is a lack of training on how to teach these skills, and uncertainty about where to access relevant instructional methods (Cho et al., 2011). Furthermore, the literature and relevant resources primarily focus on the development of self-determination skills at the secondary education level (Danneker & Bottge, 2009; Palmer & Wehmeyer, 2003). Yet, the development of self-determination occurs across the lifespan and, as highlighted by Wehmeyer and Palmer (2000), students with disabilities will not be ready to take control over their lives unless this process starts early in their schooling years. Furthermore, many students with disabilities need support with and explicit instruction in acquiring relevant self-determination skills (Campbell-Whatley, 2008).

One of the essential elements of self-determination is choice making, which needs to be encouraged and developed in children with disabilities during transition planning and during the actual transition to primary school. There are a number of barriers for students with disabilities that prevent them from developing choice-making skills (Sparks & Cote, 2012). These include a child's low self-esteem, lack of awareness about his/her own strengths and areas that need to be developed and, in some cases, a child's learned helplessness. There are many ways that primary school teachers can support the development of choice-making skills in students with disabilities. Sparks and Cote suggest that teachers use a six-sequential-step intervention, described in Figure 4.1.

Supporting self-advocacy

A crucial element of self-determination is self-advocacy. O'Regan Kleinert et al. (2010) highlight the importance of starting self-advocacy skills development and training as early as possible. One possible model for developing self-advocacy in young students with disabilities is provided by the Kentucky Youth Advocacy Project (KYAP), which was designed for students aged 7–18 years of age. A key component of the project was 'I Can' day at school. On this day mentors and speakers/self-advocates with disabilities were invited to a school to share their experiences. During the 'I Can' day, students with disabilities worked through their KYAP My Goal Book, and with the support of their parents and teachers, ended the day by identifying one goal they wished to achieve. Students also developed

> 1. Create short-story scenarios relevant to the student.
> 2. Provide three choices to the student (the best solution, an acceptable solution and the worst possible solution).
> 3. Recycle the first choice (i.e. teacher reads the options and asks the student which choice is best).
> 4. Provide the student with the opportunity to re-evaluate his/her choice.
> 5. If a student did not select the best option, the scenario is revisited, as well as the two remaining options, which is followed by:
> 6. The final re-evaluation of the student's choice.

FIGURE 4.1 The six-sequential-step intervention (adapted from Sparks & Cote, 2012)

a plan to achieve that goal, as well as identifying potential barriers to achieving it. Later, an 'I Did It' day provides an opportunity for students to celebrate their successes in achieving their goals, along with all involved stakeholders in the process.

The Self-Determined Model of Learning Instruction is particularly useful when teaching goal-setting and problem-solving skills to the youngest primary school students (K-3). It is implemented in three instructional phases, and in each of these phases a teacher supports the student to solve one problem by asking her/him four questions, which guide her/him through a problem-solving sequence (Palmer & Wehmeyer, 2003). Murawski and Wilshinsky (2005) have combined the Self-determined Model of Learning Instruction with The Mind That's Mine: A Program to Help Young Learners Learn about Learning (Levine et al., 1997) to create an intervention programme for students with disabilities attending early primary classes. The intervention focused on supporting students to explore the ways people learn, and which of these best suit themselves. This programme provided useful tools to support primary teachers in developing students' self-determination skills.

Active family involvement

There are many approaches to developing self-determination, and all include family involvement as a critical component. When involving families, cultural background must be taken into account, because families' understanding of self-determination, and the value they assign to it, vary and are greatly influenced by culture (Shogren & Turnbull, 2006). As Grigal et al. (2003: p. 98) put it, 'the success of self-determination depends on parents' views of its appropriateness and desirability'. There are a number of different strategies that families can use to promote some of the key elements of self-determination in young children with disabilities (Table 4.2).

Individualised educational plans

IEP meetings are one way in which the diverse stakeholders involved in a child's transition can collaborate. They also provide an excellent opportunity for students

TABLE 4.2 Strategies for families of young children to develop self-determination skills

Elements of self-determination	Promoting capacity development	Structuring the home environment	Providing accommodations and supports
Autonomy	Support children to explore, manipulate and play with materials that hold their interest	Place artwork and photos at eye level	Evaluate need for assistive technology to promote communication and mobility in the home
	Support children to express their preferences, verbally and non-verbally	Ensure that children have a 'private area' that they can call their own	Work with professionals to access assistive technology and modify the home environment
Self-regulation	Ensure there are predictable routines that children can discover and learn to anticipate	Set regular routines to provide predictability and consistency	Provide structured support to enable children to develop an understanding of causality (e.g. the Parent's Guide to the Self-Determined Learning Model of Instruction)
	Encourage children to set and work toward simple goals	Create a safe, child-proof space where children can explore and experiment and develop a sense of control over their environment	
Psychological empowerment	Encourage children to try new things and work through challenging tasks	Support children to engage in age-appropriate risk taking	Work with professionals to identify effective strategies to create child-proof spaces that are accessible to children with disabilities
	Talk through the process of making decisions and achieving desired outcomes	Be careful not to overprotect children with disabilities relative to their siblings and peers	

| Self-realisation | Communicate with children about their strengths and special qualities | Set up social and environmental reinforcers for appropriate behaviour | Work with professionals to develop appropriate expectations for young children with disabilities and strategies to provide supportive, positive feedback |
| | Model optimism and positive self-esteem | Set up opportunities for children to engage in self-evaluation of their strengths and abilities | |

Reproduced from Shogren and Turnbull (2006: p. 342), with permission from Wolters Kluwer Health.

with disabilities to develop further their self-determination, especially goal-setting, problem-solving, self-awareness and self-advocacy skills (Test & Neale, 2004). Neale and Test (2010) stress that the involvement of primary school students with disabilities in the development and implementation of their IEPs is important. However, in order for students with disabilities to be meaningfully involved, specific instruction in this area may be required.

Danneker and Bottge (2009) used a multiple case study approach to investigate the ways in which primary school teachers can prepare students with disabilities to participate meaningfully in IEP meetings. The results of their study, which was conducted in the USA, suggest that involving students in IEP meetings considerably contributed to the meetings being student-centred, while providing opportunities to develop their self-determination skills further. Hart and Brehm (2013) developed The Self-Advocacy Model for Obtaining IEP Accommodations for primary school students. It contains a ten-step process that includes involving students in academic goal setting, and their understanding of and asking for accommodations. Transition planning is an important part of IEPs, both in the sense of transitioning from a kindergarten to a primary school and getting used to a new setting, and also in a sense of preparing a child with disabilities and his/her family for transition to a secondary level.

Grace

Holly and Rachel, and Grace, following the advice from Grace's teacher Mr White, prepared a PowerPoint presentation for their first IEP meeting. They

(continued)

(continued)

used their photos and information about their home environment, favourite activities and plans for future. At the IEP meeting, Grace talked about her wish to have more friends who would play with her not only at school, but also after school. She admitted that she often felt lonely. Mr White suggested that Grace join one of the extracurricular activities run by the school, which might allow her to meet friends with similar interests. After discussing her preferences, Grace decided she wanted to join the music extracurricular class. Mr White asked Grace what her educational goal was. Grace said she would like to improve her writing. When Mr White asked her what made writing difficult for her, she answered that it was difficult for her to hold a pencil. Mr White, and Ms Baker, a school occupational therapist, discussed possible accommodations with Grace and her parents. A decision was made that Grace would use a pencil grip, to see whether her writing improved.

Conclusion

Transition to primary school is both an exciting and challenging step in the lives of students with disabilities and their families. The amount and level of interaction taking place during this transition are enormous. Viewed through the lens offered by Bronfenbrenner's (1994) Ecological Model, a child's microsystem becomes more complex, with a child's family, early childhood education providers and primary school personnel being progressively involved. This complexity also impacts on the mesosystem of the child, as many partners need to interact within the mesosystem (e.g. interaction between child's previous and current educational setting, interaction between a child's family and each of these settings). If the interactions and links between all involved are supportive and strong, this will likely have a positive impact on a student's development.

There are a number of ways in which a child with disabilities and his/her family can be supported. These include a focus on developing quality home–school relationships and collaboration, student and family-centred transition planning, as well as using evidence-based practices. When considering which of the evidence-based practices can be implemented during transition to a primary school, the development of a child's self-determination skills should not be ignored, because of their crucial importance for the child's future success.

Note

1 Grace's case study was based partially on the following journal article: Ross-Watt (2005).

5
TRANSITION FROM PRIMARY SCHOOL TO SECONDARY SCHOOL

> **Jérémy**
>
> Jérémy is a 10-year-old boy living in Toronto, Ontario, Canada. He is an only child and lives with his mother, Katherine, and stepfather, Joseph. Joseph holds a managerial position at an accounting firm in the city, and makes a large enough salary that Katherine is able to be a stay-at-home mother. The family is able to afford all of the basics, along with a few luxury items.
>
> Jérémy was first diagnosed with a learning disability in third grade, when he was making little progress in reading and other academic areas. He also demonstrates significant difficulties with organisation and socialisation with peers. He frequently loses letters that are to go home to be signed by his parents and forgets things such as his lunch money or homework. Jérémy currently participates in general education classes for physical education, art and music. He receives all of his academic instruction in a specialised classroom setting. At Jérémy's annual individualised education plan (IEP) meeting in November, the team discussed his transition to middle school the following September, so that they could begin planning his instruction to prepare him for this major transition.

Introduction

The transition from primary to secondary school brings many new experiences and transitions for all students, but may be particularly challenging for those with disabilities (Sitlington et al., 2010). There are many differences between the two settings, which can bring about many changes, most notably in the increased size of the student's mesosystem (Bronfenbrenner, 1994). This is evident in the typically larger size of the school and increased demands academically, socially and behaviourally (Adreon & Stella, 2001). One of the most obvious changes that many students experience when leaving primary school is that they now have to move among a series of different teachers for each class. Secondary school campuses are typically bigger and may even involve students moving from one building to another each day. Students are also expected to be more independent in their studies, with less guidance and reminding from their teacher. Some students may also be experiencing changes in their microsystems by way of family transitions (divorces, remarriages, blending families, foster care) and others are being given more responsibilities, such as staying at home alone after school (Sitlington et al., 2010). The effects of these changes can be far-reaching when viewed through the lens of the Ecological Model (Bronfenbrenner, 1994), affecting all systems, from the individual to the chronosystem. Changes in family status and school environments will have far-reaching effects in the areas of communication, collaboration, funding, teaching methods, support and individual self-efficacy. This has the potential to cause quite a bit of anxiety on the part of the student with disabilities.

Students typically experience a loss of achievement during the transition from primary to secondary. Those who have made two transitions due to the existence of middle school or junior high school experience this loss twice, and may experience increased high school drop-out rates and difficulty with self-esteem (Sitlington et al., 2010). Cohen and Smerdon (2009) pointed out that, due to these discouraging statistics, the need for high school improvement has received much attention and funding in the past decade, especially in the USA. Drop-outs are especially prevalent in the first year of high school – in low-socio-economic status communities, 40 per cent of students with disabilities drop out after the first year. If the transition from primary to secondary school does not go smoothly, the student may present with inappropriate behaviour, disengagement from his environment, chronic illness and negative effects on academic study, self-perception and perception of school (Maras & Aveling, 2006). These negative outcomes underscore the importance of supporting the transition to high school for all students, but particularly those with disabilities.

While there are normally no formal transition processes/plans for students moving to this new environment, transition at this stage can nevertheless be addressed through the IEP process. This is important to continuity, coordination, seamless/cohesive services, parent involvement and outcome orientation. Transition planning through the IEP has the potential to support students in coping with the current transition, as well as to prepare them for their post-school future.

Assessment

Transition assessment is recommended in order to plan instructional strategies and accommodations to meet the student's needs, while capitalising on his or her strengths. Students may be supported in understanding the results of assessment so that they can see the connection between their education and their post-school goals. As such, assessment information can then be used to plan post-secondary goals in education or training, employment and independent living (National Secondary Transition Technical Assistance Center (NSTTAC), 2013). The transition from primary to secondary school is equally important, as the success of this transition heavily influences the student's success in secondary school, which, in turn, is a strong predictor of post-school success.

It is imperative that the IEP team conduct age-appropriate assessments for the transition from primary to secondary school. An important point to remember when assessing a student is that she or he should be afforded the opportunity to use any assistive technology (AT) or accommodations needed during the assessment itself to maximise his/her potential. In order to obtain a full understanding of the student's abilities and the supports that may be necessary, assessments need to be conducted across each of a variety of domains, namely: school performance, self-determination, adaptive behaviour and independent living, supports intensity scale and ecological assessment of the new environment.

School performance measures include traditional curriculum-based assessments, along with an examination of the student's grades and scores on high-stakes achievement tests. Other factors that affect school performance, such as behavioural observations and attendance, also need to be taken into account. The student (with the assistance of a teacher and/or parent) can be encouraged to create a portfolio that demonstrates his or her strengths, needs and interests in regard to academic matters (NSTTAC, 2013). This will allow the student a voice in the assessment process, which will support his or her self-determination skills.

The student's level of self-determination should also be assessed at this time. His or her ability to set goals will become even more important in the secondary setting, where students are expected to choose many of their courses. Related to this are skills of persistence, self-advocacy and self-evaluation. Evaluating support needs in the areas of problem solving, persistence and self-confidence is also important, as there are likely to be new social demands in the secondary environment (NSTTAC, 2013).

NSTTAC (2013) suggests that transition assessment and skills integration begin in the primary grades. As a part of this, assessments of the student's adaptive behaviour and independent living skills can be undertaken. This will provide education staff at both the primary and the secondary school with the information needed to plan for training in skills acquisition in these areas. Since the secondary school environment is typically larger and more demanding, the student's support needs in these areas may be different during and after the transition, so ongoing assessment may be called for.

Lastly, in addition to student-centred assessments, an ecological assessment can be conducted to examine the environments in the new setting that the student will participate in. The IEP team will need thorough knowledge of the whole school environment, including areas such as academic classrooms, specialist classrooms (industrial arts (craft, design, and technology), art, home economics, music), and unstructured areas such as the hallways, the cafeteria, the gym and sports facilities. The academic, social and behavioural demands associated with these areas also are examined, in addition to assessing the physical demands of each. For example, what materials will the student be required to have for each of his classes? Are there lockers in which to store his materials, or will he need to carry a book bag with everything in it? How much homework will be assigned? What is the routine in the cafeteria? The results of the ecological assessment are then examined in conjunction with the results of the other assessments to help the team plan for any environmental changes and supports that may be required. Completing and analysing the results of a supports intensity scale, such as the Supports Intensity Scale (American Association on Intellectual and Developmental Disabilities, 2008), may also be beneficial when planning future support.

Jérémy

Jérémy's IEP team completed a battery of assessments to gain a complete picture of his abilities, the requirements of the middle school environment he will be entering, and the level of support he will need to be successful while participating in that environment. Jérémy voiced both excitement and apprehension about his move to a new school. He was excited to be at a bigger school and have more independence, but he was apprehensive about finding his way around and making new friends. He was nervous about doing well in higher-level classes, but expressed both ability and interest in mathematics. The assessment results revealed that Jérémy would most likely need support with social skills and organisation.

The team determined that Jérémy would continue to receive academic instruction in a special education setting and attend general education classes for his specialist subjects, but would also be capable of participating in a general education mathematics class. To acclimate him to this, it was decided that he would participate in mathematics with the peers in his current class, beginning when the new semester started in January. Jérémy's classroom teacher explained her expectations for the mathematics class: Jérémy would be required to complete homework four times a week, come to class prepared with a pencil and paper and be able to work both independently and with his classmates in groups. After liaising with the middle school mathematics teacher, the team discovered that these were the same expectations that would be required of Jérémy the following year, so they decided to design a plan that would support Jérémy both in the next semester as well as preparing him for his transition to middle school next September.

Typical student needs for the transition from primary school to secondary school

One of the main purposes of transition assessment is to identify a student's needs as he or she is transitioning to the next setting (NSTTAC, 2013). Although each student will have a unique set of abilities and need for support, there are several characteristics that are common to students with disabilities transitioning from primary to secondary school. It is important to examine these and plan the transition accordingly, because students with disabilities often experience decreased achievement and motivation during this time (Milsom, 2007).

In a study conducted in the USA, Knesting et al. (2008) found that students with disabilities took significantly longer to learn about and become comfortable with school routines than their typically developing peers. This caused some of them to feel less successful at school. The students in their study felt that moving to different classrooms was difficult, but also exciting. They also reported having difficulties with keeping track of and complying with the different academic, procedural and behavioural expectations each teacher had, when even the smallest of routines, such as having the right book for the right class, were stressful. Smith et al. (2008) reviewed a series of studies in English-speaking countries and found similar results, with students reporting some anxiety about classes being difficult and organisational issues, such as getting lost, but also said that they looked forward to increased independence and being able to choose their courses.

In secondary school, social expectations increase and peer relationships become more complex. Peer groups often begin to supersede the family in importance in the young person's social circle (Sitlington et al., 2010). The priority of microsystems (Bronfenbrenner, 1994) may change at this stage. For example, peer groups often take precedence over family when it comes to decision making on the part of the student, thereby shifting peers from the mesosystem to the microsystem in the student's view. Social conformity is paramount to many adolescents, but the quest to 'fit in' is just too stressful for some students, who experience significant increases in psychological distress and a decrease in academic achievement (Adreon & Stella, 2001). Students with emotional and behavioural disorders or those on the autism spectrum find these social demands especially difficult, as their impairments in social skills, communication and behaviour often lead to a mismatch between the required skills for secondary school and their abilities. To compound the problem, the secondary school environment is often more impersonal than the primary school setting, which may be difficult for students with disabilities, who typically require higher levels of social support (Adreon & Stella, 2001).

Sitlington et al. (2010) explored the expectation in secondary school that students are more independent in their studies, with less guidance and fewer reminders from their teacher. This stresses the need for student self-determination and choice making. Self-determination development is important throughout primary through secondary school, especially for students with disabilities. The goal is for students to learn to accept themselves, advocate for themselves and participate in meetings and decision making about their education and futures, for example, in IEP meetings. It is imperative that self-determination be taught, practised and reinforced from a very early age.

Cohen and Smerdon (2009) divide group transition needs at this stage into those that are social, academic and organisational in character. Social issues include students' excitement about making new friends, along with fear that they will have no friends, especially if they are going to a different high school than their primary school peer group. In addition, playground and lunchtime activities may be different in secondary school; sports and games may be less formally organised and socialising is more informal. Communication is also a factor at this stage. Because of teacher expectations of increased student independence, students may be hesitant to ask for assistance. Forlin et al. (2013) suggest that students with disabilities often require explicit instruction in self-management and how to ask for help and environmental adjustments. In addition, having many teachers rather than just one makes it more difficult for students to get to know and trust their teachers. In addition to this, parental involvement in their child's education typically decreases as their children enter high school. These two points can result in less effective communication and collaboration between students, teachers, home and school.

Organisational issues to be planned for and addressed include the overall organisation of the school. How students are organised within the school (ability streaming, inclusivity) will be a determining factor of support needs. In turn, how student support is implemented will be affected by the organisation of the school and the responsibilities of teaching staff, counsellors, principals and paraprofessionals. These may cause variations in the level and quality of support from the primary to secondary school setting and may also result in a lack of communication across stakeholders. Other school organisation factors that affect student needs include the size of the school and the complexity of the daily schedule (block schedules, start and end times). The absence or presence of year groups is also a consideration. Student support needs may also be affected by the location of special education services, how related services are provided and any provision for extracurricular activities. Many students with disabilities will have needs focused on each of these basic school organisational factors (Cohen & Smerdon, 2009).

Students with disabilities will typically also have transition needs related to academic matters, including in respect of the curriculum, accessibility, academic achievement and high-stakes testing (Cohen & Smerdon, 2009). Secondary students typically are afforded the opportunity to choose at least some of their subjects. Students with disabilities may require assistance in the form of information, so that their choices are not based solely on a perception that the work in certain subjects is much easier or harder. Students may also notice that having a variety of teachers results in an increase in homework, as each teacher tends to assign homework for each subject (Chambers & Coffey, 2013). To compound this issue, as students enter secondary school, parents may feel that their own academic abilities are not strong enough to support their children in homework and other academic matters.

Because secondary school students with disabilities often exhibit poorer academic achievement and increased behaviour problems when compared to their typically developing peers, their academic needs must be identified and supported. Students with disabilities may feel isolation at their high school, because that point in adolescence is a time when students are preoccupied with social status, and they may be less likely to befriend other students with disabilities for fear that this would negatively affect their own standing among peers.

Evidence-based interventions

The importance of school collaboration and communication, as well as students and their families having a voice and choice about issues that affect them, cannot be overstated in planning the transition from primary to secondary school. One of the best ways to accomplish this is to acknowledge student preferences when designing a service delivery plan. Choice-making skills are important, particularly when students are having a say about the special education services they would like to receive and where they would like to receive them. Choice making is enhanced when students have self-determination skills (Knesting et al., 2008). Student and family involvement in transition planning allows parents to voice their concerns about social pressures, academic matters, peer relationships and their children's attitudes about school, which is important, as students with disabilities are more at risk for difficulty than their peers during this transition (Carter et al., 2005).

Proactive planning and involvement in several transition activities increase the likelihood that the transition to high school will be successful (Adreon & Stella, 2001). Transition-planning meetings should ideally involve teachers from both schools. The transition plan includes supports for the first few weeks of school and how and who will implement any strategies prescribed by the plan. This includes the provision of any necessary training for school personnel well ahead of time. Student orientation activities are covered in the plan, as well as procedures for unstructured times, such as transport to school, class changing times, lunch and physical education, as students often have the most trouble with these.

A number of research-based strategies have been shown to contribute to successful transitions for students with disabilities from primary to secondary school (Carter et al., 2005). It may be helpful for the team to begin early when looking at the student's successes to date and places where support is necessary. They can also look ahead to the middle school environment and determine what supports will be continued, discontinued or commenced to ensure a successful transition to the next educational setting. This is best accomplished through collaboration between schools, with transition being viewed as a shared responsibility (Carter et al., 2005). It is helpful for staff from both schools to be familiar with the academic, social and behavioural demands of the other. Joint transition planning may be a good way to foster collaboration. To ensure successful collaboration, the roles and responsibilities of all stakeholders should be made explicit.

Spencer (2005) recommends that the primary school invite the high school special education professional to attend the student's last primary school IEP meeting. During this meeting, the team can share details of the student's current modifications and accommodations with the secondary school, to facilitate everything being in effect on the first day of school. The student's behaviour plan can also be introduced to the receiving school ahead of time. It is imperative that everyone on the team understands what is required. Professional development can then be provided to any teachers or paraprofessionals who need training in any specific strategies or techniques. Other suggestions by Spencer (2005) include collaboration between the primary school teacher or counsellor and the high school teacher or counsellor to discuss the student's interests and talents and how these relate to extracurricular activities. The primary school physical education teacher can speak to his or her secondary school counterpart if the student requires any specific accommodation or assistance during physical education class. Lastly, but importantly, it is vital that all physical accessibility issues are addressed before the start of school. For example, if the student requires access to an elevator, a key needs to be provided as well as providing the student with instructions and practice using it.

Students can prepare for this transition ahead of time by attending activities like orientation, open houses, social activities and sporting events throughout the year before the transition, in order to become comfortable with the school. Secondary school teachers and leadership staff, acting as middle school ambassadors, can visit the primary school to speak to students ahead of time and provide them with valuable information. Towards the end of their last year in primary school, students could spend a few part-days at the new school, shadowing a secondary school student. Cohen and Smerdon (2009) recommend the use of welcome packages to orient students to the school-wide rules, expectations and policies. These packages could also contain photos of different areas of the school, teachers and other important staff members.

Carter et al. (2005) recommend encouraging family involvement with the secondary school by establishing and maintaining communication with families as soon as possible. Although all educators involved with the child should have open communication with parents, it can be easier for parents if there is one point of contact for when they are seeking assistance from the school. This open communication may be a helpful strategy to use with the student also, because if s/he is having difficulties, they are best addressed early on. Ask the student to share any questions, concerns or anxieties and address them before the first day of school (Spencer, 2005). Cohen and Smerdon (2009) suggest providing a specific counsellor, transition specialist or special educator to give academic advice and mentoring.

Students with disabilities will often need assistance with organisation. Finding and operating lockers, locating classes and toilets, and keeping track of books and assignments can be overwhelming for students at the beginning. A peer support person, particularly for the first few weeks of school, can be invaluable helping the student navigate through procedures in the lunchroom and playground. Students who use mobile technology may find mobile applications (apps) helpful for keeping track of assignments and important dates, and to assist with mobility. Other helpful strategies include posting navigational signs around the school, and having staff wear name badges for the first couple of weeks (Cohen & Smerdon, 2009).

Cohen and Smerdon (2009) encourage supporting students with disabilities in joining clubs and sports and other school activities that align with their interests. This will assist them in making friends and they will also learn valuable skills that will help them during their transition to post-school settings. These opportunities and any supports that students require to participate successfully may be written into the IEP if there is one. Students with disabilities may need support in the areas of independence and self-determination. Picture schedules and lists may be helpful to support students in managing their time and assignments. Augmentative and alternative communication can provide the freedom to communicate for students who are non-verbal. Students must have information in order to make informed decisions, therefore provide detailed materials about the subjects offered, including expectations.

The role of school counsellors

School counsellors, where they exist, have an important role to play in this transition by facilitating collaboration with other school staff, families and staff from the school the student will be transitioning to (Milsom, 2007). This is especially important in those mainstream schools that do not have full-time special education teachers on staff. In line with the suggestions given previously, counsellors can work with the IEP team to build skills in areas that are important for successful transition, including social skills, organisational skills, communication, and self-awareness and determination.

It is essential that the classroom that the student is transitioning into is prepared for the student; school counsellors can conduct small-group diversity appreciation lessons to promote a more accepting environment/classroom culture. Teachers must also be prepared to meet the academic and social needs of students with disabilities. This can be accomplished through professional development and collaboration with special education professionals. Portfolios and/or student profiles are a good way of alerting future teachers about any modifications the student requires, as well as learning styles, environmental requirements and behaviour support plans (Milsom, 2007). These profiles typically contain, in addition to academic and behavioural information, student interests, likes and dislikes, and a summary of interventions that have been attempted, and whether they were successful or unsuccessful.

Technology and the transition to secondary school

One of the best ways to foster self-determination in students with disabilities is to involve them fully in their IEPs and transition planning. Many students have difficulty learning how to do this, as much of the materials for these two documents are print-based. Universally designed materials or materials that are usable by as many students as possible, regardless of ability, can assist in presenting this information to students. These include text to speech, multimedia and computer-based reading support programmes (Lee et al., 2011). Introducing AT interventions early will ensure that students are equipped to participate in team meetings when the time comes for transition planning.

Chambers and Coffey (2013) recommend the use of technology to support students in accessing the curriculum, in addition to managing the increased organisational and social interaction demands that come with this transition. They developed a mobile-optimised website covering six key areas of support. The first, Getting Ready, focuses on preparing students for new settings through the use of a social story designed to ease anxiety. The second area, Friendships, provides information about how to make and keep friends. The third, Planning and Organisation, offers students information on study skills, homework tips and how to read and use timetables. A section on Cyber Safety is considered crucial, as it teaches students how to stay safe online, by providing tips and links to other websites. Students also access a Frequently Asked Questions section, which is updated regularly. The final section, My Info, affords students the capability of inputting information about subjects, teachers and equipment to help with organisation. Key people and school rules can also be kept here for quick reference. Early research on using mobile devices as AT to support students with social skills, schedules and organisation has also been promising (Cumming & Strnadová, 2012).

Some primary school students may already use AT on a daily basis. Some examples of these for mobility are wheelchairs, walkers, canes, and prosthetic and orthotic devices. Students with hearing impairments may use hearing aids, amplification systems or closed captioning devices. Adaptive switches make it possible for a child with limited motor skills to play with toys and games. Computers and mobile devices can be used for text to speech, screen readers and screen enlargers. Other forms of AT are considered 'low-tech' and may include pencil grips, book holders and reading windows, which allow students with dyslexia to block out the majority of a page of text and focus on one line at a time. Additionally there are a number of adaptive devices that help students with disabilities perform tasks such as cooking, dressing and grooming.

Little research exists on what is done to support students with disabilities during the transition from primary to secondary school; however, those with specialised accommodations, such as AT, may have a more challenging time with this (Specht et al., 2007). Ideally, any AT that the student is using will transfer seamlessly from one setting to another. Specht et al. (2007) advocate that transition teams examine AT from the perspectives of the environment, training, advocacy and assessment. The environments in which the student will be using AT need to be assessed for how well the technology is accepted and supported, both for learning and for technical assistance. Technical issues can be extremely problematic; often when a device stops working and there is no assistance, the student loses an important source of support. It is best if training in the use of the device is ongoing and matched to individual needs. Training should not be limited to the student, but extended to his/her teachers, peers and family members. Time to practise is also crucial.

When the team evaluates and plans for AT advocacy, they should look at the types and amount of support and encouragement the student receives in the primary setting for the use of his/her AT. This can be addressed from the perspective of the Ecological Model (Bronfenbrenner, 2005), looking at the changes that are predicted to occur across the student's systems, and how AT figures into each of these. The focus then becomes how best to support the transition of AT, including ways to address any real or perceived stigma of entering a high school classroom with AT. Typically the student's parent or a teacher has taken on the role of advocate when transitioning AT to a new school, but the process may be more formal, part of the IEP/transition plan, to ensure that the student's AT needs are not overlooked. Lastly, the team assesses how well the student is using the AT and if it is positively impacting learning. This assessment occurs periodically and continues into the next setting, as students' needs for AT evolve as they mature and develop skills. Simply providing the AT is not enough; the student's needs must be accommodated.

Professional development

The transitions literature emphasises the importance of professional development for school staff to support students during transitions (Chambers & Coffey, 2013; Motoca et al., 2014; Topping, 2011). Hanewald (2013) stresses the important of professional development, as teacher attitudes and behaviours are critical to the success of the transition. Unhelpful attitudes and behaviours may simply be the result of secondary teachers' lack of knowledge of how best to include and support new students with disabilities in the classroom.

Motoca et al. (2014) developed a professional development model, Supporting Early Adolescent Learning and Social Support (SEALS), to create supportive environments for students transitioning from primary to secondary school. The approach is based on Bronfenbrenner's Ecological Model (1994). Motoca et al. (2014) suggest this model is a good lens through which to view teacher activities, because it offers a reminder that teachers never work in isolation, therefore must have the support of the wider ecology. Teachers' own microsystems include their students, students' parents and teachers' colleagues. The linkages among the teachers and these parts of the microsystem make up the mesosystem, which may extend beyond the school environment. The exosystem comprises the policies, rules and resources that impact classroom practices. The macrosystem is the culture of the school.

The SEALS model endeavours to strengthen both the microsystem and mesosystem, and involves three different categories, each with its own set of strategies: academic engagement enhancement, competence enhancement behaviour management and social dynamics management. When implemented with fidelity, SEALS can support teachers in promoting classroom cultures that assist students in adapting to their new environment (Motoca et al., 2014).

It is clear from both the literature and resources that are available on the topic of professional development for transitions from primary to secondary schools that teachers and other stakeholders may require training in more than one area. The professional development needs of all stakeholders (such as teachers, speech therapists and counsellors) can be determined and planned during transition team meetings. Training is then tailored to individual needs and offered in several areas, such as transition processes, inclusive education/teaching students with disabilities, AT and creating a positive, supportive culture.

> **Jérémy**
>
> Jérémy's transition team consisted of Jérémy, his parents, his primary school special education teacher and the school counsellors from both the primary school and the secondary school. The team met face to face four times throughout the school year (once each term). During these meetings, the team arranged for Jérémy and his family to attend several activities during the year at the secondary school so they would become more comfortable with the school. They attended a football game, a school play, a spaghetti dinner and a high school orientation night. The new school's special education teacher visited the primary school to observe Jérémy in class and speak to his teachers. He also had a chat with Jérémy to give him some information and answer questions. Jérémy attended his new school for a few half-days at the end of the year. During these visits, he shadowed a student who would be his peer mentor when school started the following year.
>
> The new school provided Jérémy and his family with a welcome package that contained the school's important contacts (with pictures), rules, policies and a map. The counsellor from Jérémy's old school kept in touch with the counsellor from the new school throughout the first term to ensure that Jérémy was adjusting well to his new environment. When Jérémy began having difficulties in his mathematics class, the team met and discussed providing him with a school–home note to assist Jérémy and his parents to monitor his behaviour in class and his assignments. This arrangement worked very well, and Jérémy was successful in that class. At the end of the first term the team met and decided that Jérémy was adjusting very well, and the responsibility for his academic and behavioural support would be completely transferred over to the new school.

Conclusion

Although education systems vary, several characteristics of transition are surprisingly similar (Chambers & Coffey, 2013), allowing a more global perspective on the transition from primary to secondary school. Differences between primary and secondary schools and their cultures can pose a challenge, especially when the secondary school is much larger, serving students from a wider geographic area. This means students form many new relationships, which may be difficult for some students with disabilities. Hanewald (2013) posits that this transition is a disruptive process, with many factors that can potentially have either positive or negative effects on the student's success. Some secondary schools may not encourage the inclusion of students with disabilities, as doing so may lower their reputation when high-stakes test scores are published (Forlin et al., 2013). While these and other issues can pose difficulties, well-planned and implemented transition programmes can successfully support students, families and school staff during the transition process.

It is helpful to look at the transition from primary to secondary school through the lens of Bronfenbrenner's Ecological Model (Bronfenbrenner, 1994). Milsom (2007) suggests examining the relationships between the microsystems before the transition, particularly between the primary and secondary teachers. The more the primary teacher knows about secondary school expectations, the more likely s/he can prepare students both socially and academically. Transitioning to a new microsystem that requires skills that the student already has will make the transition less challenging. Milsom further states that transition should be viewed as a process, not a one-off occurrence that happens at the end of the year.

When students feel included in the school community, their self-esteem is likely to be positively affected (Forlin et al., 2013). It is critical to implement good practice for this transition in order to ensure good outcomes for students with disabilities. Broadly this means several things. First, there needs to be a framework or policy for schools to follow so that effective processes are implemented. This should include strategically planning for the transition well ahead of time. Second, in line with Bronfenbrenner's Ecological Model (1994), collaboration and communication are needed between schools and families, with the student having a central role and a voice in the planning of his or her education and longer-term future.

6

TRANSITIONS TO AND FROM SPECIAL SETTINGS

Ajay

Ajay is a 12-year-old boy living in London. He was born in the west of the city shortly after his parents, Yadunath and Malati, emigrated from India. He has an older brother, Raj, who is 15 and a younger sister, Manshi, who is 10. Together, they live above their family-owned restaurant in Southall, a London borough popular with the south Asian community. The restaurant is popular and busy, so everyone pitches in to help daily. The family are Hindus and worship both in their home and at the local temple. Ajay attends the local school and is one of the top students in his year 7 class.

Ajay was hit by a car one afternoon while running an errand for Yadunath after school. The accident resulted in several injuries: a severely damaged left arm, a broken right wrist and ankle and a traumatic brain injury. He spent 10 days in a drug-induced coma, a total of 3 weeks in intensive care and then another 2 weeks in the hospital's neurological ward. He then spent 4 months in a rehabilitation centre. He suffered post-traumatic amnesia for 14 weeks, which left him unable to perform even the simplest daily routines. He was discharged from the rehabilitation centre with the understanding that, although he would return to the family home and school, he would continue to attend rehabilitation sessions at the centre as an outpatient.

Grace

Grace is a 16-year-old girl living in London with her father, Tim, and her 8-year-old brother, Liam. Grace's school contacted Tim with concerns about some changes in her behaviour. Tim himself had noticed strange behaviour and speech patterns from Grace during the past 3 months. These behaviours included Grace talking to herself, alternating between crying and laughing without any reason, having trouble in her relationship with her brother, and an increased level of hyperactivity. She also started speaking about death and her friends dying, unexpectedly and out of context. As time progressed, she demonstrated other behaviours at school and home, such as swearing frequently without any reason, talking to herself until late at night instead of sleeping, and being aggressive towards her belongings, her peers and Liam. She eventually became extremely withdrawn, not eating or dressing herself, and losing interest in her friends and hobbies.

One day at school Grace started talking to herself, quietly at first, but then she began to scream in the middle of class. She crawled under her desk and refused to move, yelling that everyone in the room was going to die. Tim was called to pick her up, and he took her to their family doctor. Grace became violent during the examination and was subsequently admitted to a mental healthcare centre for observation and evaluation. Grace spent 2 weeks at the centre, during which the psychologist diagnosed her as having early-onset schizophrenia. He determined that the best course of action would be for Grace to be treated with medication and outpatient therapy. Arrangements were made to discharge Grace from the centre and send her home.

Introduction

The typical educational transitions experienced by the majority of students include: home to school, primary school to secondary school and secondary school to post-school life (Sitlington et al., 2010). There are, however, some other important transitions experienced by students with special needs, particularly those who have medical or mental health needs. These include transitions in and out of hospitals, specialised mental healthcare settings and different special education settings. There is a paucity of literature describing some of these transitions. The majority of the literature about the transition to and from services or systems outside of education focuses on the transfer of care of students in and out of hospital and mental health settings (Stewart et al., 2010). The literature describing student transitions from special to general education settings (and vice versa) is more limited and mostly anecdotal (Inclusive Classrooms Project, 2013; Sharpe & Hawes, 2003). Although these unconventional transitions, such as the transition from a residential mental healthcare facility back to home, the community and school, are not often mentioned in the educational literature, they have the potential to have a substantial impact on the students experiencing them.

Transitions in and out of special settings may have a large effect on a student's ecological systems (Bronfenbrenner, 1994), as new settings, particularly those that are residential, introduce new environments, people, organisations, policies and laws to the student's systems. The macrosystem in particular may be highlighted at this time, especially when one looks at how care and support for the student are affected by the overarching values and beliefs about chronic illness, mental health issues and individuals with disabilities in society's views, theories, research and evidence-based practices. Students' microsystems and mesosystems may also evolve, as the role of primary caregiver may temporarily change due to hospitalisation and friends/peers become the other young people in the hospital or treatment centre.

Transition from hospital to home and school

The healthcare literature documents the importance of transition planning for children and young people who move in and out of hospitals. Students who have an ongoing medical condition or disease or who are medically fragile are said to have chronic illness. Shaw and McCabe (2008: p. 74) define chronic illness as: 'a medical condition of extended duration that creates impairment in adaptive behaviour and socially defined roles'. In the USA, some 18 per cent of all children are reported to have a chronic illness and 1.5 per cent of children are unable to attend school regularly because of illness (American Academy of Pediatrics Council on Children with Disabilities, 2005). Much of the literature in this area is centred on students who have experienced a traumatic brain injury. More than 60,000 young people are hospitalised each year because of this (Glang et al., 2012). Other chronic illnesses that may limit a child's educational participation include asthma, cancer, cystic fibrosis and diabetes.

Changes in the way in which care and support are given make transition planning all the more important. Funding cuts have caused many hospital stays to be shorter, and have resulted in fewer services for families and rehabilitative care, leaving parents to organise rehabilitative care themselves. This has caused a shift in the primary service provider from the hospital to the school setting. This puts the education system in the position of needing to organise and integrate student learning and support with medical care (Glang et al., 2012).

Schools need to consider that certain characteristics of a student's chronic illness may affect his/her ability to learn. Glang et al. (2012), for example, have described some of the characteristics of traumatic brain injury that may interfere with school success. These include problems with academic achievement, executive function and social/behavioural difficulties. The severity of this interference is mediated by the age of the student at injury, the severity of injury and the family environment.

Many students with chronic illness report that they experience difficulties in attention, memory, processing speed and cognitive deficits. A number of them have difficulty returning to school after their health improved, having fallen so far behind their peers academically. School refusal is common, and homebound instruction is required for some students to allow them to catch up (Shaw & McCabe, 2008). Their research, conducted in the USA, also suggests that lack of academic motivation may be another issue. Chronic illnesses such as cancer, asthma, cystic fibrosis, diabetes and epilepsy may cause fatigue, lethargy, irritability and depression.

Post-school outcomes differ by age group and medical condition, but Glang et al. (2012) provided evidence of poor post-high school outcomes for students with chronic illnesses across the board. They identified school-related contributors to poor outcomes as including: lack of teacher awareness, under-identification or misidentification of the problem, lack of hospital–school communication and poor parent–educator relationships.

Students who have a chronic illness and transition from a hospital setting back to home and school often do not receive the educational supports and services they need because they are not always identified as students eligible for special education provision (Dettmer et al., 2014). Students who participate in systematic transition planning from hospital to school, on the other hand, are more likely to be identified for and receive special education services (Glang et al., 2011). Shaw and McCabe (2008) determined that many students with chronic illnesses have social and emotional needs that are related to medical conditions, and these can affect their motivation and performance academically. Behaviour problems are also not uncommon, as students with chronic illness often struggle with depression, withdrawal, anger control, anxiety and social rejection. Shaw and McCabe (2008) argued, however, that this group of young people also possessed stronger coping skills and were less aggressive than their peers, more altruistic and more resilient.

Transition processes for chronically ill young people have garnered increasing attention recently, as children with chronic illness now have longer lifespans due to advances in medical care. Nearly 90 per cent of such children now live to adulthood and beyond. Betz and Redcay (2002) have explored some of the obstacles that young people with chronic illness encounter as they become adults. Some may experience psychological stress and mental health problems as a result of living with a chronic illness on a daily basis. Betz and Redcay (2002) concluded that the responsibility for barriers to success could be classified as systemic (related to the service systems themselves); provider (attitudes of doctors and educational providers); familial (low expectations and poor family choice making); or individual (the student herself might not be motivated to engage with education). They identified obstacles within each of these classifications and separated them into six categories: (1) healthcare; (2) employment; (3) education; (4) independent living; (5) social and recreational; and (6) general. They also outline a number of interventions to moderate these obstacles as part of the Creating Healthy Futures programme (see Table 6.1 for a summary).

Many of the challenges in moving from a hospital environment back into school can be ameliorated with collaboration among parents, healthcare staff and schools. The effects of chronic illness on school outcomes can be mitigated by linking students and their families to follow-up and ongoing services through well-designed and implemented hospital to school transition plans (Shaw & McCabe, 2008).

TABLE 6.1 Obstacles facing adolescents with chronic illnesses and potential solutions

	Obstacles	Solution
Healthcare	Lack of health insurance	Refer to public or private insurance
	Lack of adult healthcare provider	Refer to Internet resources, insurer or local free clinic or confer with case manager
	No healthcare input in IEP; school has no knowledge of healthcare needs	Educate student and parent about their rights regarding IEPs; teach them to communicate with school personnel and coordinate services
	Student is dependent upon others for health and self-care	Impress upon student and parent the importance of self-determination skills and learning to care for oneself
	Lack of follow-through by family; loss of contact with family	Evaluate plan's suitability for student/family; educate family as to the importance and health consequences of not following plans
	Healthcare provider has no knowledge of agencies for transition	Use resource directories, Internet, to put together a referral pamphlet that families can access
	Healthcare provider emphasises negative aspects of condition instead of student's abilities and strengths, leading to discouragement	Education for healthcare providers to operate from a strengths-based perspective
Employment	Lack of referrals to agencies	Make referrals to 'one-stops' in the community, rehabilitation centres, case manager of disability agency
	Fear of loss of disability payment	Educate student and family about employment incentive programmes
	Lack of accommodations at job sites	Educate employer and make suggestions for accommodations/modifications
	Student has no self-advocacy skills	Advocacy programs, self-advocacy skills training
	Mental health issues	Refer to counsellor or psychologist
	Lack of participation in transition activities due to absences from school	Plan accommodations to ensure student is not penalised for absences due to illness
	Lack of a mentor	Refer to programmes such as Big Brothers/Big Sisters; refer to condition-specific agencies which may have mentor programmes
	Lack of a career goal	Include career awareness and planning activities in IEP, including school-to-work programmes

Education	Low expectations of teachers, student, parents	Self-determination training; develop self-care responsibilities
	Low student motivation	Determine reasons; suggest meeting with school personnel; counselling; mental health services; peer support groups
	School testing not appropriate for student with that particular condition	IEP testing accommodations; health advocate to attend IEP meetings
	Lack of student participation in IEP	Educate student and parent about roles in IEP planning; have an advocate attend the meetings
	Student dropped out of school due to being overwhelmed by illness	School reintegration programmes, alternative route to diploma programmes, healthcare provider liaises with school
	Educators lack training in transition and in the student's condition	Educate teachers in IEP and transition planning, particularly on the rights of the student and family
	Lack of contact with school counsellor or transition specialist	Recommend that family make these contacts; have school initiate
	Absences due to multiple hospitalisations	Encourage healthcare professionals to communicate student's needs to educators; recommend school and family meet to formulate plan of care; health needs included in IEP
Independent living	Social isolation	Support groups; volunteer work, employment
	Lack of independent and community living skills	Independent living centre; community living skills training; community-based training; IEP and transition goals
	Lack of referral to an agency that can assist/lack of case management	Community-based agency; wraparound services; resource list
	Parental overprotection or underinvolvement	Family counselling; family support groups; independent living centre
	Dysfunctional family relationships	Counselling; identify stressors and supports
	Lack of transportation	Refer to paratransportation services; disability support services, public transport travel training
Social and recreational	Lack of friends/friendship skills	Refer to support groups and community agencies; join community groups; join disability peer groups; online peer support groups; social skills training; social skills IEP goals; counselling

(continued)

TABLE 6.1 *(continued)*

	Obstacles	Solution
	Mobility problems	Assistive technology services; referral to mobility specialist
	Poor self-image	Refer to counselling
	Lack of knowledge of community social and recreational resources	Educate student and family on available community, social and recreation resources.
	Language/communication barriers	Provide resources in other languages; use a translator; augmentative and alternative communication systems
General	Lack of consistent agency participation	Interagency team participation coordination, including education
	Difficulty in obtaining health records	Persistent coordinator to request records; have student or family ask for copies of records and maintain themselves

Transition from mental health settings to home and school

Students with mental healthcare needs also may experience multiple transitions from mental healthcare facilities to home and school. This is partially due to the fact that the average duration of hospital stays has decreased, requiring quick transitions back and forth (Clemens et al., 2011). A large number of young people with mental health problems spend time in residential treatment centres each year, and 30 per cent of these students in the USA have an individualised educational plan (IEP) when they are admitted, with more being referred for special education services after they are discharged (Simon & Savina, 2010).

Clemens et al. (2011) described some of the barriers to successful transition back to school by students with mental health needs. These include negative experiences when teachers are unwilling to make accommodations and adjustments, when there is a lack of family involvement, when there are unsatisfactory educational services, when re-entry plans are not followed through and when there are inconsistent or inflexible school policies. Students with mental health problems also may experience social isolation, as peers may not understand mental health issues or know how to help, and may be fearful as a result of this lack of understanding. The ongoing medical management of the student's mental health problems may cause inconsistent attendance due to doctor and hospital appointments, and the side effects of medication may lead to missing school, sleepiness or difficulty concentrating. Students with mental health problems may experience different challenges that are dependent upon whether or not the student also has a disability or unrelated medical condition (Clemens et al., 2011). In addition, young people with mental health needs are often especially susceptible to peer pressure and may display antisocial behaviour or try out illegal substances. Suicide attempts are also an occasional possibility (National Collaborative on Workforce and Disability (NCWD), 2009).

Much of the literature on transitions involving students with mental health needs is focused on the transition to adulthood, because young people with mental health needs often face unemployment, underemployment and discrimination when they enter the workforce (NCWD, 2009). As they enter adulthood, it is often challenging for them to find the services they need, including mental health treatment, employment and vocational rehabilitation, and housing. Members of this group have significantly lower rates of high school completion and post-secondary education compared to other individuals their age without serious mental health problems. These characteristics illustrate the importance of effective transition processes, particularly those that involve youth service professionals helping young people navigate uncoordinated service provision and connecting them to people and needed systems of support.

Evidence-based interventions for the transition from hospital to home and school

Hospital–school transition services are a strong determinant of whether students are identified as having a health impairment at school and receive any necessary support (Glang et al., 2012). One of the most effective interventions for students with chronic illness is the provision of coordinated hospital-to-school transition planning. Communication and collaboration between staff in both settings are key to successful transition (Betz & Redcay, 2002; Glang et al., 2011, 2012; Shaw & McCabe, 2008). Glang et al. (2012) suggested that, wherever possible, educators should take an active role in school re-entry planning, including school personnel observing the prospective student beforehand in the hospital setting, attending pre-discharge meetings and gathering information from the hospital before the student is discharged and re-enters school. Communication between hospitals and schools should begin early, ideally from the time the student is admitted to the hospital.

Glang et al. (2012) has outlined the School Transition Re-entry Programme (STEP), to facilitate hospital-to-school transition. The programme is fairly simple in its structure, and includes the following steps:

1. Hospital staff obtain permission from parents to release health information to school authorities and do so.
2. School authorities assign the case to a transition specialist (this may be a counsellor or special education teacher).
3. The transition specialist contacts the child's school and family to offer support and resources.

Students receiving this type of transition support are more likely to be identified as eligible for special education services. Glang et al. (2012: p. 6) claim, 'the STEP intervention appears to provide the essential link from hospital to school previously available only to students receiving rehabilitation services'.

More recently, Dettmer et al. (2014) stressed the need for professional development for teachers to assist them in providing appropriate support for students during transitions in and out of special settings. They suggest that this includes training on the best strategies to adopt for students with specific impairments or conditions. Training should include hands-on instruction in the natural setting, so that teachers have the opportunity to consult with experts and learn through modelling, rehearsal and feedback. Teachers and classroom assistants may also require training in administering treatments when a nurse or nursing assistant is not available (Shaw & McCabe, 2008).

Shaw and McCabe (2008) have outlined a series of possible supports that schools can provide for students with chronic illnesses. Many chronically ill young people will need support with attendance, especially if they are discharged and returned home before their treatment is finished. Flexible attendance, such as half-days, or a combination of homebound and partial school attendance, may help the student to stay caught up and involved. Technology can help with this, through the use of phone calls, online chats, emails and instant messaging. Home instruction may facilitate a good transition from hospital to school, as it allows a student one-to-one support in catching up. Differentiated instruction can help ensure that the student is reaching academic goals. In contexts where students only receive a small amount of home instruction, parents need to be very involved, and the use of email and Internet resources can assist with this.

Physical support, in the form of physiotherapy, special equipment or consultation with an occupational therapist, may be necessary. Some students may need quiet space or naps, reduced physical activities or study carrels to eliminate distractions. All health and medical accommodations need to be noted on the student's IEP if there is one in existence, so that all school personnel are aware of the student's needs and planned supports.

To foster communication and collaboration between school and home, teachers can try to make themselves available by email or phone in case the parents have questions. They can also call the student and the parents to remind them of deadlines, see how things are going and answer any questions. Social support from teachers, parents and close friends is very important, and online chat sessions with the entire class can make the student feel more involved (Shaw & McCabe, 2008). Support groups consisting of other children of the same age with the same condition can also be very valuable.

Lastly, Shaw and McCabe (2008) suggested that teachers developing a hospital-to-school transition plan develop collaborative relationships with healthcare system personnel and form transdisciplinary teams. They need to remember that the student is an individual and not a medical 'condition', and treat him or her accordingly. The transition team should regularly monitor the effectiveness of the transition plan in case there is a change in the student's condition. During the planning, implementation and evaluation of the plan, teachers can support parents and listen to the student, so that both students and their families have a voice and a choice. Betz and Redcay (2002) advised that specific approaches be used to overcome some of the typical barriers that can arise at this stage. See Table 6.1 for more detail.

Ajay

When Ajay was first admitted to the hospital, the hospital called the school authorities, which promptly assigned a transition specialist. The transition specialist contacted the hospital administration staff, who then obtained permission for information about Ajay's condition and progress to be shared between the hospital and the school. The transition specialist then liaised with the school counsellor, who let Ajay's teacher and classmates know that he was in the hospital. They sent cards and gifts, and a few of his closer friends visited him during his stay. As Ajay's health improved, he was able to keep in touch with everyone by contributing to the class blog on his iPad. Ajay's classmates were given information about traumatic brain injury so they would have a better understanding of his needs and behaviours.

Ajay's parents, Yadunath and Malati, communicated with both the hospital and the school to ensure that Ajay was getting the care and rehabilitation necessary for his recovery. They also participated in team meetings to facilitate a smooth transition back to home and school for Ajay. The transition team consisted of Ajay, his parents, his teachers, the school's special education teacher, his medical doctor, his therapist and a case worker. The team determined that Ajay would begin his transition back to school by attending school for half-days at first, as he tended to tire easily and lose concentration quickly. A teacher would visit him at home for an hour a day to help him catch up, as although he received instruction at the hospital and rehabilitation centre, this was mostly focused on reacquiring skills.

The school's special education teacher suggested a series of accommodations that Ajay's teachers could use to support him in the classroom. He also worked with Ajay's parents to design a series of accommodations, such as checklists, to remind Ajay what tasks needed to be done, that would allow him to return to helping out in the family restaurant. The careful planning, collaboration and cooperation of all stakeholders enabled a smooth transition back to school and home for Ajay. Although he required continuing support, he was able to return to his normal activities while he continued to convalesce.

Research-based interventions for the transition from mental health facilities to home and school

Simon and Savina (2010) have examined the role of the special educator in students' transitions from in-patient mental health settings to regular school settings. One of their major findings was that the amount and quality of communication between hospital and education professionals influenced the student's need to return to the hospital setting post-discharge. This communication is crucial in providing the support the student needs to return to school successfully. Effective communication addresses school staff members' knowledge and perceptions of, and attitudes towards, the disease or disorder. It is helpful to provide the school staff members with information about the disease/disorder and its influence on the student's psychological and academic well-being. Other facets of communication may include parent involvement and the expectations of the student.

Clemens et al. (2011) have also stressed the need for communication and collaboration, and added the requisite of an individualised re-entry (transition) plan that fully considers the student's and family's needs and preferences. They further suggest guidance for parents to support them in accessing school-based services such as special education, alongside education for teachers and the student's peers so that they can develop an understanding of the condition and its effects on academic performance and behaviour.

Because this particular transition includes a number of organisations and their representatives, it is truly a multisystemic transition, from the individual up to the chronosystem, when viewed through the lens of the Ecological Model (Bronfenbrenner, 1994). Although the focus at this point in time is mainly on the mesosystem due to all of the necessary collaboration, the exosystem comes into play in terms of laws, regulation and policy, both in the healthcare system and the education system. The strength of the macrosystem may play a large part in whether or not the student receives the support and evidence-based strategies necessary for successful transition, and how others view him or her throughout the process. The entire experience of residing in and receiving his or her education in alternative settings has an effect on the chronosystem, as all experiences contribute to who the individual is over time.

Although many stakeholders participate in the planning for the transition from mental health facility to home, school and the community, Simon and Savina (2010) claimed that special educators are uniquely qualified to assist, as they have both knowledge and experience working with students with mental health issues, and are used to transdisciplinary collaboration. In addition to the student and his/her family, stakeholders who may possibly participate in hospital-to-school transitions include: special and general education teachers, counsellors, psychotherapists, social workers, school psychologists, psychiatrists, medical doctors, case managers and nurses.

Successful transition back to the home requires that parents be invested in their child's recovery, follow through on aftercare and treatment and be involved with reintegration to school (Clemens et al., 2011). Stakeholders who are part of the mental healthcare system also have responsibilities to fulfil in order to support the student in transitioning effectively. These include planning for continuity of care, which can be accomplished by the therapist participating in the transition meeting, and procuring the release of medical information that facilitates mental health staff in speaking with school staff.

Schools have important responsibilities in this process, and ideally have a knowledgeable person acting as a re-entry coordinator, as many hospitalisations are short, and students may be forced to reintegrate too quickly (Clemens et al., 2011). To facilitate this transition, one person can be the main point of contact for the student, family and other stakeholders. He or she can then coordinate the sharing of information and intervention planning, not as the sole person responsible, but as a facilitator, developing a team plan to meet academic, social and emotional student needs.

Simon and Savina (2010) suggest that special education teachers may be ideally suited for this role. The results of their U.S. study indicated that most teachers had contact with parents before students re-entered the school setting, but less than half had contact with other professionals, which places most of the responsibility on the parents for providing information and assisting with the transition process. Teachers in their study felt that they needed to have more information about the disorder that the student was hospitalised for, more consultation with treatment centre personnel and the ability to obtain discharge summaries. Teacher self-efficacy in this area may be improved if pre-service teacher programmes train special education teachers to engage in this kind of collaborative transition planning.

Simon and Savina (2010) also found that the first 2 weeks were a critical period after the student's return to school. In order to make this time a success, educational and hospital personnel can work with parents to create a detailed plan to support students in having their needs met as they re-enter school, in order to lessen the probability that they will be rehospitalised. Overall, results of the study demonstrate that the key to successful re-entry into school and providing students with necessary support is close collaboration among medical, mental health and educational personnel.

The US NCWD (2009) developed the Guideposts for Success for Youth with Mental Health Needs. The Guideposts encourage the adoption of the previously mentioned strategies along with several other considerations. Because of the episodic nature of mental health disabilities, young people with mental health needs require flexible and stable educational environments that allow them to learn responsibilities, and to become engaged and empowered. The NCWD advocates comprehensive transition plans (including school-based behaviour plans) linked across systems, and with an avoidance of stigmatising language. These plans typically identify goals, objectives, strategies, supports and outcomes that address individual mental health needs in the context of education. Mental health problems may cause some students to become disengaged from their education, and schools can assist by providing them with academically challenging educational programmes and general education supports that engage and re-engage them in learning. The transition plan may also detail accommodations needed in both educational and workplace settings.

Strategies and supports specific to students with mental health needs suggested by the NCWD (2009) include providing them with meaningful opportunities to develop, monitor and self-direct their own treatment, recovery plans and services. The NCWD also advocates educational opportunities for young people with mental health problems to learn healthy behaviours regarding substance use and avoidance, suicide prevention and safe sexual practices. Another supportive practice is exposing the young people to factors of positive youth development, such as nutrition, exercise, recreation and spirituality. Additionally, the NCWD (2009) advocates supporting young people to gain an understanding of how disability disclosure can be used proactively, They also recommend supporting young people in understanding the dimensions of mental health treatment, including medication maintenance, outpatient and community-based services and supports.

Young people with mental health problems may benefit greatly from planning that helps them prepare for their futures. A focus on health can include several key areas, including a continuity of access to and an understanding of the requirements and procedures involved in obtaining mental health services and supports as an independent young adult. Some young people may benefit from social skills training and exposure to programmes that will help them learn to manage their disability, including strategies for addressing the negative stigma and discrimination associated with mental health needs, including cultural, racial, social and gender factors. Lastly, the importance of developing relationships and ties in the community cannot be overstated. Young people with mental health problems need opportunities to develop meaningful relationships with peers, mentors and role models with similar mental health needs, to have exposure to peer networks and adult consumers of mental health services with positive treatment and recovery outcomes, as well as the chance to give back and improve the lives of others, such as community service and civic engagement.

Grace

Just prior to Grace's discharge from the residential treatment facility, her school's special education teacher, Mrs Brownley, contacted the hospital staff, Grace and Tim. She explained that she would be facilitating Grace's reintegration to school. After meeting with each stakeholder separately, Mrs Brownley convened a team transition meeting. Grace's current needs were assessed, as were those of Tim and Liam. Grace was extremely hesitant to return to school, as she was embarrassed about her behaviour the last time she was in class. The team suggested that Mrs Brownley would speak to the students on Grace's behalf and explain a little about her condition. She also volunteered to liaise with Grace's teachers. Tim and Liam revealed that the family was taking advantage of the free family counselling provided by the centre, and learning how to support Grace as a family.

Grace would be assigned an adult mentor, her English teacher, Mrs Singh, with whom Grace had a trusting relationship. The team determined that there was a need for daily communication between the school and Tim for the first 2 weeks, after which it would take place on a weekly or as-needed basis. Grace's psychologist discussed warning signs for her teachers and father to look out for, and the importance of reporting any changes in Grace's behaviour, as several medications might need to be trialled until one was found that worked for her. Once Grace was attending school for a month, the team would reconvene to determine longer-term support.

Transitions in and out of special education settings

The call for the inclusion of individuals with disabilities, particularly in educational settings, has steadily gained momentum globally over the past three decades. It is interesting to note, however, that despite the success of these efforts, there is a dearth of literature on transitioning from special education to general education, and vice versa. The reality is that some students still require the support of a pull-out programme, or even a special school setting (Sharpe & Hawes, 2003). The goal of special education is most usually to provide the necessary supports and services to the student in the least restrictive environment possible. Due to the changing nature of support needs as students with disabilities progress through their educational careers, many undergo this type of transition several times throughout their schooling.

It would be a mistake to assume that students naturally adapt to a change in educational environments. Support during these transitions is crucial to ensure the success of the student in the new environment. Some students transition between general and special education settings daily. Careful liaison between general and special educators is integral to the success of students involved in such arrangements. Sharpe and Hawes (2003) advocate a training model that provides general and special education teachers and paraprofessionals with the collaborative planning and instructional skills necessary to meet the needs of students with disabilities. Their model, named Applied Collaboration, comprises an aggregate of collaborative and instructional strategies for general and special educators to apply as a team in the general education classroom. The model also contains a professional development component, whereby teams of general and special educators work together to identify mutual goals and use negotiation skills to address the needs of students with disabilities.

The authors describe a five-step process for effective cooperation and collaboration. The general and special education team:

1. communicate about the curriculum standards the student will encounter;
2. discuss the student's needs and available resources. Determine if modifications need to be made;
3. explore possible accommodations for the student and decide who will be responsible for implementing them;
4. decide who will monitor the accommodation. Monitor, adjust and provide formative feedback;
5. evaluate the student's progress using the established criteria.

The Inclusive Classrooms Project (2013), an online resource for teachers in New York City, also stressed the importance of collaboration between special and general educators. The Project focuses on transitions to new service delivery models, specifically out of specialised classes into inclusive classrooms. The project sought to engage with the likelihood that the new inclusive education setting will have different – usually higher – academic, social and behavioural expectations, a situation complicated by the fact that the student may have been stigmatised by an earlier segregated placement and internalised this or may have been working from a different or modified curriculum. Because of this, special and general educators may find it helpful to work together to consider both the socioemotional and academic needs of the student transitioning. The project was also based on the tenet that transitions should not happen overnight; conversations, time and support are crucial. Supports can then be set up in all of the environments that the child will participate in.

The Inclusive Classroom Project (2013) made several suggestions for successful transitions to new service delivery models. The first is the development of a school-wide plan that outlines how decisions are made when transitioning students from special education settings into the general education classroom. Secondly, school leaders can facilitate teacher collaboration and student success by making timetables more flexible to allow for co-teaching planning time and individual supports/related services. Longer transitions may be required to enable students to become familiar with, and feel successful in, the curriculum they will be using. Thirdly, teaching routines and skills ahead of the transition will increase the student's comfort level with the new environment and curriculum. Finally, the collaborative teacher team reviews the student's IEP to determine if different or additional services are needed to support the student in being successful in the new setting.

Conclusion

Transitions to and from special settings can be a stressful time for students and their families, and this stress is exacerbated by the presence of a disability, chronic illness or mental illness. Little is written from an educational standpoint on how best to facilitate these specialised transitions in order to provide students with optimal opportunities for success.

Both health and psychology have recognised the importance of these transitions for the continued success of young people and to maintain them in the least restrictive environment possible. The consensus is that successful transitions in and out of special settings are heavily dependent upon the quality of collaboration and cooperation among the various stakeholders. This aligns well with current evidence-based practices in regards to schooling transitions and also with Bronfenbrenner's Ecological Model (1994), through its focus on the student, the family and collaboration with health and education professionals, as well as the larger community.

First and foremost, the student should always be held at the centre of any transition planning and have a voice and a choice. The family as the microsystem is of the utmost importance, especially considering that transitions for students with disabilities, chronic illnesses or mental health needs often need to focus on support for all family members, as the home is where the student receives primary care. Students whose families are encouraged to be involved in their treatment and education traditionally experience more positive outcomes than those whose families are excluded (Glang et al., 2012). As described in Chapter 11, the other subsystems, from the mesosystem up to the chronosystem and their associated stakeholders, all need to be taken into account and included to the extent possible in transition planning, as a multisystem approach will likely be the most effective for the student and his/her family.

7
TRANSITIONS FROM JUVENILE JUSTICE SETTINGS BACK INTO THE COMMUNITY

Trevor

Trevor has just been released from a juvenile detention centre in the large city where he was born and raised. He is 16 years old, has a history in the social services system and made his first court appearance when he was 10 for running away from a foster home. Trevor has been detained in juvenile detention centres about ten times, ranging from 2 weeks to 4 months, for various things, including possession of stolen property and probation violations that came from drug use and running from foster homes. He has not spent longer than 5 months out of incarceration since his first arrest. Trevor has also been placed in group and foster homes after his mother declared he was not listening or following rules, and that he was at times too defiant for her to handle. She also has a history of mental health issues as well as substance abuse, and was not always available to care for him, due to being incarcerated or in treatment centres. In addition to defiance and rule breaking, Trevor has a history of alcohol and marijuana misuse. Each time Trevor was released from custody, he was either remanded to his mother's care or sent to a different foster home, if his mother was unavailable.

Education has also been an issue for Trevor. His history with the juvenile justice system and frequent change of living circumstances caused frequent changes in schools and substantial breaks in his schooling. These breaks, combined with his behavioural issues, have caused Trevor to underachieve academically. He has been labelled as a student in need of special education intermittently throughout his school career. On the occasions when he was labelled, it was as a student with a specific learning disability or an emotional/behavioural disorder. Trevor typically would not be enrolled in a school long enough for officials to locate his records from his previous school, so academic or behavioural interventions, if attempted, were sporadic and generic. Information was not shared well between schools and the juvenile detention centres either, so Trevor was not always identified as a student with a disability when he attended school while in the centres. Without any kind of documentation to alert them of Trevor's disabilities, his teachers and school officials generally reacted to his misbehaviour with punitive measures, such as suspensions and expulsions. These situations combined to leave Trevor feeling disengaged with education. Upon release, he would think, 'Another family, another school, big deal, who cares?' and proceed to break the terms of his probation by being truant, running away, using drugs or alcohol or committing some other crime. Eventually he would be caught, arrested and locked up again.

Introduction

Trevor's story is not unusual. Young people are far more likely to be incarcerated for committing a crime than adults, and, in Australia, comprise 8–21 per cent of all persons arrested (Richards, 2011). Young people with disabilities are overrepresented in the juvenile justice system, particularly those with emotional disturbance (47.4 per cent) and learning disabilities (38.6 per cent), the most highly represented disabilities in the juvenile justice system (Slaughter, 2010). Clark and Unruh (2010) detail the often dismal outcomes for this population of young people, including a 55 per cent recidivism rate in the USA. These poor outcomes are related to poor transitioning and can cost society over US$1 million per person, over the cost of a lifetime (Slaughter, 2010). Clark and Unruh (2010) also suggest that, for young people like Trevor, returning home is sometimes harder than being locked up. Schools, the community (especially employers), housing, healthcare and other treatment may not be welcoming or available. It is also difficult for many teenagers to have to return to the environment that fostered the situation and behaviours that put them there in the first place. Clark and Unruh state that one of the most effective ways to mitigate these factors, and foster positive outcomes for incarcerated youth is through transition planning. They further state that transition planning is the most critical part of the overall programme for incarcerated youth with disabilities. The need for coordinated transition planning and support is made apparent when one examines transitions in and out of the juvenile justice system through the lens of Bronfenbrenner's Ecological Model (1994).

When young people enter the juvenile justice system, all of their systems are likely to be affected. It is highly probable that an individual's emotional state, affect, self-determination skills, goals, needs and desires will change upon incarceration, as freedom and choice become severely limited. The student's microsystem changes as a result of not being able to choose whom to interact with, as well as when and how the interaction takes place. The mesosystem is changed too, as there are now more players in the game. In addition to the typical home–school dynamic, there are personnel from the juvenile justice and juvenile justice education personnel to add to the mix. How the student with disabilities is supported while incarcerated is dependent on the many different factions that now comprise his or her exosystem – the laws, policies, funding and philosophies of the geographic area and its justice system. The attitudes and beliefs of the people involved with the incarcerated young person in both his or her previous and new environment, along with society's view of the student (which may change due to the student's new status) make up the macrosystem, and may affect whether or not the student is afforded the support that he or she requires to be successful in the new environment. Lastly, the experiences that led to incarceration as well as the experience of living in a juvenile justice centre will affect who the individual ultimately becomes, or the chronosystem. All of these can be better understood by examining the typical experiences of young people with disabilities transitioning into and out of the juvenile justice system.

Assessment

When students with disabilities transition into and out of juvenile justice settings, several different kinds of assessment need to be undertaken at specific moments in the process. The first assessment usually happens on intake, and one of its purposes is to decide whether or not the young person in question has a disability. This is crucial to having the proper services provided in line with the student's individual needs, which is a practice strongly supported by research (Clark & Unruh, 2010; Drugs and Crime Prevention Committee (DCPC), 2009; Hall, 2000; Linhorst et al., 2002). Hayes (2006) developed the Hayes Ability Screening Index (HASI) for this purpose, and this measure is now widely used internationally. The HASI is not meant to determine whether or not a student has a disability, just whether further assessment should be undertaken.

Other assessments should take place shortly after the student enters the juvenile justice centre, as best practice dictates that a transition plan be developed immediately (Gagnon et al., 2008). This plan is ideally organised around student abilities, needs, interests and preferences, so the transition specialist, or whoever is creating the plan, must determine what these are (Slaughter, 2010). Lastly, in order to plan for reintegration and create an individualised instructional programme for the student while in the juvenile justice setting and beyond, an ecological assessment of the education, workplace, housing and community environments that the student will encounter upon release should be undertaken (Clark & Unruh, 2010).

Academic assessments are also needed to determine where the students are functioning educationally and what supports are necessary in order for them to participate fully in the classroom and meet their educational goals (Gagnon & Richards, 2008). A full educational assessment is particularly useful if the student's records were not forwarded to the school at the juvenile justice centre or correctional facility. The results of educational assessments provide educators with a starting point for instruction, help to determine if and what kind of supports may be necessary and assist with data-based decision making (Slaughter, 2010).

Students' vocational skills should be assessed in order to support them effectively in career exploration, development and in finding employment (Slaughter, 2010). Slaughter (2010) also recommends that student learning and progress towards the certification and/or licensing requirements of the student's chosen career should be assessed. The results of these vocational assessments can then be forwarded with the student to the next educational or vocational setting (Gagnon & Richards, 2008). Programmes such as the Vocational Competency Tracking System have been developed that assess students, assist in instructional planning, evaluate student mastery and provide accountability data (North Carolina Department of Public Instruction, Career and Technical Education (CTE) Division, 2008). These programmes also assist teachers in connecting educational and vocational skills and curricula.

Typical student needs for the transition from juvenile justice to school and/or employment

Students transitioning from juvenile justice settings back to the community have specific needs that need to be met in order to reintegrate successfully and avoid reoffending. These may include education, employment, assistance with finances, independent living skills, housing, medical, psychiatric, alcohol/substance abuse treatment, social and recreational activities, transportation, and individual and family counselling (Linhorst et al., 2002). Although not all students will need assistance with all of these, and each student's needs should be assessed and met on an individual basis, some characteristics of each of these are typical.

It is crucial to engage the student in the community immediately upon release (Clark & Unruh, 2010), and education is one way to accomplish this. One of the biggest challenges in this respect is the timely sharing of records between the juvenile justice and educational systems (Gagnon & Barber, 2010). Without records, some schools and colleges may delay the student's enrolment, which may be detrimental to the student's re-engagement with education (Mathur & Schoenfeld, 2010). Another consideration in the area of education is that it be flexible. Having a high school diploma or certificate is a large predictor of positive outcomes (Gagnon & Richards, 2008), so for students aged 15 years and older the focus is on attaining a diploma or equivalent. Students who have a history with disengagement with education may be more successful doing this in non-traditional ways (i.e. evening class or tests).

The risk of reoffending is lowered substantially when a student is still gainfully employed 6 months after release (Gagnon & Barber, 2010). This underscores the importance of finding dependable employment that is well aligned with the student's interests, abilities and preferences. Students with disabilities are likely to need assistance and support in this area, as many employers are opposed to hiring young people with a criminal record (Clark & Unruh, 2010). Close collaboration between the transition specialist, the student and potential employers may help to alleviate this. Another factor that supports continued employment for this population is having the necessary social skills to be successful in the workplace (Slaughter, 2010). The attainment of these skills is a need related to employment, and includes working with others, accepting criticism and following directions (Clark & Unruh, 2010; Gagnon & Richards, 2008; Slaughter, 2010).

Students with disabilities transitioning out of juvenile detention centres typically require support with independent living skills. This includes assistance with housing, finances, transportation and social/recreational activities (Linhorst et al., 2002). It is not unusual for young people to enter the justice system from another form of residential care, such as foster care. Upon release, a decision must be made as to where the young person will be housed. Regardless of where s/he is living, assistance with finances such as making and sticking to a budget, saving money and general banking may be necessary, as there is usually little opportunity to practise such skills while in detention. Decisions must also be made as to how the student will get to school and/or work. This will depend on the community into which s/he is reintegrating. Is there a dependable public transport system? Is car pooling or ride share an option? Perhaps the student requires support in obtaining a driving licence and a dependable vehicle. The student should be fully involved in making this important determination, as timeliness and a good attendance record are imperative for sustained employment. It is crucial to support the student in forming prosocial friendships and participating in productive activities in his or her leisure time, keeping busy and hopefully reducing the impulse to reoffend (Clark & Unruh, 2010).

Upon release, many students with disabilities will require support in accessing physical and mental health services (Simpson, 2013). Students like Trevor, in the case study above, may require both individual and family counselling services to ease the transition back into the community. A student's health has a direct impact on his or her well-being, as well as attendance and performance at school and/or work. Knowing how to access healthcare when necessary is an important independent living skill. Students who are on medication for various medical and mental health conditions need to have uninterrupted pharmacological treatment. Assisting families to support the student to access services also promotes successful transition (Garfinkel, 2010), and this can be accomplished through the coordination of wraparound services (Gagnon et al., 2008; Mathur & Schoenfeld, 2010).

Trevor

During his last intake at a juvenile justice centre, Trevor was assessed by a psychologist and it was determined that he had a learning as well as an emotional disability. His academic and vocational skills and preferences were also assessed at this time. The team, which consisted of Trevor, the juvenile justice centre's educational staff, his proposed mentor and future probation officer met to review the results of the assessments and design an individualised education plan (IEP) and an individual transition plan. His mother was invited to attend the meeting and be part of the team, but numerous attempts to reach her were unsuccessful.

The team determined that Trevor's academic goals needed to focus on literacy and functional skills. Trevor expressed interest in attending and finishing high school upon his release, then a vocational school to obtain his qualification to be an electrician. With this information, the team were able to align the IEP and the transition plan, so that Trevor's academic plan was focused on the skills he would need to have in order to reach his goals. The centre would also provide him with therapy for his emotional disability and substance abuse issues. Finally, Trevor would receive instruction in the area of independent living skills, as, due to his current family situation, the team decided that a supported independent living arrangement would be the best option for him upon release.

Evidence-based interventions

A clear set of evidence-based educational and transition processes and practices for young people with disabilities in juvenile justice facilities does not exist. As indicated earlier, educational outcomes have a positive effect on successful transition and recidivism (Gagnon et al., 2006); therefore it is important to include these. Mathur and Schoenfeld (2010) suggest that, in the absence of research-based practices for this specific population, practices that have been shown to be effective for students with emotional/behavioural disorder and learning disability would be a logical place to start, particularly in the areas of academics, behaviour and social/emotional interventions.

Transition practices that are commonly suggested throughout the literature for students with disabilities include: (1) transition planning that begins upon entry to the facility, and includes the writing of an IEP; (2) high levels of youth involvement in all stages of the process; (3) attention to the individual needs of the 'whole person or child'; (4) record sharing among stakeholders; (5) adequate funding to provide necessary staff to ensure dependable processes; (6) vocational training; (7) access to technology; (8) family involvement; (9) provision of wraparound services; (10) support post-release; (11) graduated release with access to off-facility work experiences; (12) social behavioural skills training; (13) processes that focus on community reintegration; and (14) well-designed tracking and monitoring systems. Each of these will be discussed in the context of the stages in which they typically occur.

Transition in the context of the juvenile justice system can be defined as, 'a coordinated set of activities for the youth, designed within an outcome-oriented process, which promotes successful movement from the community to a correctional programme setting, and from a correctional programme setting to post-incarceration activities' (Brock et al., 2008: p. 3). Transitioning in and out of the juvenile justice system is a complicated, challenging process for any young person, and having a disability may exacerbate these challenges (Clark & Unruh, 2010). There has been some research in the area of transitioning youth from juvenile justice facilities back into society (Brock et al., 2008; DCPC, 2009; Gagnon & Richards, 2008; Slaughter, 2010). Many of these studies have resulted in 'best practice guides'. There have been fewer studies focused specifically on young people with disabilities experiencing these transitions, but there is general agreement that recommendations for students without disabilities also apply to those with disabilities, with the addition of practices and strategies that are specific to the young person with disabilities (Clark & Unruh, 2010; Garfinkel, 2010).

Stakeholders

A range of interventions and programmes have been used to support students in transitioning into and out of the juvenile justice system, but many times these are not systematic and evidence-based (Sprague et al., 2013). In order for transition support to be effective, a comprehensive, coordinated, systematic approach should be taken. The first thing that must be accomplished in order to make this happen is to decide who the stakeholders are, so that a team can be built.

The first people to consider are the young person and his or her family. Family involvement may be difficult, as family members often do not have the skills or receive the necessary guidance to participate in the process and advocate for their children (Garfinkel, 2010). Professionals from the justice facility will also be part of the team. These may include individuals involved in the student's assessment, a transition specialist, education personnel, behaviour management staff, mental health professionals, medical staff and any administrative staff who are responsible for keeping and maintaining the student's records. Individuals from the school system that the student is transitioning out of/back into are also part of the team, both for the sake of continuity and to stay informed. These individuals could be regular or special education teachers, counsellors, principals or related service personnel. Lastly, members of the receiving community should be invited to be involved as early on as possible. These community members may include probation officers, vocational education service personnel, disability service personnel, family or individual counsellors, previous or future employers and individuals from welfare and other community agencies.

Transition stages

There is general agreement among researchers that the transition process in this context begins at the time of entry into the juvenile justice system, and does not end abruptly upon release (Brock et al., 2008; Clark & Unruh, 2010; DCPC, 2009; Gagnon & Richards, 2008; Garfinkel, 2010; Slaughter, 2010). This is due to the fact that, once the young person becomes involved in the system, there are a series of transitions that he or she typically experiences. Brock et al. (2008) divide the transition process into four stages: (1) entry into the justice system; (2) residence; (3) exit from incarceration; and (4) aftercare.

Entry into the justice system

Communication is the key to successful collaboration, especially when there are such a large number of stakeholders. Thus a transition plan is usually created immediately upon the young person entering the juvenile justice facility. Someone is selected to chair the transition team, usually a transition officer or specialist. The transition specialist's job is to coordinate communication among stakeholders, ensure the timely transfer of records, ensure the assessment of the student, write the transition plan, oversee the plan's implementation and coordinate any after release (wraparound – see Chapter 11) services.

The family has a vital role to play in tackling the student's problems and helping him or her build a 'non-offender identity', so high levels of family and youth involvement should begin early and be fostered throughout the transition process (McAra & McVie, 2010). Garfinkel (2010) advocates the early promotion of communication between families and police, since they are often the first point of contact into the juvenile justice for the young person. Efforts to foster communication with parents ideally include culturally and linguistically sensitive practices (Brock et al., 2008). Families may know little about the police and court process and may require guidance by court personnel who are trained to work with parents. Brock et al. (2008) also recommend that parent advocates be integrated into the juvenile justice system in order to encourage family-friendly sentencing options, such as graduated-release programmes.

Residence: education

Brock et al. (2008) recognise that students entering the juvenile justice system have varied needs, and that initial assessment will most likely indicate the need for one or more of the following types of instruction: (1) English language; (2) self-determination skills; (3) social skills; (4) vocational skills; and (5) intensive literacy. Mathur and Schoenfeld (2010) outline a number of ways in which instruction in each of these areas can be provided effectively. They begin by emphasising the importance of a positive classroom culture, characterised by positive teacher–student relationships and positive peer relationships. Such a culture should promote and foster diversity and one way of accomplishing this is by employing culturally responsive instruction, with a focus on literacy (Brock et al., 2008).

Students who are educated in an effective instructional environment are more likely to develop a personal sense of self-worth and the ability to manage their own emotions. Instruction in an effective instructional climate should, where possible, be individualised to meet the needs of each student. In addition to a focus on traditional academic matter, students with disabilities in juvenile justice settings will also benefit from instruction that highlights functional social, independent living and vocational skills, so they can learn to live independently, including finding and sustaining employment. Traditional academic instruction may be best focused on areas that assist students in earning their high school diploma or certificate and/or prepare them for further education.

There is a dearth of studies offering an evidence base for instructional practices in this setting, so researchers suggest that educators look toward evidence-based practices for students with emotional/behavioural disorders or learning disabilities, since their characteristics often match those of students in juvenile justice settings (Gagnon et al., 2006; Gagnon & Barber, 2010; Mathur & Schoenfeld, 2010). Response to Intervention (RtI) is a suggested framework for teaching and learning (Gagnon & Barber, 2010; Slaughter, 2010). It involves a three-tiered system of teaching and learning support based on individual student need. Mathur and Schoenfeld (2010) recommend several research-based instructional strategies that are well situated in the RtI model and are therefore a good starting point for students in juvenile justice settings. These include the use of: (1) step-by-step prompts; (2) sequencing; (3) drill and practice; (4) questioning; (5) individualised instruction; (6) breaking lessons into small segments; (7) small-group instruction; (8) the provision of opportunities for active responding; (9) peer tutoring; and (10) integrating technology.

Residence: behaviour

Gagnon and Richards (2008) stress the value of positive behaviour supports in addition to effective classroom instruction. Teachers in juvenile justice settings cite behaviour and discipline as two of the greatest barriers to teaching and learning (Houchins et al., 2009). The typical reactions to misbehaviour in juvenile justice settings are isolation and exclusion (Gagnon et al., 2008). Those reactions are often among the reasons that young people become disengaged with schools and education and are well cited as negative factors influencing the pipeline from schools to prison (Cumming et al., 2014). Researchers widely recommend that the use of school-wide positive behaviour support (SWPBS) can ameliorate some of these factors and is appropriate and effective for use in juvenile justice settings (Brock et al., 2008; Gagnon et al., 2008; Gagnon & Barber, 2010; Gagnon & Richards, 2008; Slaughter, 2010).

The foundation of SWPBS lies in positive behavioural interventions and support (PBIS), a three-tiered intervention model that provides a range of supports to students depending on their needs, and therefore aligns well with RtI (Figure 7.1) for this population in particular, as these students often demonstrate deficits both academically and with respect to behaviour (Read & Lampron, 2012). SWPBS concentrates on modifying the context to change behaviour and promoting and supporting desired behaviour through positive reinforcement rather than more negative forms of discipline (Horner & Sugai, 2000). The approach is centred around assessment, planning, careful implementation of interventions and data-based decision making (Gagnon et al., 2008).

Read and Lampron (2012) identify six fundamental components of SWPBS: (1) setting behavioural expectations agreed upon by all stakeholders; (2) direct instruction in interpersonal skills; (3) systematic positive reinforcement for meeting and exceeding performance criteria; (4) continuous data collection and analysis to monitor the effectiveness of interventions; (5) involvement of all stakeholders in the design of interventions; and (6) replacing reactive, punitive discipline with a proactive and more preventive philosophy. In line with these, some of the features/interventions of SWPBS that have been found to be effective in juvenile justice settings include data-based decision making, the use of token economies, social skills instruction and functional behavioural assessment (Timouth, n.d.).

Implementing SWPBS in a juvenile justice setting comes with challenges related to that particular context (Nelson et al., 2009). If the juvenile justice facility is offering the range of services recommended by research (education, counselling, vocational training, recreation, substance abuse rehabilitation, mental health services), then the number of stakeholders who have contact with the students is likely to be large and varied. Extra coordination may be required to gain consensus on both behavioural expectations and systematic interventions. Another challenge involves dealing with the punitive philosophy of many juvenile justice facilities and

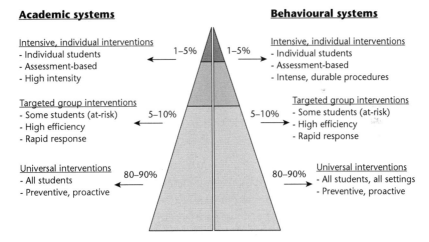

FIGURE 7.1 Response to Intervention (RtI)/positive behavioural interventions and support (PBIS) pyramid

the employees who work in them. Changing the views of staff in this regard may take some doing, and total buy-in is required for maximum effectiveness (Read & Lampron, 2012). Because many such facilities are residential settings, PBIS must be implemented consistently, 24 hours a day, 7 days a week. Although this can be a challenge, the challenge can also be a positive, as it lends itself to consistent implementation across all systems (Nelson et al., 2009). Box 7.1 provides some suggestions to promote implementation.

BOX 7.1 SUGGESTIONS TO PROMOTE IMPLEMENTATION (READ & LAMPRON, 2012)

1. Garner support at the legislative organisation level.
2. Conduct an assessment of the behaviour system and each facility in order to determine what is needed and what is available, and to set realistic goals.
3. If school-wide positive behaviour support is being implemented in feeder schools, link to them, as this will make transitions between the two settings more seamless for students.
4. Employ a data collection and data-based decision-making model.
5. Focus on the facility's current strengths by incorporating positive behaviour interventions and support into any existing treatment interventions that are compatible.

Sprague et al. (2013) conducted a study on PBIS in juvenile justice settings in the USA and found that juvenile justice staff surpassed their expectations in implementation fidelity, and that adapting PBIS for secure juvenile justice settings was beneficial to both the incarcerated youth and the facility staff members. As the global popularity of PBIS and SWPBS grows in mainstream schools, adopting this practice in alternative settings, including juvenile justice facilities, offers the chance to provide a consistent, proactive, positive alternative to zero-tolerance negative disciplinary approaches, which have been shown to exacerbate the problem (Sprague et al., 2013). The hope is that improving the conditions and quality of treatment in juvenile justice facilities will impact on students' long-term behaviour as they transition back into wider society. Transition processes and post-release support may be key in this respect (Sprague et al., 2013).

Exit from incarceration

Effective transition back to home, school and communities requires collaboration and shared accountability between different systems (familial, educational, correctional and community). Nellis and Hooks Wayman (2009) advocate certain practices during this stage. Pre-release planning is important, especially the transfer of records from the juvenile justice facility to the educational, vocational, medical and social services stakeholders in the community that the student will be returning to.

They also stress the importance of family involvement at this crucial juncture. It is likely that the student will have gone through some changes while residing in a juvenile justice facility, and acknowledging and adapting to these will require some adjustment on the part of the family. Families may require assistance and support during the student's reintegration, and this can take the form of family therapy, family-focused mental health treatment or organised family-integrated transition programmes (Garfinkel, 2010).

A graduated release is often a good strategy, as it gives the student, family and community stakeholders the opportunity to become acquainted with and accustomed to the changes brought on by this transition. Brock et al. (2008) suggest a pre-release visit to the educational setting in which the student is expected to enrol. They recommend the visit be conducted as a team, including the student, key family members and a juvenile justice representative, and take the form of an admission interview. This gives the young person the opportunity to become acquainted with the new environment and with the principal and teachers. At the same time, it is also appropriate for the school to explain the school's expectations and disciplinary procedures, as well as provide the family with the school handbook. This meeting can go a long way in mending fences and demonstrating growth and rehabilitation if the student is returning to a previously attended setting.

Setting up the appropriate wraparound service is crucial at this point (Slaughter, 2010). Wraparound services (discussed in greater detail in Chapter 11) are individualised services based on the student's strengths, challenges and needs (Brock et al., 2008). Individually tailored wraparound services may include: (1) mental healthcare; (2) financial assistance; (3) vocational/employment assistance; (4) education; (5) housing; (6) substance abuse treatment; (7) juvenile justice/probation; and (8) recreational opportunities. Ideally, they are planned and implemented with the student's new context in mind and should aim to be both comprehensive and coordinated. This can be done either by transition specialist, or by a wraparound coordinator who is employed by one of the systems involved, such as education. Brock et al. (2008) stress the importance of proper management of these services, particularly in role definition and responsibilities to provide planned and organised comprehensive services.

Aftercare

In order for reintegration to be successful, transition must not end when the young person leaves the juvenile justice facility. It is especially important for the transition plan to contain plans for follow-up counselling, particularly in the first few weeks after release to make sure that the student is supported (Brock et al., 2008). This can be done by a counsellor, a previously assigned mentor or a probation officer. Such support will help to address issues or difficulties the student might be experiencing early on. Clark and Unruh (2010) suggest instituting a formal data management system to track young people's progress for at least 6 months after release. The information tracked typically includes the school he or she is enrolled in, the employer and the hours worked. This ensures that the young person is receiving all necessary services, and identifies those who are not engaged and who may need more intensive intervention/involvement. The family may require continued support during this stage. Brock et al. (2008) suggest home visits to monitor how the student and the family are adjusting, as well as counselling, intervention services, training and parent support groups.

Formal structured aftercare programmes do exist. The Youth Justice Service Delivery Model (DCPC, 2009) is a programme in Victoria, Australia, which offers a coordinated, integrated and holistic model addressing social inclusion, economic inclusion, health and well-being, gender, developmental needs and the individual dreams and aspirations of each young person. The service focuses on building resilience, wellness and self-determination, giving young people the means to participate more fully in their community. Youth Justice Support Services' teams of caseworkers from across each agency provide individualised counselling and support in areas of student need. In the USA, the Intensive Aftercare Programme has similar goals and focuses on preparing the student for increased responsibility and participation in the community. It also works to provide the necessary support systems and facilitates collaboration among them.

Trevor

Trevor's release from the juvenile justice centre on this occasion was different from his previous experiences. Trevor's mother was now living at home, successfully participating in a substance abuse programme and accessing mental health services, so instead of Trevor just being released to his mother or a foster home and assigning him a probation officer, Trevor and his family worked together with a court-ordered family therapist, Dr Nagi, who began working with Trevor on a weekly basis just prior to his release. In addition to providing family therapy, she helped to coordinate Trevor's records being provided to his new school, as well as a school–home communication programme. Trevor has been clear of drugs and alcohol for a year, attending school on a regular basis and doing well with his studies. He plans to finish high school, then enrol in a vocational school to study to be an electrician.

Conclusion

The complexity of the transition from juvenile justice settings back into the community and its effects on the development of the young person concerned can best be summarised by viewing Trevor's story through the lens of the Ecological Model. Trevor's encounters with the juvenile justice system over the years have negatively affected every system in the model, as each system is interconnected, and all of Trevor's experiences ultimately affected who he was as an individual.

Lack of proper support over the years caused a vicious cycle of poor behaviour, educational issues and a lack of acceptance and understanding of Trevor by people in both his microsystem and mesosystem. Although the situation once seemed hopeless, the positive involvement of people in both Trevor's and his mother's mesosystems proved successful in interrupting this cycle. Dr Nagi intervened in Trevor's life during his last transition out of the juvenile justice centre by taking a holistic systems approach to supporting him in having many of his needs met. She began at the centre of the Ecological Model, with Trevor himself, and worked her way out through the microsystem and mesosystem, to establish a solid base of collaboration and support for Trevor's continued success.

The diversity of young offenders invalidates the effectiveness of 'one size fits all' transition programmes, particularly for students with disabilities. Although there is currently a lack of evidence with respect to specific programmes that have been shown to be effective, a range of practices and strategies developed in different but related contexts are underpinned by research to demonstrate their efficacy. Overall, it is an individualised, holistic, student-focused, family-involved, collaborative systems approach that is most likely to produce the desired result of transitioning a young person with disabilities from a juvenile justice setting back into the wider community.

8

TRANSITIONS FROM SCHOOL TO WORK

> **Mark**[1]
>
> Mark is a student of Italian background, attending a special unit at St Mary's High School in Sydney. He is 16 years old, and has Down syndrome, a moderate level of intellectual disabilities and autism. He lives with his parents and 8-year-old twin sisters. His family is from a lower socio-economic background. Mark's father is employed in a cafe and his mother stays at home. The family lives in a public housing complex with Mark's paternal grandparents, neither of whom work. Mark's mother is feeling overwhelmed and feels that her husband does not provide enough emotional support to her. She is concerned about Mark's future, as she feels that he is capable of many things and does not wish to see him staying at home, watching television and collecting a disability payment. She is teaching him to do household chores such as laundry, light cooking and washing up. She is also concerned about the challenging behaviours displayed by Mark, especially in relation to his future. Due to his very challenging behaviours, Mark's educational history includes attendance at two primary schools and two secondary schools. As Mark's mother is worried that history might repeat itself, she arranged a meeting with Mrs Green, Mark's classroom teacher, to discuss how her concerns might be addressed. They both agreed that Mark's individualised education plan (IEP)/individualised transition plan (ITP) meetings need to focus more on his future transition to post-school life.

Introduction

The situation that Mark and his family face is not a unique one. A number of students with disabilities and their families experience anxiety about 'what will life after school be like?', and to what extent formal education prepares young people for post-school life. While students with disabilities are a very diverse group, there are issues related to their transition from secondary schools to post-school life that many have in common. These include negative post-secondary outcomes, such as poor rates of high school graduation and low levels of post-secondary education (Noonan et al., 2013; Shogren & Plotner, 2012) and poor transition planning (Winn and Hay, 2009). It has also been highlighted by numerous researchers (e.g. Noonan et al., 2013; Shogren & Plotner, 2012) and in a number of reports (e.g. Organisation for Economic Co-operation and Development, 2010; World Health Organization, 2011) that people with disabilities are much less likely to be employed than their peers without disabilities.

The quality of the transition process and availability of supports and adequate services, as well as effective collaboration among all relevant stakeholders, is crucial for future success and the quality of life of students with disabilities (Wehman et al., 2014). Thus, focusing on improving transition processes brings considerable economic value on a national and international level. One issue that has been widely discussed is the question of how best to improve the secondary school curriculum to prepare all students better for post-school life. Traditionally many students with disabilities, especially those with intellectual disabilities and autism spectrum disorders, followed life skills curricula at secondary school level (Bouck, 2012). However, many Western countries have put forth great effort over the last two decades to make the curriculum accessible to all students, in ways that balance academic rigour with the development of social and work-related skills. Examples of these efforts include the Australian National Curriculum, and the Individuals with Disabilities Education Improvement Act (2004) in the USA.

Wehman et al. (2014: p. 36) call for using 'paid employment with intensive job coaching and support' as a part of high school curricula. Students' work-related experiences during their secondary school studies are among the strongest predictors of post-school employment outcomes (Carter et al., 2010; Wehman, 2013). Carter et al. (2010) argue that one of the factors influencing different post-school employment outcomes of students with disabilities may be the availability of career development and vocational experiences. Vocational experiences are incorporated in national educational systems worldwide and in diverse ways. For example, the vocational education and training (VET) in Australia are studies nationally recognised under the Australian Qualifications Framework, which offer three options to students: (1) a VET qualification without undertaking any work placement; (2) participation in a school-based apprentice or traineeship;

or (3) undertaking structured workplace learning as part of their study (Gemici & Curtis, 2012: p. 37).

While the importance of vocational experiences during high school studies has been established, schools continue to struggle to provide these kinds of experience for their students (Carter et al., 2009). There are a number of reasons for this, such as employers' reluctance to provide work experience for students with disabilities (Carter et al., 2009), or financial constraints resulting in limited resources (e.g. lack of staff to accompany students in their work placement). As one of the participants in a survey study of transitions for students with developmental disabilities in New South Wales, Australia, commented, there is 'not enough funding to hire staff to support more students attending work experience programmes outside of school' (SRS7 in Strnadová & Cumming, 2014: p. 10). Importantly, from an Ecological Model perspective (Bronfenbrenner, 1994), vocational experiences bring more complexity into a student's mesosystem, as it is a student's school, an employer and a student's family that interrelate in this matter. One of the solutions suggested by Carter et al. (2009), among others, is a development of strong linkages between high schools and the local businesses.

Transition to post-school life takes time. Preparation for adulthood evolves from an early age through primary, middle and high school (Carter et al., 2010). Transition-related activities and processes need to start as early as possible, and not be left until one or two terms prior to the transition point itself. Researchers in the transition field usually refer to the age of 14–16 years as an optimal time to begin transition processes (Neubert & Leconte, 2013) through transition assessment (TA), student-centred transition planning and by focusing on a student's development and monitoring his/her progress and changing needs, strengths and preferences. Quality transition processes are also characterised by family involvement in this process, as well as interagency collaboration. All these approaches require time and commitment from all parties involved.

Improving the quality of transition processes has been an ongoing focus of researchers and educational professionals for the last three decades; however there are still a number of issues that need to be resolved. Bullis (2013) highlights the changing nature of employment and education (e.g. online learning, linking through Internet and social media, use of technology in diverse work positions), which is too often not reflected in transition programmes and processes. He further states:

> If we return to the purpose of public education in general – to prepare the next generation of citizens to be successful – and acknowledge that the transition field should provide services to adolescents and young adults with disabilities, then it seems clear that schools and transition programmes should be designed to prepare students to engage in the emerging world economy. Speaking another language and having international travel experiences will not just be 'hip'; those experiences will be necessary for success in the new world order (p. 33).

There are clearly emerging challenges ahead for educators, communities and other relevant stakeholders in finding new ways to address these. These challenges can be found at – amongst others – the macrosystem level (Bronfenbrenner, 1994), as it is new theories of learning, as well as government policies and directions in the area of education that often drive the changes implemented on a school level. New directions to address these challenges are emerging, such as using mobile learning with students with disabilities to support their acquisition of transition-related skills, and to smoothen the transition process itself.

Assessment

Assessment is one of the building blocks of any successful transition process (Cobb & Alwell, 2009; Milsom, 2007; Test et al., 2009). Age-appropriate TA aims to identify measurable goals for post-school life, as well as the services necessary to support a student with disabilities in reaching these goals (Neubert & Leconte, 2013). Within this innovative practice, both chronological and developmental ages of a student are considered. The TA needs to address three areas: employment, independent living and education/training.

One crucial aspect of age-appropriate transition process is an ongoing assessment, which involves a student with disabilities, his or her family, teachers, relevant outside agencies and other personnel from outside school (such as job coach). A key element of conducting successful TA is gathering and integrating perspectives from multiple people who know the student well. Carter et al. (2014: p. 246) highlighted that TA is a broad endeavour, which allows multiple transition domains, contexts, time points and support systems to be addressed.

Once a student's strengths, needs, preferences and interests have been identified for the purpose of transition planning (usually at the age of 14–16 years), monitoring of the student's changing needs and preferences in relation to employment, independent living and community involvement takes place. Data on a student's progress are also collected and gradually evaluated. Furthermore, a student and family are instructed as to how they could use the TA's results in an IEP (Neubert & Leconte, 2013). Making the Match, a framework for TA and for facilitation of its processes, considers three dimensions that need to be addressed. The individual dimension includes methods to assess a student with disabilities, such as interviews, formal and informal assessments, curriculum-based assessments and behaviour observation techniques. The environmental dimension focuses on methods to assess the current and future environments (e.g. job analysis, vocational training assessment). The congruence dimension is about making the match between a student and his/her environment (for more information about TA, see Neubert & Leconte, 2013).

The importance of environment when examining the needs of students during the transition from school to employment cannot be understated. Students move across many environments, including school, home, community and employment, so all of these environments must be included when assessing transition needs and planning for the future. The stakeholders from these environments are ideally involved, as collaboration between these different microsystems is vital (Bronfenbrenner, 1994).

> **Mark**
>
> Mrs Green interviewed Mark's parents to gain more information on Mark's strengths, needs, preferences and interests. She also talked several times with Mark about his likes and dislikes. Mrs Green and Mark's parents independently completed the Transition Planning Inventory to gather information about his transition-related knowledge, behaviour and skills. Mrs Green used a behaviour observation given Mark's challenging behaviours in unstructured and unpredictable situations. After the assessment data were collected, the whole IEP/ITP team met to discuss the results in accordance with Mark's and his family's vision for his future.

Typical student needs for the transition from school to work

In order for students with disabilities to transition successfully from school to work, there are a number of skills that need to be focused upon. Besides academic skills relevant to the curriculum, it is essential to address life skills and employment skills. Life skills instructions commonly include purchasing skills, banking skills, cooking skills, food preparation skills, functional mathematics and reading skills, grocery shopping skills, home maintenance skills, leisure skills, safety skills, self-advocacy skills, self-determination skills and social skills (Test et al., 2009). While all of these skills are crucial for an individual's independent functioning in post-school life, self-determination skills hold a special place among them. Wehmeyer (1996: p. 24) defines self-determination as 'acting as the primary causal agent in one's life and making choices and decisions regarding one's quality of life free from undue influence or interference'. Self-determination skills develop during childhood and adolescence, in relation to taking more responsibility as individuals grow up (Wehman, 2013). While many students with disabilities learn these skills, some need support to acquire them. Providing students with a choice is one of many ways through which self-determination skills can be increased.

The employment skills that need to be targeted for many students with disabilities include completing a job application, job-specific employment skills, job-related social communication skills and self-management for employment skills (Test et al., 2009). There are a number of ways these skills can be developed, through vocational education training as well as by incorporating them into curricula-related activities.

Social skills are yet another skills area of vital importance. Alwell and Cobb (2009: p. 95) define these skills as 'behaviours that may be taught, learned and performed', and distinguish these skills from a broader concept of social competence. Students with disabilities who lack social skills are more likely to drop out of school, experience social isolation and to be less successful in employment and/ or further education (Alwell & Cobb, 2009). While social interaction comes to many students naturally, a number of students with disabilities (such as students with autism spectrum disorders, intellectual disabilities, emotional and behavioural disorders), but also students from low socio-economic backgrounds often struggle to engage in these interactions (Coles-Janess & Griffin, 2009). The majority of students without disabilities learn social norms and rules through their interactions with others, and thus their need for explicit instruction in this area is minimal. However a number of students with disabilities need to be taught this 'hidden curriculum' more explicitly. The hidden curriculum usually refers to 'rules or guidelines that are often not directly taught but assumed to be known' (Smith Myles et al., 2004: p. 5). Among these belong metaphors, body language and social situations. In order to develop social skills, ongoing assessment is essential. Coles-Janess and Griffin (2009) developed a questionnaire allowing for assessment of interpersonal skills, which teachers can easily use, together with their observations and functional behavioural assessment.

Evidence-based interventions

Test et al. (2009) conducted a review to identify secondary transition evidence-based practices (EBPs). The practices were categorised using the Taxonomy for Transition Programming (Kohler, 1996) into the following categories: student-focused planning, student development, interagency collaboration, family involvement and programme structures. The literature review resulted in 2 practices, for which there was strong evidence, 28 with moderate evidence and 2 with potential evidence. Most EBPs were from the category 'student development' (25/32), followed by 'student-focused planning' and 'programme structures' (both 3/32), 'family involvement' (1/32) and 'interagency collaboration' (0/32). According to Mazzotti et al. (2014: p. 7), 'as a result of the systematic review to date, 64 practices have been identified to support students in the area of secondary transition'. An overview of the secondary transition EBPs by skills taught is presented in Table 8.1. As highlighted by Mazzotti et al. (2014), identifying EBPs by skills taught aimed to 'provide secondary transition teachers with a practical method for incorporating EBPs into their teaching' (p. 7). When using secondary transition EBPs, teachers and other stakeholders need to remember that 'not enough EBPs have been identified to meet every skill need of every student a teacher encounters' (p. 9). This is why professional judgement, as well as continuing professional development, in the area of EBPs is crucial.

The following secondary transition EBPs are discussed within the Taxonomy for Transition Programming (Kohler, 1996), in relation to taught skills. The authors do

TABLE 8.1 Evidence-based practices organised by Kohler's taxonomy, and the skill taught (Mazzotti et al., 2014: p. 8)

Taxonomy category	Skill taught	Examples of instructional strategies
Student-focused planning	Student knowledge of transition planning	Whose future is it anyway?
	Student participation in the IEP meeting	Check and connect Technology Self-advocacy strategies
Student development	Academic skills	Mnemonics Peer-assisted instruction Self-management instruction Technology Visual displays
	Functional life skills	Forward or backward chaining Constant time delay Progressive time delay Self-monitoring instruction System of prompts
	Banking skills	CBI Constant time delay Simulations
	Community integration skills	CBI
	Food preparation and cooking skills	Technology Constant time delay Response prompting Video modelling System of prompts
	Grocery shopping skills	Computer-assisted instruction CBI Response prompting System of prompts
	Home maintenance skills	Response prompting Video modelling
	Laundry tasks	Response prompting
	Leisure skills	Response prompting Constant time delay
	Safety skills	CBI Progressive time delay System of prompts
	Counting money	One more than strategy
	Increased finance skills	Extension of career planning services after graduation
	Purchasing skills	CBI Progressive time delay Response prompting Simulations

		System of prompts
	Self-determination	Whose future is it anyway?
	Goal attainment	Self-determined learning model of instruction
	Social skills	Response prompting
		Self-management instruction
		Simulations
	Communication skills	CBI
		System of prompts
	Employment skills	CBI
		Response prompting
	Job specific skills	Computer-assisted instruction
		Constant time delay
		Self-management instruction
		System of prompts
	Completing a job application	Using mnemonics
Family involvement	Parent involvement in the transition process	Training modules
Programme structure	Student participation in the IEP meeting	Check and connect
	Banking skills	CBI
	Grocery shopping skills	CBI
	Community integration skills	CBI
	Purchasing skills	CBI
	Safety skills	CBI
	Communication skills	CBI
	Employment skills	CBI
	Increased finance skills	Extension of career planning services after graduation

Notes: IEP, individualised educational plan; CBI, community-based instruction.

not aim to provide an exhaustive analysis of every identified EBP, which is beyond the scope of this chapter. The aim is to describe a couple of EBPs addressing some of the transition-related skills taught per each taxonomy category, and discuss how these practices can be used in everyday life to allow for successful transition to work for students with disabilities.

Student-focused planning

Planning is a key aspect of any transition, especially when started as early as possible (Riches, 1996). It is fundamental, though, that the planning process is not carried out in a spirit of 'About us without us!' In other words, the active involvement of a student with disabilities in transition planning is essential (Bhaumik et al., 2011; Wagner et al., 2012). Student-focused planning falls under the umbrella of person-centred planning, which with time has become the prominent and preferred format of transition planning, as it proposes that post-schooling options need to be relevant to the student's needs, strengths and preferences (Kaehne & Beyer, 2009).

An important skill allowing a student with disabilities to partake actively in planning is student participation in the IEP/ITP meeting. There are several EBPs for developing students' participation in the IEP/ITP meeting, including self-advocacy strategies, the use of self-directed IEPs/ITPs (Mazzotti et al., 2014; Test et al., 2009), and curricula such as Whose future is it anyway? (Mazzotti et al., 2014). Self-advocacy strategy is an evidence-based motivation and self-determination strategy, which was developed for a purpose to prepare students with disabilities to participate in IEP/ITP meetings (National Secondary Transition Technical Assistance Center (NSTTAC) 1). It uses the acronym I PLAN (Flexer et al., 2013). The first letters of this acronym stand for individual steps within this strategy, which are as follows:

> I: Inventory – completed by students listing their strengths, weaknesses, learning needs, goals and choices to prepare them for their upcoming IEP conference.
>
> P: Provide your inventory – involves identifying appropriate time for individual to share information during the conference, speaking clearly and completely and referring to inventory as needed.
>
> L: Listen and respond – addresses being an active listener and responding to statements made by others in a positive manner.
>
> A: Ask questions – focuses on asking appropriate questions to gather needed information.
>
> N: Name your goals to communicate goals and ideas on actions to be taken (NSTTAC 1).

Self-directed IEP is an evidence-based programme consisting of 11 lessons aimed at teaching students with disabilities how to participate actively in their IEP/ITP meetings, and to chair them as much as possible (Flexer et al., 2013).

Whose future is it anyway? is a 'student-directed transition planning curriculum' (NSTTAC 2: p.1) aimed at supporting students to become involved in the IEP/ITP process. It has been implemented with students with diverse disabilities, ranging from attention-deficit hyperactivity disorder and learning disabilities to intellectual disabilities and autism spectrum disorders. The main areas of this curriculum include: (1) self and disability awareness; (2) decision making about transition-related outcomes; (3) identifying relevant community resources; (4) developing goals and objectives; (5) effective communication; and (6) becoming a team member, leader and self-advocate (NSTTAC 2: pp. 1–2).

An important part of transition planning is a focus on improving employment outcomes for students. Westbrook et al. (2012) have identified a number of key elements potentially leading to the successful employment of students with disabilities, many of which relate to transition planning. These include the need to identify the most appropriate work settings and placements and effective on-the-job supports, as well as the long-term support services for the employer and the employee that may need to be provided. In order to involve students with disabilities actively in these activities, and to make the transition-planning process truly student-centred, students need to have adequate knowledge about their post-schooling options and learn to make informed choices. In order to develop students' choice making and decision making, methods such as task analysis, picture books or computer-assisted instruction (CAI) are frequently used (Mazzotti et al., 2010).

An integral part of transition planning is to encourage students to develop a portfolio with examples of their best work, academic successes, teachers' and peers' comments and videos or audios (Kellems & Morningstar, 2010). These portfolios are not only an important part of IEP/ITP meetings, but can also be used by students to introduce themselves to their potential employers and relevant outside agencies. Such portfolios can take different forms – from a ring binder to a PowerPoint presentation. Using mobile devices for this purpose can be especially beneficial for students with more severe disabilities, whose verbal communication skills are typically limited.

Mark

Mark, Mark's parents, the school counsellor, the school transition specialist, the career advisor, Mrs Green and the learning support teacher held an IEP meeting to discuss Mark's post-school options. The guiding questions at the IEP/ITP meeting were: 'Where do you want to live after school, Mark? Where do you want to work? Where do you want to learn after school?' When discussing Mark's interests and wishes for future, it became apparent that Mark's passion for airplanes drives his vocation preferences. After discussing Mark's motivation to become a pilot, the career advisor suggested that, as the local airplanes community museum is supportive of employing people with disabilities, it might be suitable and potential employment for Mark. Mark liked the idea, and the IEP/ITP team identified the main employment tasks that need to be targeted: maintenance skills, and keeping the men's room clean. The development of skills necessary for these tasks was incorporated into Mark's IEP/ITP and the main goals, including designed responsibilities, relevant tasks and important resources, were identified. Positive behaviour supports already in place were revised to address Mark's challenging behaviours. Furthermore, the team agreed that vocational placement would be of a great benefit.

Student development

Skills that are of specific focus when preparing students with disabilities for transition to work are especially life skills, employment skills and social skills. There are a number of EBPs that can assist in supporting student development in these areas. Using CAI is an EBP which requires the use of computers or other associated technologies to teach a specific skill (NSTTAC 3). The main advantage of CAI in supporting students with disabilities in learning transition-related skills is the interactive nature of the technology, which allows for providing students with individually paced examples and feedback (NSTTAC 3). According to Mazzotti et al. (2010), the main advantages of CAI include promoting students' active engagement, and increasing their motivation and on-task behaviour.

Video modelling is a form of CAI that has steadily gained momentum as an EBP (NSTTAC 3). One of the advantages of video modelling is that it 'allows teaching skills by video recording someone performing the desired skill correctly in a controlled natural setting' (Kellems & Morningstar, 2012). Preliminary studies about using mobile devices (tablets, etc.) for video modelling have had promising results. Compared to computers, where a video camera, computer, editing software and a DVD player may be needed, mobile devices provide an 'all in one' platform, and therefore a more convenient and accessible platform for students with disabilities, their families, teachers and other relevant stakeholders (Cumming et al., 2013).

Mark

In order to develop vocational skills relevant to his envisioned employment in the local airplanes community museum, Mrs Green used video modelling to teach Mark sweeping with a manual sweeper, accompanied with a written task analysis.

Another area, which Mark's parents, Mrs Green, and to some extent Mark felt needed to be targeted, was the hidden curriculum. Following Mrs Green's recommendation, Mark started to use an iPad application for adolescents called Hidden Curriculum on the go! This application proved to be especially useful as it covers topics such as community, workplace or money matters, and it includes real-life examples with suggestions.

Programme structures

In order for any educational instruction to be effective, it needs to be related to real-life experiences (Kellems & Morningstar, 2010). Community-based instruction (CBI) is a commonly used EBP to teach students relevant skills in the community where they will be using these skills (Test et al., 2009). CBI programmes often focus on development of skills essential for engagement in the community, including employment skills. CBI was effectively used when teaching students with disabilities to cash a cheque, send a letter from a post office, or, for example, to operate a copy machine (NSTTAC 4).

> **Mark**
>
> The local airplane museum agreed to take Mark for an internship with three 12-week rotations. This was crucial for Mark, as such an arrangement allowed him to show his potential. The staff members were briefed about Mark's challenging behaviours, most commonly triggered by unexpected changes in his routines. Peter, one of the museum staff members, volunteered to become a key support person for Mark. He was briefed about Mark's strengths and needs, and met with Mark for a coffee to talk about his work placement. Mark's job coach gradually decreased his support and input, as Mark settled into his job well.

Family involvement

Active family involvement in the transition process is important for the successful transition of students with disabilities to post-school life. It is also one of the quality indicators of high-quality services provided to young people aged 18–21 years (Wehmeyer et al., 2006). As indicated by Gillan and Coughlan (2010), one of the identified barriers to a successful transition process in their Irish study was a lack of parent involvement in decision making and planning. Similarly, Davies and Beamish (2009), in an Australian study, concluded that parents indicated low levels of participation in the transition process, despite the results of research studies indicating that parents are essential stakeholders in this process. In order to be effectively involved, parents need to have information about available supports, as well as about post-schooling options for their child. There are existing transition brochures or tip sheets to provide families with explanations of what is involved in a complex transition process to post-school life, and how families and students can be involved in this process. However, a number of states lack national databases with information about available services and post-school options. Developing these should become a priority for educational systems worldwide.

Among EBPs focused on parent involvement in the transition process belong different training modules developed to provide parents with understanding of what is involved in the transition process, what supports are available to them, and how parents themselves can get actively involved. Another common practice is to organise transition-related information evenings for parents (ideally prior to their child's 16th birthday) or weekly/biweekly futures night (Kellems & Morningstar, 2010).

Teachers and other relevant stakeholders need to be aware of the impact the family's culture (Flexer et al., 2013) and socio-economic status (Atkins et al., 2007) have on transition outcomes. Family culture may influence whether a family relies more on informal resources of support (such as extended family, friends and neighbours) or rather on formal ones (service providers). As Bronfenbrenner (2005: p. 262) highlights, among all student's microsystems the family is 'the most humane, the most powerful, and by far the most economical system known for making and keeping human beings human'. Anything that happens in this microsystem thus has far-reaching effects on a child's development.

> **Mark**
>
> Mark's parents are from an Italian background. Relying on family members rather than reaching out to official authorities for support is something they have been used to for generations. Mark's mother is, however, aware that providing support to Mark during the transition process is above his family's capacity, and Mrs Green (Mark's classroom teacher) is aware of this delicate situation. She makes sure that Mark's parents have a leadership role in the IEP/ITP meetings. She encourages them to develop an agenda prior to every meeting. Mark's parents do so together with Mark. They found that preparing the agenda as well as their transition goals and thoughts about the ways these can be accomplished in PowerPoint works very well.

Interagency collaboration

Interagency collaboration can be crucial when it comes to securing students' post-school outcomes (Carter et al., 2009). Furthermore, its existence is one of the essential indicators of quality transition services (Noonan et al., 2013). There are a number of ways in which relationships with outside agencies can be established. Kellems and Morningstar (2010) recommend that schools hold a transition fair once a year, where all relevant outside agencies are invited.

Schools, and especially school transition specialists, may wish to address diverse areas in building the post-school linkages, such as employment, independent living, further education and community inclusion. Developing interagency transition teams is a critical component of a quality transition process (Flexer et al., 2013). An interagency transition team usually reviews a student's IEP/ITPs and other relevant information, and discusses a student's current work experience. The team may also revisit what services need to be approached outside of school, in order best to facilitate a student's transition to post-school life. Interagency transition teams can further promote important linkages between a student and relevant services, which can promote better continuity in services long term (Lee & Carter, 2012).

> **Mark**
>
> St Mary's High School had developed a number of linkages with outside agencies over the years, which is highly appreciated and further built on by Mark's IEP/ITP team. This team became an interagency transition team in its nature, as representatives of services relevant to Mark's post-school life joined the team. As developing Mark's self-determination and advocacy skills became one of the foci of Mark's IEP/ITP, Mr Grey from the People First Self Advocacy group was invited to join the team. Mr Grey is a young man with intellectual disabilities, who works for a local cafeteria. While sharing his experiences with employment and using self-advocacy skills there, he also highlighted the need for Mark to learn how to request reasonable work accommodations. Mark insisted these skills to be added to his IEP/ITP.

Conclusion

Transition to post-school life happens within a complex interaction of micro-, meso-, chrono- and macrosystems (Bronfenbrenner, 1994). During this transition, a student's microsystems (such as family, school, peers) are affected. The school environment is changing with incorporating transition-related activities, such as vocational education. The family environment is changing as well, with the increasing focus of the family members on 'what will happen after school?'. Becoming an adult means changes in family dynamics, often accompanied by tensions. A young person with a disability is often viewed as more vulnerable than his/her peers without such disabilities, which may make it difficult for parents to allow for their child's increasing independence.

Mesosystems, such as home–school collaboration or collaboration between school and the post-school setting, become more critical than ever in order to allow for a successful transition. Therefore the student's and the family's active involvement in this process, as well as interagency collaboration are essential. Students' IEP/ITP meetings provide a space for such collaboration. National and international transition-related policies are an integral part of a student's exosystem. States with legislatively mandated transitions and with mechanisms supporting successful transitions in place present environments in which a quality transition is more likely to occur.

Macrosystems can have a great influence on the smoothness of the transition itself. Societal attitudes prevailing in society, and specifically the prejudice of potential employers, can be a strong – although not the only – contributing factor to poor post-school outcomes, such as unemployment. While existing prejudice towards people with disabilities is being addressed in a number of countries by mandating antidiscriminatory legislation, grounded in international documents such as the United Nations Convention on the Rights of Persons with Disabilities

(United Nations, 2007), there is still much be done to change the prevailing negative and patronising attitudes in society. The level of success of this transition in particular greatly affects the student's chronosystem, as transitioning from school to work or further education followed by a career greatly shapes the developing persona of the student.

Note

1 Mark's case study was partially based on accounts and descriptions contained in the following journal articles: Carter et al. (2014); Flexer et al. (2013); Kellems and Morningstar (2012); Neubert and Leconte (2013); and Wehman (2013).

9
TRANSITIONS FROM SCHOOL TO FURTHER EDUCATION OR TRAINING

Jack and Lucy[1]

Jack and Lucy are siblings. They have an East Asian background, and live with their father, Mr Lee, in a family house in Toronto, Canada. Their father is a university professor in biology. Their mother died of cancer while they were in primary school. Grandparents from both their mother's and father's side greatly support Jack and Lucy, which allows their father to continue his demanding work.

Jack is a 19-year-old university student with high-functioning autism. He has a great passion for mathematics and physics, and is studying for a Bachelor's degree. His dream is to win a Nobel Prize for a ground-breaking discovery in the field of physics. His main areas of difficulty are sensory sensitivities and social relationships. His sister Lucy is a 17-year-old secondary school student with dyslexia and attention-deficit hyperactivity disorder (ADHD). Spelling is one of the areas where she struggles. This impacts on her memory – she focuses so much on spelling that she forgets what she wanted to write, which makes taking notes very difficult. She also has low self-esteem as a result of being bullied throughout her schooling. Her dream is to become a special education teacher in order to support students with disabilities.

Their father is worried about his children's future. Although Jack is already studying at university, his father is concerned about his vulnerability in social relationships and his ability to function independently. While Jack's IQ is 160

(continued)

(continued)

and he is far beyond his classmates, he needs support in decisions such as what to wear, or taking a shower frequently. Jack wants to find a girlfriend, and feels unhappy about not being successful in this area. Lucy is a determined student, who knows what she wants to do with her life.

Introduction

Globally, diverse terminology is used to describe different types of post-secondary settings. For the purpose of these chapters, the authors use the term *university* to describe university, community college and 4-year college settings, and *vocational school* to denote vocational schools, business schools, training centres and technical colleges.

Successful participation in post-secondary education carries with it a number of benefits, which include: increased prospects in the job market; better health and higher reported happiness; development of independence; higher self-esteem; richer social networks, such as friendships and professional relationships; and a broadened view of the world (Folk et al., 2012; Thoma et al., 2011). These benefits also include a widening range of people introduced into the young adult's microsystem and mesosystem (Bronfenbrenner, 1994). While a number of students with disabilities want to continue their studies beyond secondary school, their participation rate in post-secondary education has until recently been lower than that of the mainstream population (Karpur et al., 2014). Ideals of inclusive education, as well as policies on international and national levels, are undoubtedly contributing to the increasing number of students with disabilities in higher education. According to Barnard-Brak et al. (2010), the number of such students attending institutions of higher education increased three to four times in the last 25 years. As a result, students with diverse kinds of disabilities access post-secondary education: students with learning disabilities, emotional and behavioural disorders, sensory and speech/language impairments, physical disabilities and other health impairments (Flexer et al., 2013).

There are likely to be a number of supports available for students with disabilities once they sign in with the university/vocational school's disability support centre. The most common accommodations at the post-secondary level include specialised orientation programmes, reduced course load, course substitutions, extended time for completing a test or handing in an assignment and/or alternative forms of testing (i.e. an oral examination instead of written one), services offered by adjunct personnel (note takers, proof readers, interpreters) and availability of audio-recorded lectures (Flexer et al., 2013; Squelch, 2010). However there are still a number of individual, institutional and policy barriers that students with disabilities experience when accessing post-secondary education (U.S. Department of Education, 2010: see Table 9.1 for more details).

TABLE 9.1 Potential barriers to post-secondary education experienced by individuals with disabilities

Individual barriers	Institutional barriers	Policy barriers
Lacking a high school diploma	Instruction or curricula not suitable	Limits on financial aid available to part-time students
Lack of academic preparation	Lack of support and counselling services	Post-secondary funding formulas
Knowledge of helpful resources, and where to find information		Lack of alignment among various levels of education

Reproduced from U.S. Department of Education, Office of Vocational and Adult Education (2010).

Although opportunities to access post-secondary education have increased for students with disabilities in the last decade, students with intellectual disabilities are still the least likely to participate in post-secondary education (Griffin et al., 2010; Neubert et al., 2001). A recent literature review on the participation of students with intellectual disabilities in post-secondary education revealed that post-secondary education for this cohort of students has been defined mostly as programmes for students who are 18–21 years old and receive education in their local school (Thoma et al., 2011). This is cause for concern, as people with intellectual disabilities have the same right to access lifelong learning opportunities as people without disabilities. Probably the most common argument against students with intellectual disabilities attending college is that the academic content would have to be 'watered down' for these students (Hart et al., 2010).

However, inclusive education at the tertiary (or any) level is not about compromising the academic curriculum. There are a number of ways in which students with intellectual disabilities can participate in post-secondary education, with appropriate accommodations and/or modifications. Hart et al. (2010: p. 139) identified some of the non-traditional pathways that students with intellectual disabilities might take in colleges, such as 'audit courses, take credit and noncredit courses, . . . or participate in a totally separate curriculum designed for students with disabilities'. These authors also identify alternative pathways to accessing college for both students with autism spectrum disorders and intellectual disabilities: dual/concurrent enrolment for secondary school students, college-initiated programmes designed for this cohort of students and individual/family-initiated supports. Folk et al. (2012) described preliminary outcomes of the Dual Enrolment with Individualised Supports Project model, within which four students with intellectual disabilities enrolled in a college in the USA. The participating students appreciated this opportunity to learn in a new social environment. Other benefits of having an access to post-secondary education for students with intellectual disabilities include increased self-determination and self-esteem, reduced feeling of 'otherness', as well as the further development of academic, social and vocational skills (Hart et al., 2010).

Within the group of students with intellectual disabilities is a cohort of students who continue to be consistently marginalised when it comes to opportunities for mainstream post-secondary education – students with high support needs (Causton-Theoharis et al., 2009; Uditsky & Hughson, 2012). A lack of further education options and options for lifelong learning for this population of students may be viewed as a human rights issue.

Assessment

As discussed in Chapter 8, age-appropriate assessment prior to transition to post-secondary life is of crucial importance for students' future success. The ongoing aspect of transition assessment is critical, as it allows for the capturing of students' changing needs, strengths, interests and preferences (Neubert & Leconte, 2013). Age-appropriate transition assessment also leads to identifying relevant transition and other services, accommodations and supports. The transition assessment process usually focuses on students' academic and social skills, their self-determination skills and vocational skills. These may be measured both formally and informally. Among formal assessments used to determine skills crucial for post-secondary education belong academic achievement tests (Mazzotti et al., 2009), social skills assessments, adaptive skills checklists (e.g. the Vineland's Adaptive Behaviour Scales – Vineland-II) and learning styles inventories (Gill, 2007). Informal assessments, which are more subjective in nature, include observations, talking with students about their interests and preferences, or for example portfolio assessment (Mazzotti et al., 2009). Gill (2007) highlights the importance of students keeping a portfolio with the results of their career interest inventories and learning styles assessments, as these can be helpful when discussing necessary accommodations with university disability officers. Transition assessments are ideally completed at least once per year from the age of 14 onwards (Martin & Williams-Diehm, 2013; Neubert & Leconte, 2013).

The results of transition assessment inform the development of individualised education plan/individualised transition plan (IEP/ITP) goals, and ultimately assist students with disabilities to make informed choices about their future (Mazzotti et al., 2009). Post-secondary measurable and observable education goals may include university, technical college, vocational school or employment training programmes (Mazzotti et al., 2009). Following transition assessment, the IEP/ITP team needs to focus on developing annual goals, which ultimately lead on to post-secondary education goals. As highlighted by Mazzotti et al. (2009), annual IEP/ITP goals need to include reference to transitions services, and how students will access or complete these.

Planning for transition assessment includes the identification of a person (or persons) responsible for reviewing a student's records on academic performance, assessment results, development and changes in IEP annual goals. This is usually a role of the school's special educator or school counsellor, who is a member of the IEP/ITP team. Environmental analysis (i.e. assessment of a student's current and future settings) is important, yet is often part of the transition assessment that is omitted. Assessment of a student's current setting may include extracurricular activities or courses to prepare for university/vocational school, which can ultimately lead to achieving post-secondary education goals (Neubert & Leconte, 2013). Assessment of a student's future settings in relation to his/her post-secondary education goals likely covers exploring local vocational programmes, technical colleges and universities, including available disability-related supports. Environmental analyses can be conducted using a Community Analysis approach (Neubert & Leconte, 2013), where the IEP/ITP team uses the Internet and/or visiting programmes to analyse post-secondary education options, available supports at educational settings of interest (such as university/vocational school) and transport options.

Lucy

Lucy and her IEP/ITP team discussed Lucy's vision for the future in terms of educational and career plans. Lucy wants to be a special educator, and to focus on supporting students with disabilities. Her motivation is to use her own experiences to support and encourage other students with disabilities to achieve their dreams. Based on this, Lucy's post-secondary educational goal was developed: Upon graduation from secondary school, Lucy aspires to attend St Ives University, and complete the Bachelor's of Special Education programme, meeting the requirements to attain her Bachelor's degree. As mentioned above, however, Lucy struggles with spelling, which is an area that she – as a future teacher – needs to focus on. Therefore spelling became a focus area of Lucy's annual goals. In order to facilitate the attainment of this goal, the plan included provision for Lucy to participate in peer tutoring sessions. A peer tutor, Rebecca, was identified among Lucy's classmates and she was excited to take on this role. Lucy's English teacher trained Rebecca to develop lesson formats with clear goals, as well as instructing her in strategies she can use (such as modelling and giving constructive feedback). The peer tutoring sessions were planned to last 15 minutes per session, twice a week for a period of 3 weeks. Lucy's progress was evaluated after this period, and as the sessions were found to be beneficial for improving her spelling, with both Rebecca and Lucy enjoying this experience, Lucy continued in the peer tutoring sessions.

Typical student needs for the transition from school to further education or training

In order to transition successfully to post-secondary education, students with disabilities need to gain an understanding of their disabilities, including both strengths and areas of needed support. They also need to be aware of the accommodations and modifications available to them (Garner, 2008), and to develop self-awareness, especially in relation to preferred learning strategies and coping skills. While certain learning strategies may have worked for students with disabilities during their secondary school studies, given the more complex nature of post-secondary education, these strategies might not work any more.

It is important for students with disabilities to become self-advocates (Hewitt, 2011; Webb et al., 2008), which requires an understanding of personal strengths and weaknesses (Roberts, 2010). Developing self-awareness is a critical part of a transition process, as students need to understand their disability and how it impacts on their learning. Flexer et al. (2013) point out that this can be an uncomfortable topic for parents and teachers to address, who thus might tend to omit it with their children/students.

When students with disabilities enter post-secondary education, they are often required to self-identify their disabilities in order to receive appropriate services and supports. To do this, they may need to contact a college or university disability officer and provide that person with appropriate documentation, as well as request relevant accommodations (Dente & Parkinson Coles, 2012). This requires self-advocacy skills, which not all students with disabilities will have developed by this stage, particularly as it is usually parents who act as their advocates during their time in secondary school. This is why involving students in the decision-making process about issues related to them as soon and as often as possible is so crucial, yet it is so commonly ignored (Strnadová & Cumming, 2014).

Gill (2007) highlights that entering a post-secondary education institution (university/vocational school) brings a new set of responsibilities for a student, which s/he was not accustomed to in secondary school. For example, while a disability office may send a letter to tutors and lecturers asking for identified accommodations for a student, it is the student's responsibility to follow up on these with each of his or her instructors and advocate for their provision. Similarly, while making lecture handouts accessible for all students prior to lectures is now a common practice at universities in Western countries, it is not always the case (Hanafin et al., 2006; Hopkins, 2011; Moriña et al., 2014; Strnadová et al., under review). In situations when such a provision is not made, a student with disabilities needs to have the skills to approach a course instructor appropriately and ask for what is needed. To do so requires not only skills in self-advocacy, but also a degree of self-determination.

Self-determination

Wehmeyer (2004: p. 339) suggests that, given the different meanings attached to the term self-determination, there is a need 'to move from discourse with regard to global "self-determination" to consider how and why people become "self-determined"'. According to Wehmeyer (2004: p. 352), 'self-determined people are *causal agents* in their lives', meaning that 'they act "with authority" to make or cause something to happen in their lives'. Self-determination involves a complex set of skills, such as problem-solving skills, decision making, self-awareness and self-management. Self-awareness is very important, as students need to have an awareness of their disabilities and how these impact on their academic and social skills, in order to apply for suitable accommodations. They also need to develop compensatory strategies in order to use their strengths to compensate for their weaknesses (Gill, 2007).

There are a number of ways in which students' self-determination can be developed throughout the secondary school years. Among these is a student's active involvement in IEP/ITP meetings (Morningstar et al., 2010). However, in order to be actively involved in an IEP/ITP meeting, it is crucial for a student to understand the purpose of such a meeting, as well as his/her role within it. Some students with disabilities may need to be educated as to the purpose of an IEP/ITP team, and their role as a team member (including language and expected behaviour) (Martin et al., 2006). Students should ideally be taught to run the meeting, and help the team with establishing goals and objectives, based not only on assessment results, but also on their own preferences regarding learning strategies and styles (Martin et al., 2006). Such meetings provide a remarkable opportunity for a student to engage, interrelate and potentially influence his/her microsystems.

Academic preparation

One of many skills that students with and without disabilities need to acquire and/or further develop in post-secondary environments is time management. This may be particularly challenging for students with disabilities, for example, students with high-functioning autism (Hewitt, 2011; Roberts, 2010), dyslexia (Mortimore & Crozier, 2006) and ADHD (DuPaul et al., 2009). In their study of learning strategies and study approaches of university students with and without dyslexia in Canada, Kirby et al. (2008) concluded that students with dyslexia self-reported greater use of time management strategies than their counterparts without dyslexia. Time management was a major issue also for students with Asperger's syndrome in the UK, in a study conducted by Knott and Taylor (2014). Participating students highlighted that they needed support in order to avoid procrastination or not completing their assignments.

Given the overall environment in most post-secondary education institutions, which is often complex, one area that might be particularly demanding for students with executive functioning deficits (such as students with high-functioning autism) is problem solving (Hewitt, 2011). According to Grandin (2008), problem-solving instruction should consist of 'training the brain to be organized, break down tasks into step-by-step sequences, relate parts to the whole, stay on task, and experience a sense of personal accomplishment once the problem is solved'. These skills can be taught in several ways, and several problem-solving curricula are available commercially. Computer-assisted problem-solving instruction has been shown to be an effective way to foster this skill in children with autism from an early age (Bernard-Opitz et al., 2001).

Students with disabilities may also have problems with planning, note taking, study skills, memory strategies, organisation skills, self-monitoring and timetabling (Adreon & Durocher, 2007; Simmeborn Fleischer, 2012a, 2012b; Webb et al., 2008). Roberts (2010) points out that, while students with autism spectrum disorders have a need for routines and schedules, timetables at universities/vocational schools seem to be more bound to change than those at secondary schools. Therefore it is advisable to prepare these students for possible timetable changes at the secondary school level, by using role plays, for example. Orientation in a new environment can be another challenge, therefore becoming familiar with the campus before semester commences needs to be considered (Adreon & Durocher, 2007). Planning ahead and allowing for collaboration and relationship building before the student officially enters the new environment will contribute to the quality of the student's mesosystem (Bronfenbrenner, 1994).

Social skills

Some students with disabilities (for example, students with high-functioning autism, learning disabilities or emotional and behavioural disorders) are likely to have learned appropriate rules of social interaction within the secondary school environment. However these rules become different once students enter post-secondary education. Social skills can be crucial for the completion of some assignments, especially those that require group work. Furthermore, post-secondary education environments may have their own hidden curriculum, which can be very different than that found at secondary schools (Hewitt, 2011). Post-secondary students are often encouraged to engage with other students, which from the perspective of the Ecological Model (Bronfenbrenner, 1994) further expands students' microsystems and mesosystems. While this can contribute to strengthening the campus community as well as possibly developing professional relationships for the future (Dente & Parkinson Coles, 2012), it can also be a demanding task for students with social skills issues.

One possible approach to teaching post-secondary students with disabilities relevant academic and social skills is a first-year experience seminar. Wenzel and Rowley (2010), both based in the USA, developed a first-year experience course designed specifically for students with Asperger's syndrome, with a focus on the typical first-year experience and social skills instruction. The course included both in- and out-of-class experiences and included topics such as services available for students with disabilities, social life, personal boundaries, conversational skills, time management, registering for the course, balancing school with social activities, stress management, and giving and accepting criticism in a positive way. The course ran for 14 weeks (1 hour per week). The authors used social stories and paired video-based instruction with descriptions of social situations, including people's facial expressions and other non-verbal cues, to teach social skills.

> **Jack**
>
> Jack's transition to university was successful due to intensive collaboration between his IEP/ITP team and a university disability support centre. Jack and his father visited the university prior to enrolment and met Rachel, a disability support officer. Rachel explained the available accommodations, such as extra time and recording of lectures, which might be particularly useful for Jack. Rachel also suggested that, given Jack's passion for mathematics, he could join the university students' maths team. Jack became a close friend with one of the team members, Johnny, who also became his life skills coach. He continuously explained some of the social behaviour rules in the university environment to Jack. He also invited Jack to join him and his friends for their bike rides on the weekends.
>
> Jack commenced his university studies by enrolling on a first-year experience course for students with disabilities. This course was particularly useful in helping him to understand the subtle nuances of the hidden curriculum in the post-secondary environment. For example, learning about turn taking during tutorial discussions, using good listening skills and respecting others' opinions during these discussions helped him understand better what was going on in his courses. He learned how to ask for accommodations for his courses, as well as about the best places to eat and meet people on campus.

Evidence-based interventions

Evidence-based practices related to secondary transition for students with disabilities have been discussed in Chapter 8. These practices have relevance both for transitions to work, as well as transitions to post-secondary education. The authors use Test et al.'s (2009) categorisation of evidence-based practices in line with the Taxonomy for Transition Programming (Kohler, 1996), as discussed in Chapter 8. In this chapter, the categories of evidence-based practices follow the structure of Chapter 8, and further discuss these evidence-based practices in relation to post-secondary provision.

Student-focused planning

The IEP and ITP preferably include a wide range areas, such as present levels of academic performance, related services, community and vocational experiences, and objectives for post-secondary education, employment and independent living. Both secondary school students and their parents need to understand the various types of post-secondary education institutions that are available. They may need support and guidance in navigating the maze of available universities, vocational schools and further education centres (Shaw et al., 2009).

When deciding on the most suitable post-secondary educational setting, there are a number of issues that a student with disabilities, his/her family and a whole IEP/ITP team may need to take into consideration. These include the type and size of the educational setting and transport-related issues (Adreon & Durocher, 2007; VanBergeijk et al., 2008). Some students with disabilities may find a big campus and large classes overwhelming, and thus may prefer to attend a smaller college. On the other hand, larger universities/vocational schools may be better equipped to address students' diversity, for example, by having learning centres for students which focus on the remediation of academic skills (VanBergeijk et al., 2008). Hewitt (2011) recommends that secondary school students with disabilities and their families organise an on-site visit of the post-secondary institutions that were shortlisted.

Transport to a new educational setting is also important, as some students may not cope well with public transport or may not be able to drive. For example, many students with high-functioning autism have sensory sensitivities (such as sensitivity to noises or smells), which make it challenging for them to use public transport (Adreon & Durocher, 2007). Similarly, student living arrangements need to be considered – such as whether a student will stay in dormitory, rent an apartment or stay with his or her family. As VanBergeijk et al. (2008: p. 1363) point out, dormitories can present a 'less structured and more socially complex nature of communal living'. Students with high-functioning autism can struggle in dormitories due to their difficulties in sensory processing.

The development of a student's self-determination needs to be a significant part of IEP/ITP meetings. Because it is important for the student with disabilities to seek out available supports in post-secondary educational settings, and advocate for him/herself, these skills need to be learned prior to enrolment at the post-secondary institution. IEP/ITP members should not assume that self-determination and self-advocacy skills come naturally to students. It is important therefore that the transition plan and process include strategies for supporting the student's self-determination, for example, scaffolding: (1) how to take leadership during the IEP/ITP meetings; (2) how to articulate his/her needs; and (3) how to identify relevant accommodations and modifications. Examples of instructional programmes that can be used to support students with disabilities in active engagement and leadership in transition planning include Whose Future Is It Anyway?, Take Charge for the Future, Student-Led IEPs: A Guide for Student Involvement, and Student-Directed Transition Planning (Martin & Williams-Diehm, 2013). Students with disabilities also need to have the opportunity to try out a variety of possible accommodations in the secondary school environment, in order to find out what works best for them (Shaw et al., 2009). It is important for the IEP/ITP team to discuss in advance possible barriers to accessing these accommodations at post-secondary education level. These may include issues related to a student him/herself (such as feeling of embarrassment, lack of awareness, failure to advocate), to a teaching staff (lack of awareness and knowledge) or to a system-level problem such as the unavailability of certain accommodations locally (Bolt et al., 2011). The IEP/ITP team can use these discussions to plan in advance how such barriers might be overcome.

> **Jack**
>
> One of the major focus areas of Jack's IEP/ITP team was his wish to live independently. While Jack appreciates his father's support, he wants to live as other peers of his age, who move out of their parents' homes. Jack has always wanted to have friends; however his efforts have not been successful so far. He hoped that moving to a dormitory would assist him to build new friendships. Prior to enrolment, members of Jack's IEP/ITP team discussed the pros and cons of his wish with him. While the pros were obvious to Jack, he did not consider the cons brought up by the team, such as the possibility that living in a dormitory would challenge his sensory processing issues. Jack and his father visited the university's disability support office and asked the disability officer for advice in regard to accommodations. In the end Jack decided to stay in the dormitory, and based on his needs, the planned accommodation was that he stayed in a single room in the quietest part of campus, which would help minimise his sensory sensitivities.

Student development

Skills that are critical when preparing students with disabilities for transition to post-secondary education include academic, social and vocational skills, as well as self-awareness, self-determination and self-advocacy skills. Some of the evidence-based practices identified in Chapter 8 (such as computer-assisted instructions and video modelling) can be used to develop these skills.

Another useful practice for skills development and for supporting students with disabilities during the transition process is mentoring, though evidence-based support for the efficacy of this practice is still needed. Brown et al. (2010: p. 100) define mentoring as 'a dynamic, reciprocal, long-term formal or informal relationship that focuses on personal and/or professional development'. According to these authors, a mentor acts as 'a sounding board and guide', offers perspectives and resources and asks thought-provoking questions (p. 100). There are different types of mentoring, such as face-to-face, group, community-based, electronic and peer mentoring, which are all usually part of a larger system of services (Brown et al., 2010). One possible approach to mentoring can be involving successful people with disabilities to share their experiences with students undergoing this transition. For example, Bell (2012) designed a mentoring programme for young people with blindness, which included participation by adults with blindness who had been successful in their life both academically and career-wise, and with secondary school students with blindness. The results of the study conducted in the USA indicated that students increased their career decision-making efficiency and positive hopes for life after school. As mentioned earlier, mentoring can be instrumental for students' skills development. Hart et al. (2010) suggested that mentors for students with autism spectrum disorders or intellectual disabilities can role-model appropriate social behaviour in the university/vocational school environment.

Incorporating the use of appropriate technology during the transition process is another way in which to assist students' development in diverse areas (such as development of academic, social and vocational skills). The IEP/ITP team needs to explore the post-secondary setting's technology expectations for students (Shaw et al., 2009). For example, university students commonly pursue their courses in virtual learning environments such as Moodle or Blackboard, and are expected to have the skills and knowledge to navigate these quickly and efficiently. They are also required to be able to use the Internet to search for relevant information. These areas need to become a focus in preparing students for transition to post-secondary education.

Assistive technology can be a critical support to further developing the skills of students with disabilities. When determining whether the use of assistive technology would be beneficial for a particular student, there are a number of issues that need to be considered, such as the student's knowledge of how to use a particular technology and the availability of an IT person who can assist the student with any potential assistive technology-relevant problems in the post-secondary education setting (Roberts, 2010). While the use of assistive technology has traditionally been accepted as a support for students with disabilities (Ayres & Langone, 2008), it is mobile technology – accepted at an even more rapid pace – that deserves special attention. Due to its portability and availability to be used across diverse environments, mobile technology in the form of tablets and smart phones presents a useful tool to be used by post-secondary students with disabilities. These kinds of technology have the potential to be used by students with disabilities to learn academic, social and communication skills (Cumming et al., under review).

Jack

Mobile technology has been extremely useful in Jack's working and limited social life. Like many other persons with high-functioning autism, Jack finds personal interaction with other people overwhelming. Thus he prefers the use of emails and short message services (SMS) as a way to communicate and socially engage with people, as, in his own words, 'it is an act of social interaction, where I do not have to engage in preliminary social niceties or chitchat before and after coming straight to the point of the communication itself'. Jack uses his iPad to access books and academic journals and to be organised. He uses applications such as Reminders and MyProject to keep him on track with tasks and activities. iCalendar assists him with being on time for appointments.

Family involvement

As discussed in Chapter 8, it is essential that a student's family is involved in a process of transition to post-secondary education. For this to happen, a good-quality home–school collaboration needs to be a focus of all parties. There may be several barriers to parents' involvement in IEP/ITP meetings and in transition planning in general. These include transport-related issues, unsuitable meeting time and childcare conflicts, but also language barriers or the overuse of professional jargon during the IEP/ITP meetings, which can be offputting for parents (Flexer et al., 2013). Furthermore, parents are often not informed about students' transition plan (Martinez et al., 2012), and may lack awareness about the post-secondary education options available for their children (Strnadová & Cumming, 2014). Schools need to be aware of these issues and barriers, and take proactive steps to prevent difficulties arising. Information materials detailing existing post-secondary options and relevant services need to be available in multiple formats (Martinez et al., 2012). For example, it is important for schools to have information available in plain English, which is more accessible for parents with disabilities or parents coming from non-English-speaking countries). The transitions to post-secondary education settings and to post-secondary life in general can be overwhelming for some parents. Providing them with an explanation of the whole process (possibly using schemes/charts) while avoiding the use of professional jargon can be a useful strategy to adopt.

Family involvement in post-secondary education is usually not expected (Dente & Parkinson Coles, 2012). Students with disabilities in colleges and universities are usually treated as independent adults and their parents need to obtain permission from them in order to intervene in any way (Hewitt, 2011). According to Hewitt (2011: p. 278) 'the difficulty of achieving such major change while being away from home in a novel environment is at the heart of the college transition'. Nevertheless, the relationships that students with disabilities have with their families can range from independent to semidependent and dependent, and need to be considered by disability support services. In other words, while a student's family usually continues to be an important microsystem, it is that period of a student's life when this role becomes less prominent, which is also reflected in some of the student's mesosystems.

Interagency collaboration

The IEP/ITP team needs to involve not only a student with disabilities and his/her family and relevant school staff members (classroom teacher, school counsellor), but also representatives from other relevant agencies, whose support may benefit the student in his/her post-secondary life (Roberts, 2010). The key elements of successful interagency collaboration are: (1) forms of collaboration that are systematic and evolve over time; (2) availability of training opportunities across agencies; (3) the interagency transition team meets regularly (ideally on a monthly basis);

and (4) the interagency transition team has made team building an integral part of their operation (Noonan et al., 2012). Collaborative strategies used by members of a state-level transition team in Noonan et al.'s study (2012) included site visits at vocational training centres, technical schools or a school store run by students with disabilities in the USA, all of which were found to be eye opening for the team members. Other key strategies identified during the focus groups were joint planning, joint training and sharing information.

The IEP/ITP team may need to consider to what extent a post-secondary educational institution is supportive of students with different needs and abilities. One way to do this is to seek advance information about the disability support centre at the post-school educational setting by examining their website and/or scheduling a meeting about how many students with disabilities the centre currently supports (VanBergeijk et al., 2008), the types of support available (Hewitt, 2011) and the percentage of students with disabilities who successfully graduate. Another issue that the IEP/ITP team may need to be mindful of is that only a limited percentage of students disclose their disabilities at post-secondary level. Non-disclosure is a right of any student; however, students also need to understand the consequences of such decision (e.g. the disability support office cannot provide students with services and support unless the student asks for assistance). Some of the questions that may be asked by the IEP/ITP team are discussed in Table 9.2. Inviting a representative from the disability support unit from a preferred post-secondary educational institution to join an IEP/ITP meeting could be beneficial to future student success.

TABLE 9.2 Questions about the teaching approaches used by a preferred post-secondary educational setting

Question to ask	Ways to find out	What to look for
Does the educational institution have a disability support centre?	Check university/college website	Services provided by the disability support centre, number of students using these services, student feedback on services provided
Are there supports in place if a student needs to develop his or her study skills further?	Search university/college website, and look to see what a student learning centre provides	Services provided by a student learning centre (tutorials, one-to-one sessions, etc.)
Do course convenors in a study programme considered by the student use the principles of Universal Design for Learning in their classes?	See course outlines on the university/vocational school website	Diverse means of representation, expression and engagement used in teaching modalities and/or assignments

Conclusion

The transition to post-secondary education is a complex process which needs to start as early as possible, and which needs to be well planned and thought through within a well-rounded interagency IEP/ITP team. The difference between secondary and post-secondary education settings can be overwhelming if a student with disabilities is not prepared. Self-determination and self-advocacy skills have an important role to play in students' success in post-secondary education settings. Therefore members of the student's IEP/ITP team need to ensure that the student is provided with enough opportunities to practise these skills across diverse environments.

The successful transition to a post-school educational environment, like other transitions, is largely dependent on successful interactions among the student, family, school and systems. These are represented by the nested systems represented by Bronfenbrenner's (1989) Ecological Model. The main purpose behind post-school educational transition planning is to foster successful relationships and collaborations across these different domains. To do this, it is important that all aspects of the process, from assessment to planning to implementation, are carried out with fidelity. This will ensure that the demands of the new environment and expectations of the educators involved are identified, and appropriate preparation and support are provided to the student.

Note

1 Jack's and Lucy's case study was partially based on the following journal articles: Mazzotti et al. (2009); Mitchell (2014); Strnadová et al. (2014a); VanBergeijk et al. (2008); and Webb et al. (2008).

10
TRANSITION TO RETIREMENT

Rose[1]

Rose is a 60-year-old woman with intellectual disabilities. She lives with her 79-year-old mother in a small house in Melbourne, Australia. She has been working in a textile division of Newland Industries, a sheltered employment provider, for the last 15 years. She enjoys her work and she has made many friends there, with both her co-workers and support staff members. In the last 2 years however her arthritis has worsened, and she is in lot of pain. She gets tired more easily, and her beloved work is more and more taxing. Rose is determined to keep on working in spite of her health issues. Her elderly mother is worried about Rose and she has had a number of conversations with her about possible retirement. Rose is not happy about the prospect of not working any more, as she cannot imagine what her life would be like without her work.

Rose's mother has also talked to a member of support staff at Newland Industries, Michael, about her concerns regarding Rose's health. Michael values Rose as one of the most dedicated and dependable employees. He agreed that Rose is getting tired more easily lately, and that it takes her longer to do her usual work. He told Rose's mother that he has already talked to Rose about possibly changing to part-time employment. However Rose reacted anxiously, worried that she is not wanted at Newland Industries any more.

Introduction

Retirement has become a common experience for an increasing number of people in industrialised countries, due to increases in life expectancy (Fouquereau et al., 2005). People are also experiencing retirement for an increasing amount of time (Pinquart & Schindler, 2007). The transition to retirement is one of the most significant and demanding life transitions for many people. The shift from being valued as an employee or even being 'an expert in their field of work, to beginner retirees' is demanding for older adults with or without disabilities (Wilson et al., 2013b: p. 2). This shift, while predictable, often happens in a relatively short time and it can radically affect an individual's life, given the changes in his/her daily routines, income, social roles and possibly social networks (Pinquart & Schindler, 2007).

In this chapter, we explore similarities and differences experienced by people with and without disabilities during the transition to retirement. While transition planning and diverse forms of support during transition to retirement benefit any older worker with disabilities, people with developmental disabilities such as intellectual disabilities and autism spectrum disorders may need extra support in this process. Most research in the field of disability studies has been conducted with a focus on this population, using diverse terminology, such as intellectual, developmental or lifelong disabilities. This chapter therefore focuses on the transition to retirement for people with lifelong disabilities (mainly intellectual disabilities), and contains suggestions for supporting members of this population during this transition.

There are diverse factors influencing individuals' coping with retirement and general satisfaction with life. Fouquereau et al. (2005) recognise four key sets of factors: (1) sociodemographic factors (age, gender, marital status, previous occupational status); (2) individual characteristics (personality, mental and physical health, acceptance of a retiree role); (3) the way in which working life ended (reasons for retirement, whether the retirement was voluntary or involuntary, whether the retiree planned and prepared for retirement); and (4) cultural, economic and social factors. The way people retire can be a significant factor influencing their life satisfaction in retirement. Reasons for retirement range from unplanned/involuntary retirement due to health problems, to other reasons such as voluntary redundancy and retrenchment, to expected and planned retirement. Unplanned and/or involuntary retirement often causes grief, anxiety and reduced self-esteem, which can lead to social isolation (ARTD Consultants, 2012). Furthermore, unplanned/involuntary retirement is commonly associated with economic disadvantage (Noone et al., 2013; Petkoska & Earl, 2009) and poor health (Noone et al., 2013). The number of retirees exiting their work involuntarily is quite high – for example, it may be up to 20–30 per cent in the USA and Australia (Noone et al., 2013).

In addition to the four sets of factors influencing satisfaction in retirement, Pinquart and Schindler (2007) highlight the role of coping responses, and situational variables. Satisfaction with retirement may also be influenced by lifestyle choices, as identified in the retirement literature by Hopkins et al. (2006). Some retirees, especially people most commonly engaged in unsatisfactory employment and who wish to focus on self-actualisation, may perceive retirement as an opportunity for a new start. Meeting new people and becoming part of a new environment may be very satisfactory and sought-after experiences for them. The change and the widening of one's microsystems can thus act as an incentive (Bronfenbrenner, 1994). Other retirees may view retirement as a continuation of their pre-retirement. Some may not have been very invested in their work, with retirement allowing them to continue with some of their favourite activities in 'a more self-chosen way' (Hopkins et al., 2006: p. 90). Then there are retirees who may view retirement as an unwanted and imposed part of life. For such individuals, work was perhaps a primary source of self-identity; hence these retirees tend to look for ways in which they could replace their employment. Last but not least, there is a group of retirees who perceive their retirement as a transition to the last stage of their life, and tend to use this opportunity to self-reflect, while decreasing their activity levels (Hopkins et al., 2006).

Van Solinge and Henkens (2008) have identified two main developmental challenges in managing the transition to retirement: (1) social and psychological detachment from employment; and (2) the development of a suitable retirement lifestyle. The latter involves acquiring new daily routines, reorganising activities and leisure time, and possibly becoming more involved in volunteer work (Van Solinge & Henkens, 2008).

Transition to retirement can be especially challenging for people with disabilities, as many have fewer financial and personal resources with which to find optimal solutions for retirement (ARTD Consultants, 2012). Furthermore, retirement is yet another area in which people with disabilities are disadvantaged. According to Denton et al. (2013), 39 per cent of people with disabilities in Canada retired involuntarily. While all older people hope for an active retirement with choices of what they do and control of the retirement process (Buys et al., 2008), people with disabilities often have only limited say and control over what happens to them (ARTD Consultants, 2012). Moreover they have limited choices in regard to service providers, and they tend to experience problems with navigating health and social welfare systems (ARTD Consultants, 2012). Other challenges include the fact that reaching retirement age also means that people with disabilities in assisted living situations have to move from disability to aged care sectors. They may also be experiencing additional health conditions, both those related to disability and/or those related to ageing in general. Declining health can also result in a decrease in social relationships, thus increasing the chance of loneliness (Ballin & Balandin, 2007).

An especially vulnerable population from a retirement perspective are people with intellectual disabilities. They are among the lowest represented in the labour market and those that are employed are most commonly employed part-time or in supported employment (Wilson et al., 2010). Alongside their limited choices in living arrangements, employment and leisure time activities, members of this population may also face restricted opportunities with respect to when and how they retire, and what to do next. As highlighted by Judge et al. (2010), the concept of retirement can be especially problematic when applied to those with intellectual disabilities. This is due to a number of factors, such as the limited control individuals may have over their own lives (ARTD Consultants, 2012; Judge et al., 2010; Strnadová & Evans, 2012), as well as having difficulty envisaging a different lifestyle from the one they are experiencing at the present moment (Wilson et al., 2010). According to the Evaluation of the Australian Disability Enterprise Transition to Retirement Pilot (ARTD Consultants, 2012), people with intellectual disabilities working in supported employment may be more reluctant to retire. This can be the result of employment (even if only part-time or working in sheltered workshop) providing them with meaningful activities and routines, social networks and at least some income (Wilson et al., 2010).

Typical needs during the transition from work to retirement

Retirement, as perceived from the perspective of active and successful ageing, is a time when people 'actively engage, or indeed re-engage, with meaningful and active pursuits' (Bigby et al., 2011: pp. 167–168). People with intellectual disabilities often prefer to continue living an active life, rather than switching to a slower-paced life (Fesko et al., 2012). In a recent study, a cohort of 16 Australian older adults with this disability revealed that they preferred being active and they wished to avoid boredom in their lives (Buys et al., 2008). Similarly, the cohort of older people with intellectual disabilities in Judge et al.'s (2010) study in Scotland indicated that they enjoyed living an active life and contributing to society, and hoped that this would not change as they aged.

In retirement, people often seek to develop further the social networks they created earlier in their lives. However, people with intellectual disabilities not only have narrower social networks (Fesko et al., 2012), but also fewer opportunities and skills to maintain their social networks and/or to develop new ones after retiring. The more limited social networks experienced by people with intellectual disabilities can contribute to a reluctance to retire, with employment or day care activities being the most common source of their social relationships (Forrester-Jones et al., 2006; Stancliffe et al., 2013a). The loss of such well-developed social networks when retiring can sometimes cause depression and anxiety (Hartley & MacLean, 2009).

Wilson et al. (2010) have highlighted how the functional skills of people with intellectual disabilities commonly differ from those of people without disability. These skills include money management, travel-related skills and communication skills (Stancliffe et al., 2013b). Acquiring functional life skills is important for living a good-quality life in retirement. Some people with intellectual disabilities struggle with independent travel, and may thus find themselves even more dependent on their family members or support staff. Lacking independence in this area can also contribute to social isolation, as older adults with intellectual disabilities often depend on others when they want to go out and meet their friends (Strnadová et al., 2014b). Fesko et al. (2012) observed that travel costs may sometimes be too expensive for retired people with intellectual disabilities. Transportation costs as well as limited skills in negotiating transport systems can also constrain opportunities for social networking in retirement. This is not surprising, as travel costs (among other factors) are commonly a limiting factor when searching for employment opportunities (Lysaght et al., 2009).

Assessment

The importance of age-appropriate assessment in relation to different life stages and diverse transitions has been well established (Neubert & Leconte, 2013), and is no different for the transition to retirement. Age-appropriate assessment focuses on an individual's strengths, areas of need (including health), goals and priorities, all in the context of an individual's living arrangements, community and networks. Knowing one's personal strengths, needs, interests and aspirations is an important prerequisite to transition planning.

It is good practice to establish an interagency transition team to support the transition process. In the transition to retirement, the transition coordinator is usually a staff member of a main service provider institution (e.g. sheltered workshop, day centre, group home). Lack of clarity about who fulfils this role, what the role entails and the composition of the transition team can be a substantial obstacle to transition planning. The transition coordinator needs to become acquainted with an individual's preferences, which can be done through interview and conversation with the individual, as well as with family members and support staff. Learning as much as possible about an individual's life, from the perspectives of past experiences and memories, present situation, as well as future plans, is essential (Stancliffe et al., 2013b).

Rather than using a traditional assessment approach, which 'aims to diagnose and classify, to identify a problem and predict its future course', a functional approach to assessment, which identifies and accommodates for the relationship between an individual and his/her environment, is needed (Walsh, 2005: p. 27). The assessment of functional skills, such as money management, communication, health, behaviour and self-care skills, is important to determine what level of support will be needed (Stancliffe et al., 2013b). Assessment of these skills is best conducted in real-world settings and in real time, using some of the methods of functional assessment, such as repeated observation and an ecological inventory conducted across the diverse settings that a retiring person with disabilities is likely to find him/herself in (such as employment, home and the community group) (Walsh, 2005: p. 27).

Health assessment is also important, given that health problems often arise with ageing. In addition to age-related health issues, some medical conditions experienced by people with developmental disabilities appear over the course of the lifetime, and may be syndrome-specific. For example, people with Down syndrome are at risk of an early onset of Alzheimer's disease, as well as hearing and visual impairments. Therefore health and medical assessment in regard to planning their support needs during retirement is of vital importance (Henderson & Davidson, 2000).

> **Rose**
>
> Michael invited Rose and her mother for a meeting to discuss and address Rose's anxieties about retirement. He talked about different ways in which people can prepare for retirement without immediately retiring. He also talked about different transition to retirement (TTR) programmes that he had learned about during a staff professional development day. He reassured Rose that Newland Industries is not trying to get rid of her, that the main purpose of their meeting was to offer her support in preparing for the next stage in life, and that talking about retirement does not mean that she has to leave her employment. Michael elaborated that he would mainly support her in finding more friends and activities in her local community. Following this meeting, Rose discussed this more with her mother and decided to meet again with Michael and her mother to discuss and plan further for her transition to retirement.
>
> In order to provide tailored support for Rose, Michael, with help from Rose's mother, explored Rose's neighbourhood, as well as existing volunteering and community groups. Michael, Rose and her mother also met on a regular basis to talk about Rose's interests, preferred activities and wishes. Michael talked with Rose not only about her present situation, but also about her past, which helped him to get to know her much better. Rose is fond of cooking and gardening; however gardening is becoming increasingly difficult for her. Michael told Rose that a local charity delivers meals to seniors' homes and that they are looking for volunteers to help in the kitchen. Rose is excited about the proposition of volunteering in this area, as she had this experience as a young adult, and felt fulfilled by volunteering.

Evidence-based interventions

A number of evidence-based practices applicable across the lifespan have special relevance at this stage. They include transition planning, discussed in all earlier chapters, and interagency collaboration, which was discussed in detail in Chapters 8 and 9. To these general principles may be added the need to personalise retirement planning where possible. This is due to a change in the sectors (perhaps moving from the disability sector to elder care sector) within which they receive services, as well as the need to provide the additional support as experienced by a number of people with disabilities.

Person-centred retirement planning

Early planning is crucial for a successful transition to retirement, as it results in less preretirement anxiety and better adjustment and satisfaction in retirement

(Bigby et al., 2011; Petkoska & Earl, 2009). The *Evaluation of the Australian Disability Enterprise Transition to Retirement Pilot* (ARTD Consultants, 2012) found that lifelong person-centred planning may be valuable to ensure that older people with disabilities are at a lower risk of social isolation. Many members of the mainstream population plan for retirement throughout their working life, especially in the later stages of employment. Transition planning commonly includes attention to financial considerations, as well as planning for leisure and volunteer activities, all of which can be associated with life satisfaction in retirement (Noone et al., 2013). Lack of planning for retirement by people with disabilities may result in insufficient social connections in the community; 'not knowing what life after work could be like'; or a lack of life skills (ARTD Consultants, 2012: p. iii).

A person-centred approach to transition planning for retirement is important, as it allows for making sure that the wishes, needs and choices of older adults with disabilities can be taken into account. Furthermore, person-centred transition planning allows for the support and further development of empowerment and self-determination skills (Heller, 2013; Sterns et al., 2000). That said, there is a major gap in research about the ways in which older people with intellectual disabilities can best be encouraged to make self-determined choices about their transition to retirement (McDermott & Edwards, 2012).

Person-centred transition planning needs to include open discussion about the financial implications of leaving employment or of changing from full-time to part-time employment (Fesko et al., 2012). Because money management tends to be a challenge for people with intellectual disabilities, visual support and/or assistive technology (such as relevant tablet applications) may be helpful. As discussed earlier in the chapter, social interactions are another area of focus when planning for the transition to retirement. The transition team (usually an older adult with intellectual disabilities, family member or carer, support staff member and transition coordinator) may discuss ways in which existing relationships can be further developed and nurtured after retirement, and in what ways new relationships (if wanted by the retiring adult) can be established. A person's preferred activities and community involvement in retirement need to be discussed and planned for as well. Thus the transition team will need to consider local opportunities for engagement in preferred leisure activities or community groups; issues with travel within the community (e.g. whether a support person will be needed); and whether support for engaging in local community or leisure activity will be necessary, and if so, to what extent.

One of the specific aspects of transition planning for retirement for people with developmental disabilities derives from the fact that affected individuals often live with their families (i.e. parents and siblings) until adulthood (Sterns et al., 2000). As Greenbaum (2007) highlights in this context, when the parents of these adults die or are no longer able to act as caregivers, adults with developmental disabilities often move to unfamiliar settings, which can be a traumatising experience. Planning for the transition to retirement includes addressing these issues, which can be a demanding task both for an adult with developmental disabilities, and for his or her parents. Discussing a suitable residential situation within a community that the adult is familiar with, and where there are options for preferred activities should be a priority.

An important part of planning for retirement involves also educating people with disabilities (and especially those with intellectual disabilities) about retirement. This is essential as many do not think about and/or cannot imagine life after retirement (Stancliffe et al., 2013b). In a study conducted in Australia by Bigby et al. (2011), retirement was perceived as an unwelcome, 'risky proposition' by people with lifelong disabilities, their family members and their staff. People with lifelong disabilities may also have few opportunities to experience community involvement and available leisure time activities in mainstream society, due to their experience of living a segregated life, rather than being socially included (Bigby et al., 2011; Stancliffe et al., 2013a).

Transition to retirement programmes

Active support and co-worker training are evidence-based practices relevant also for people with disabilities who are retiring, as they allow for the social inclusion of adults with disabilities, especially those with intellectual disabilities (Bigby et al., 2011). The co-worker training model has been well researched in relation to an open employment environment, when a co-worker is trained to be a mentor and a job coach for a worker with intellectual disabilities (Wilson et al., 2010). This model of a mentor who belongs to a community group that a person with a disability wishes to join was successfully used in the TTR programme developed by Stancliffe et al. (2013b). This 12-month programme allows people with lifelong disabilities who intend to retire in the near future to establish their place in a community, along with new routines and networks. It included the following stages, within which a programme participant could opt out and return to employment at any time: (1) planning a retirement lifestyle; (2) finding a suitable mainstream community or volunteering group (which meets at least weekly); (3) preparing for a new routine; (4) recruiting and training mentors; and (5) ongoing monitoring and support (Stancliffe et al., 2013b). The core idea of the TTR programmes is that participants drop one day from their typical work week, and this day is then used for preparing for changes at home, work and community, and for participating in a selected mainstream community group, with the support of a mentor.

Mentoring is an important aspect of this kind of work (Wilson et al., 2010, 2013a). Mentors are usually existing members of a community or a volunteer group, who wish to support an older adult with intellectual disabilities, and they can constitute an important microsystem (see Bronfenbrenner, 1994) in the life of a retiring person. Besides the benefits it brings from a social inclusion perspective, the financial benefits of this approach cannot be underestimated (Stancliffe et al., 2013a). Mentors within the TTR programme receive training based on evidence-based approaches of active support and co-worker training. Part of their role is to contribute to the inclusion of an older person with intellectual disabilities, both socially and in activities preferred by the supported person. A mentoring perspective in this context can be a beneficial experience for both parties involved. The overarching experience of 14 mentors in the above TTR programme was the realisation that people with intellectual disabilities are not different from the mainstream population (Wilson et al., 2013a). Such experiences can contribute to overcoming societal prejudice towards the population of people with this disability.

Lifelong learning

The desire to learn new things or to continue learning in key areas of interest (such as reading and using computers) does not decrease with age for people with intellectual disabilities. Yet opportunities for lifelong learning may be rather limited. When discussing opportunities to participate in lifelong learning for older adults with this disability, Fesko et al. (2012) suggest the use of lifelong learning programmes, day trips and involvement in leisure activities. Unfortunately, social prejudice towards people with intellectual disabilities and incorrect assumptions about their ability to learn can be a significant barrier to lifelong learning.

Participation in community groups

A wide range of community groups may be available to people with and without disabilities. They include formal groups with paid staff members, groups established by community members and informal groups established based on shared interests within local community halls or churches (Stancliffe et al., 2013a). It is of the utmost importance to find a good match between an older adult with intellectual disabilities and a community group. This can be done by considering a number of areas, such as: (1) interests of the older adult and how can these be fulfilled by participating in a community group; (2) personal characteristics (age, gender, health needs); and (3) community group culture, including the attitudes of existing group members towards social inclusion. As highlighted by Bigby et al. (2011), some mainstream community group members may express opposition to having people with intellectual disabilities join their group. They may also be worried about risk management concerning people with intellectual disabilities joining in. However this opposition can be overcome by a positive experience, with the role of mentors being especially crucial here, especially those with relevant leadership qualities (Wilson et al., 2013a).

Volunteering

There are a number of reasons why older adults, irrespective of disability or non-disability status, may be interested in volunteering during retirement. These include: (1) having the desire to feel useful; (2) having the aspiration to help others; (3) looking for an opportunity to meet new people (Balandin et al., 2006);

and (4) being interested in the area of volunteering (Stancliffe et al., 2013b). It is more likely for people in retirement to engage in volunteering if they have had this experience prior to retirement (Petkoska & Earl, 2009). Staying active as a retiree (in work, by volunteering, etc.) contributes to a decreased likelihood of depression, increased life satisfaction and better cognitive performance (Lysaght et al., 2009).

Lysaght et al. (2009) concluded that, while volunteering plays an important role for people with intellectual disabilities, a number of adult participants in their study conducted in Canada would still prefer to be paid for their work, and viewed volunteering as a passing stage in their life, leading them to a paid job. They appreciated extrinsic awards for their volunteering work, such as food or gift cards.

Rose

Michael arranged a meeting with representatives of the local charity kitchen to make sure it would be a good match for Rose. Given that two members of this kitchen had children with a disability, the level of acceptance and positive attitudes towards Rose was exceptional. One of these two members volunteered to be an on-site mentor for Rose. Michael met with the whole kitchen team to discuss the group's expectations and habits, to tell them about Rose, and to plan Rose's introduction to the group. He then met with Rose to tell her about the group. He also arranged an informal meeting with Rose, her mother and Rose's future co-worker and mentor Emma over a cup of a coffee. After Rose met her mentor Emma, she was even more excited to join the charity kitchen team.

Michael joined Rose on her first day at the local charity kitchen. After preparing meals for distribution, the group prepared a light lunch as a surprise for Rose, which allowed for a more informal meeting and getting to know each other. The only remaining concern Rose had was getting to the charity kitchen, as she felt anxious about travelling by bus. Provisions were made for Rose to be accompanied by a volunteer, who would travel with Rose and support her in developing independent travel skills. After this Rose made necessary arrangements, supported by Michael and her mother, to work only 4 days a week, while using the fifth day to engage with the local charity kitchen from 8.30 to 11.30 a.m. Her main responsibilities were cutting and cleaning vegetables, and helping to clean the kitchen.

One year after planning for retirement and changing from working full-time to working part-time (4 days a week), Rose made another change to work only 2 days a week at Newland Industries. She continued volunteering in the local charity kitchen and she also joined a local knitting group, where she utilises her skills from the textile division employment. She made a couple of new friends in this group, and meets them outside the group for a coffee or lunch.

Conclusion

Transition to retirement is a time of substantial changes in several different environments. An individual's microsystem includes his or her most immediate environment, such as family, peers and workplace (Bronfenbrenner, 1994). However with family members and peers growing older or dying, retirement and joining new environments such as community and/or volunteering groups, or a retirement village, an ageing individual's microsystems change considerably. Given that a mesosystem is 'a system of two or more microsystems' and the relationships existing between these (Bronfenbrenner, 1999: p. 17), changes in microsystems affect an individual's mesosystem too. As previously mentioned, interagency collaboration is very important in the planning for transition to retirement. The microsystems in which a retiring person with disabilities exists, such as his/her family, his/her service provider, should ideally be involved and collaborate in this process.

The exosystems of retiring people with disabilities (such as spouse's or adult children's work context) also deserve the attention of service providers (Löckenhoff, 2012). In this context, Jacobson and Wilhite (1999) highlighted the effects of legal policies, which underpin and shape the service provision provided to the retiring population of people with disabilities. Lack of policies regarding transition planning and transition to retirement programming for ageing people with disabilities is a serious oversight that can negatively impact the quality of life of members of this population.

Retiring people with disabilities may face a number of challenges at the macrosystem level (cultural and societal factors), such as prejudice and misconceptions about them, their abilities and needs. People with developmental disabilities may be especially vulnerable from this perspective, as it is commonly assumed that they are not able to have control over their lives and make important decisions, including when to retire, and what to do following their retirement.

The transition to retirement is one of the major life transitions in life for any person, yet it is more demanding for people with disabilities. There is a great need to raise awareness about people with disabilities retiring, in order to facilitate their participation in the community. The same applies to employment providers and employees in group homes and sheltered workshops. Stancliffe et al. (2013b) suggest the provision of seminars and workshops for employers to address this lack of awareness.

Note

1 This case study is fictional. However, the approaches and strategies used in the process of supporting Rose's transition to retirement are based on suggestions in the following resource: Stancliffe, R.J., Wilson, N.J., Gambin, N., Bigby, C., & Balandin, S. (2013). *Transition to Retirement. A guide to inclusive practice.* Sydney: Sydney University Press.

11
WRAPAROUND SERVICES TO SUPPORT LIFESPAN TRANSITIONS

> **Gerald**
>
> Gerald is a 17-year old African American with a learning disability who is half-way through his final year of secondary school. His teachers are concerned about his transition from secondary school, as he is 2 years behind his peers academically and has significant behaviour problems. His behaviour may have contributed to the academic problems he has encountered, as he has a history of running away from class and school, throwing furniture around and breaking things when upset at school. He has also had a history of drug and alcohol abuse, and physically aggressive behaviour towards peers and adults (punching, kicking, spitting). In the community, he has demonstrated behaviours that have required police involvement, such as painting graffiti and fire lighting.
>
> Gerald's mother, Maryann, also has an intellectual disability and the family has a history of learning disabilities. He has experienced neglect and malnourishment and has been placed in various foster homes over the years. He is currently living at home with his mother and younger sister, Maggie, who is 6. Historically, there has been no father figure present. Maryann does not work and receives financial and housing assistance from the government.

Introduction

Internationally, there is a high prevalence of young people with disabilities who also have significant mental health issues (Einfeld et al., 2011; White et al., 2005).

These mental health issues have the potential to affect the behaviour of individuals severely, thus negatively impacting on their quality of life. What is called a 'wraparound' process has emerged in recent years as best practice for these students (Walker & Sanders, 2011). Bertram et al. (2010: p. 713) define wraparound services as involving 'a community-based, family-driven collaborative team planning process that engages informal supports and formal services with families in culturally competent, individualized, strengths-based assessment and interventions'.

Young people with disabilities and concurrent mental health diagnoses may require support in several areas of their life: school, home, community and medical. It can be difficult and overwhelming for both the individual and his or her family to coordinate all of these services (McKay & Bannon, 2004). It becomes even more challenging when these services have competing agendas or offer contradictory advice. Wraparound is a process that is designed to assist with these challenges by providing an individualised comprehensive plan to support the behaviours of the student in all arenas. To be successful, this requires the process to be managed collaboratively.

There is a large body of literature describing wraparound services for individuals with disabilities and behavioural health issues (Bruns et al., 2005; Scott & Eber, 2005; Walker & Schutte, 2004), most of it originating from the USA. While there is a high percentage of children and adolescents with mental illness globally (World Health Organization, 2011), a review of the current literature yields few studies about wraparound services as yet in other settings (Morgan Disney & Associates, 2006; New Zealand Ministry of Education, 2014). Einfeld et al. (2011) point to the need for service providers to be aware of this comorbidity and to identify and provide support for individuals who are affected.

The importance of high-quality wraparound services cannot be overstated, especially when one examines the involvement of individuals with disabilities and complex needs in the criminal justice system. Such young people are overrepresented in the courts and prison system as both victims and offenders (Vermeiren et al., 2006). For many of them, the trajectory into the criminal justice system begins very early in life, so cooperation between schools and social welfare systems is crucial in diverting from these pathways.

Due to the collaborative nature of this process among families, schools, community organisations and government agencies, implementing and maintaining an individualised wraparound system can be both complex and challenging. For the individuals managing this collaboration, it can be difficult to determine the adequacy of the plan, where exactly different systems of provision should focus and, in some cases, what services are available in the first place. Wraparound services therefore require careful evidence-based planning, implementation and assessment.

History of wraparound

Over 30 years ago, Jane Knitzer recognised the need for a system of care (SOC) approach to support young people with mental health needs and their families in the USA (Knitzer, 1982). She recommended that SOC approaches make provision for a continuum of strength-based services and supports. Other essential features are a focus on cultural relevance and natural supports that are designed based on the preferences of the child and the family. This was, in effect, the beginning of what is now known as wraparound. Achieving this level of integration has been an uphill battle, as coordinating services and supports across and among systems is a complex task, and one that is inconsistent with most traditional models of intervention and service delivery.

Stroul and Friedman (1986), who approached this issue from a mental health services perspective, further developed and refined the process of implementing and expanding integrated SOCs. As state and local systems embraced this new philosophy of community-based interventions and natural supports that kept students out of costly, ineffective and restrictive placements away from home, the elements of SOC became more refined and operationalised, developing into what is now referred to as the wraparound approach (Eber et al., 2013).

The focal point of this SOC approach is the wraparound team. This team usually consists of the student, family members, teachers and other school personnel, natural support providers such as friends and community members, and professional support providers. The philosophy behind the team composition is that the student and family should have a voice, as well as the presence of natural support providers, to increase the likelihood that the individualised plan will be accepted by the student and family, and therefore be more effective in providing strategies and supports that will support them in reaching their goals in school, home and the community (Eber et al., 2013).

Wraparound had its beginnings in the mental health and child welfare systems, but continues to evolve. It is now commonly used in schools in the USA as a tier 3 intensive behavioural support, as one element of school-wide positive behaviour interventions and supports (SWPBIS) (Eber et al., 2009). This third, or most intensive, support tier, is usually only required by 2–3 per cent of the school population, usually those with emotional and behavioural disorders. Eber et al. (2013) describe what wraparound looks like in a school setting as part of SWPBIS process: 'These school-initiated wraparound plans typically include lower-tiered interventions (e.g., high-frequency reinforcers, daily check-in/check-out systems, social skills instruction, function-based behavioural interventions) all integrated through a person-centred wraparound' (p. 380).

The school-based team is usually led by a school counsellor or psychologist, who facilitates the team throughout the process, including a commitment to persist, despite any challenges or setbacks that may occur. School-based wraparound is a person- and family-centred strengths-based approach that aims to focus on quality-of-life goals for students and families. Each team member has a specifically defined role and the implementation of any planned interventions is very detailed. Implementation guidelines and practice standards continue to evolve today. Having a solid theoretical framework will go a long way to guiding the implementation and practice of wraparound systems.

Theoretical framework

The existing literature in the field of wraparound services has mainly addressed the definition of the model, the fidelity of the model and intervention outcomes. Bertram et al. (2010) suggest that more investigation is necessary in the area of constructing a theory base for the wraparound process. Eber et al. (2009) suggest that the reason that wraparound has been implemented in numerous forms is a lack of consistency due to no established theoretical framework. Having a sound theoretical base is important because clarity about this will positively influence the focus of team assessments, the design of interventions and the selection of formal services. Three theoretical perspectives have been most associated with wraparound in the literature: (1) ecological theory; (2) social learning theory; and (3) the theory of change.

Bronfenbrenner's ecological systems theory frames wraparound well, since it is consistent with wraparound's individual and family-centred strengths-based approach. Rather than being expert-driven, wraparound is person-centred and family-focused. Ecological theory focuses on reciprocal interactions over time, and the success of the wraparound process hinges on the unique ecological environment of the child and family, with change or adjustment taking place within the natural settings of the school, home and community, but in close interaction with those contexts (Eber et al., 2013).

Wraparound also seeks to work with elements of Bandura's (1977) social learning theory, which states that both adaptive and maladaptive behaviour are learned through the reciprocal relationships that occur within the child's environment over time. This theory supports change in the environment to support the individual in learning to behave in a more acceptable manner. This is evident in the individualisation of wraparound services – each person has different strengths and needs according to his or her environment, with some families requiring formal supports and others benefitting from more informal interventions (Burchard et al., 2002).

Currently the most widely accepted theoretical framework informing the notion of wraparound is the theory of change (Walker, 2008). Here, the focus is on goals and an outcomes pathway that recognises and identifies linkages between short-term, intermediate and long-term outcomes. Just as this theory calls on stakeholders to determine specific forms of intervention to achieve the outcomes, the wraparound process demonstrates that there are several routes by which the process may lead to desired outcomes. Both require a team of stakeholders to design an individualised outcomes-based plan, evaluate it regularly and make informed decisions about its effectiveness. Lastly, both the theory and the process are inclusive of many perspectives and participants in achieving solutions (Walker, 2008).

Walker (2008) suggests that the complex nature of the wraparound process, and especially the participatory creation, implementation, evaluation and adjustment of the plan, leads to improved coping and problem-solving abilities. Together these elements contribute to increased self-efficacy, which leads to greater success in the process. This in turn leads to increased self-efficacy – a positive spiral that should improve the effectiveness of the treatment and support. She also posits that in order for the theory to drive the practice, sound adherence to the principles and implementation model is imperative, because positive outcomes are dependent on implementation fidelity.

All three of the theories presented here have relevance to the wraparound approach and have had an influence on the history and development of the wraparound process, moving behavioural support away from a medical towards a more social perspective. Although the theory of change is currently the most acceptable framework, research still needs to test each of the theory's main assumptions, to determine what components contribute to wraparound's effectiveness and how these contributions specifically affect outcomes (Walker, 2008). This knowledge should enable practitioners to refine their wraparound practice.

Conceptual framework

Wraparound has been used in schools, child welfare, juvenile justice, health and mental health settings. In addition to a definition (Bertram et al., 2010), a conceptual framework is necessary to ensure fidelity to the essential elements of the wraparound process. The need for standards, replicability, implementation consistency and clearly defined outcomes was voiced as early as 1999 (Burns & Goldman, 1999). Burns and Goldman (1999) further stated that, in order to define wraparound thoroughly, the values associated with wraparound must first be conceptualised. The book, *Ten Principles of the Wraparound Process* (Bruns et al., 2008) provides a conceptual framework for the approach.

The first principle of wraparound (Bruns et al., 2008) focuses on voice and choice, that is, the young person and family are encouraged to share their perspectives, which are then used to ensure that the planning process includes options that are congruent with family values and preferences. This supports the development of self-determination skills and contributes to the collaborative process allowing the stakeholders who are most affected by decisions to have an active role in making them. Secondly, wraparound is team-based, with the family's needs and perspectives driving the composition of the wraparound team. Families may need support in choosing individuals who will be committed to providing them with formal and informal support and services.

The third principle of wraparound is that of using natural supports to assist the student. These include the supports the family may access outside of the formal service system. Sources of natural support may include the family's network of extended family, friends, neighbours, church, sports teams and other community organisations. Because these supports occur naturally and therefore will most likely be sustained after formal service provision ends, the individuals who provide these supports should be encouraged to participate as team members.

As these natural supports are most likely to exist within the community of the student and family, the fourth principle of wraparound is that it is community-based.

Service and supports should ideally be fully accessible and take place in the least restrictive environment possible. In other words, families should access and use the same services and activities available to other families in the community, located in the community they choose to reside in.

Due to the involvement of many different stakeholders, collaboration is the fifth principle. Team members are encouraged to listen to one another respectfully and reach agreement on what goals to pursue, the best ways of reaching them and how to assess if the plan is effective. Tension lies in being both youth- and family-centred, as well as team-driven. This tension may be resolved on an individual basis, as each family and team will have different needs and goals.

In line with this notion of collaboration is the sixth principle, namely that of cultural competency. The team needs to recognise that culture shapes each member's beliefs and actions and that the process must respect and build on the values, culture and beliefs of the young person, the family and the community. Cultural competency also recognises that traditions and values can be a source of strength for the family, and that people who share cultural identities with the family are often sources of sustainable natural support. The team needs to be aware that cultural sensitivity must extend beyond the team meetings to the actual supports and services that are part of the wraparound plan.

It is of great importance that the plan be individualised and strengths-based (principles seven and eight). In order for the plan's goals to be attainable, strategies, supports and services planned are tailored to the unique needs of the young person and family. Supports and services are built on the strengths of family members and based on available community formal and informal resources. Ideally, the wraparound plan identifies, is based on and enhances the strengths of the young person, family, wraparound team members and the wider community. The process recognises the expertise and value that each team member contributes, but is particularly focused on the young person and family. The plan is to increase the individual's knowledge, skills and capabilities, especially psychological and interpersonal assets.

The ninth principle states that, to increase effectiveness of the wraparound process, the team should work in the spirit of unconditional persistence. This means that the team does not place blame on or reject young people and their families, even when faced with challenges and setbacks. The team is committed to continuing to work to meet the needs of the young person and family until there is collective agreement that there is no more need for a formal wraparound process. Lastly, the plan is outcomes-based. The team is accountable to all stakeholders to achieve the goals that are specified in the plan. In order for the plan to be effective, the goals and strategies of the plan are tied to measurable indicators of success, progress must be monitored regularly and revisions should be made accordingly.

Together, these principles provide teams with a solid basis from which to begin their work, but in order to ensure fidelity, more specific implementation standards are necessary. The basic steps have continued to evolve over the last three decades; the following section describes the most current recommended steps for implementation.

Forming an evidence base

As wraparound has continued to evolve, practitioners and researchers alike have seen the need for an education-centred approach for transition-age youth struggling with mental health and behaviour issues. One of the earliest programmes to take a wraparound approach to transition planning was Project RENEW (Cheney et al., 1998). Named RENEW to signify the goals of the project – rehabilitation, empowerment, natural supports, education and work – the project was based in New Hampshire, USA, and its approach is still widely used and studied in the USA today (Eber et al., 2013).

The RENEW model is often used in conjunction with SWPBIS, as an intensive-tier intervention. The seven major components of the RENEW model include: (1) personal futures planning; (2) interagency coordination; (3) naturally supported employment; (4) flexible high school programming; (5) social skill building; (6) mentors; and (7) flexible funding to support successful transition (Cheney et al., 1998). These components are well aligned with wraparound's principles and elements. The RENEW model has also enjoyed decades of documented success (University of New Hampshire Institute on Disability/UCED, 2014). A brief review of literature that supports the efficacy of RENEW and other wraparound models follows.

Cheney et al. (1998) studied 18 young people with emotional or behaviour disorder who participated in the RENEW project for wraparound. They found that, at the end of 3 years' participation in the RENEW project, participating students had achieved positive outcomes such as completing high school. Nearly one-third of the participants had enrolled in post-secondary education, and 75 per cent were still employed 3 months after the end of the project. Hagner et al. (2008) found similar results 10 years later when elements of the RENEW model were used to provide wraparound services to 33 young people between the ages of 14 and 17 who were at risk of being removed from school and home to juvenile justice settings. Over half of the participants either returned to their home schools or studied for their General Equivalency Diploma, and 24 students were employed.

Burns and Goldman (1999) conducted an early meta-analysis of wraparound studies. Although the studies offered preliminary evidence of wraparound's effectiveness, the designs were mostly uncontrolled and subject to bias. Two of the studies were randomised clinical trials and showed promising results. Four of the studies were conducted in school settings. Burns and Goldman recommended that future research use larger samples and a standard set of outcome measures, which led the way to further research.

Bruns and Suter (2010) have summarised the wraparound evidence base. Their first finding was that, in the time between 2003 and 2010, the number of controlled research studies on wraparound published in peer-reviewed journals grew from three to nine. They reviewed these nine studies, seven of which were controlled studies with experimental designs that compared the outcomes for young people with emotional and behavioural disorders who were involved in the wraparound process to those who received more traditional care approaches. They found statistically significant outcomes in several areas, including: (1) reduced aggression; (2) reduced school truancy and suspensions; (3) less likely to be arrested; (4) reduced recidivism; (5) increase in permanency of residence; (6) improved moods and emotions; (7) improved school performance; (8) fewer disciplinary actions; and (9) residing in less restrictive placements.

The wraparound approach is being considered for inclusion in the Substance Abuse and Mental Health Services Administration (SAMHSA) National Registry of Evidence-based Programs and Practices (NREPP) (Bruns & Suter, 2010). In the meantime, Partners with Families and Children, which is a SOC programme that uses the basic principles of wraparound, has been included on the NREPP. In order for wraparound in general to be included, however, there needs to be agreed-upon theory, a strong research base, clear outcome evidence and connections between the process change and clinical outcomes (Bruns & Suter, 2010). Although wraparound has enough evidence of efficacy to suggest its use, a stronger evidence base will allow for listing from organisations such as SAMHSA, which will inspire the confidence required for widespread adoption.

Implementation

The National Wraparound Initiative was established in 2003 to 'promote understanding about the wraparound model and its benefits, and to provide the field with guidance that facilitates high quality and consistent wraparound implementation' (Miles et al., 2011: p. 3). Because wraparound implementation is such an individualised process, rather than develop standards for implementation, the National Wraparound Initiative has developed a guide that contains resources and practical information for service supervisors, managers and administrators (Miles et al., 2011). The following is a summary of the implementation information provided by the guide.

The first step of implementation is choosing a community structure, managing it, using it effectively and supporting stakeholder participation. From a school-based perspective, there often exist collaborations that can be built upon, such as relationships with mental health services, social work provision and juvenile justice. School personnel often have connections with stakeholders in each of these areas, and can build upon these relationships to put together a representative group of stakeholders who can take responsibility for project design and guidance through obstacles and challenges. It is important to include stakeholders who have the ability to make decisions in their particular areas of expertise. Students and their families can be provided with training and support to foster their self-determination and allow them to develop these roles fully.

Once a team has been formed, stakeholders work together to set a clear purpose for the group, including who will be helped, how this will be done and what the expected outcomes are. Stakeholders benefit from having clearly defined roles and responsibilities; students and families are matched to the individuals or organisations that are most likely to provide the quality services required. Managing the quality of these services is an ongoing part of the process, and the team, including the student and family, regularly reviews the plan and tracks outcomes. Lastly, the team needs to determine how the plan will be funded. Funding is usually necessary to provide a high-quality wraparound process. It is best if funding from a variety of sources can be combined, in order to ensure flexibility and sustainability. Potential sources of funding are typically dependent on geography, politics and the services offered and needed.

Wraparound is built on the principles of individual needs and a community-based SOC. In order to provide different families with resources to suit a family's individual needs, it is best if a wide array of services and supports is available. These may include formal supports such as evidence-based treatments and practices that already exist in the system, creative interventions developed by the team to assist specific students/families and informal supports identified by the team and the family. Services can then be carefully selected to guarantee that the student and family get the services they need without being burdened with unnecessary activities. Students, families and teams can be provided with the flexibility to leave services that are not working and access alternative services. With children, especially those about to transition out of secondary school, time is of the essence, so it is important that the team endeavours to expedite waiting lists, and realign resources to fit with demand. A service provider network may be created so that available resources in the youth's community are identified. These services are not accessed until (and if) they become necessary. Although planning access to services is imperative to the process, wraparound teams must also create protocols for exiting these services.

Different roles are developed so that the team can meet the needs of the student and family. Miles et al. (2011) suggest: (1) wraparound facilitator; (2) family support partner; (3) youth advocate; (4) direct support services; (5) wraparound clinician; and (6) wraparound supervisors. Once these roles have been filled and each member's function has been determined, the time and resources necessary to fulfil each role are calculated and resources allocated. These would include time to complete necessary tasks and a manageable caseload. The student and family need to be involved in all phases of team selection and are part of the training team for new staff.

Accountability is an integral feature of the implementation process. The team can take steps to ensure wraparound fidelity, service quality and the development of the wraparound process. Establishing clear outcomes so that the team can determine whether they are getting the results they were aiming for is a good way to set up an accountability measure. Next, the team should define what processes staff and managers can use to assess whether outcomes are being achieved. Regular meetings that occur as often as necessary can assist with progress monitoring and any needed changes to the plan. Satisfaction data from families are important when determining whether their needs are being met. Finally, costs should be monitored to track whether the investment of time, money, space, resources and personnel is worth the outcomes that are being achieved.

One area that cannot be neglected is transition from wraparound. When the student and family have met the outcomes identified early on by the team and no longer require the support of the facilitator and the team, a transition plan is developed that includes less intensive forms of support. The team reviews and celebrates the accomplishments, and the student and family may be given the opportunity to mentor others who are in earlier phases of the programme.

Due to the individualised person-centred nature of wraparound, implementation will look slightly different for each team. It is important however to adhere to the core principles of wraparound (Bruns et al., 2008), whatever the approach taken, and the information presented above (Miles et al., 2011) into the process. These principles and suggestions are necessarily generic, so an example of what the wraparound process might look like when it is school-based and centred on a transition-aged student and his family is presented below.

Gerald

Gerald's teacher approached the school counsellor about her concern about his current academic and behavioural performance, and his impending transition to post-school settings. The counsellor, Jeff Bloom, collected some data and determined that Gerald and his family would benefit from the wraparound model of support to assist with his transition from high school. He scheduled a meeting with Gerald, his mother Maryann, and her social worker to gather information about the family's situation and preferences.

Gerald indicated having an interest in cooking and possibly working in a local café. He also indicated that he had no hobbies to speak of, and that he spent his leisure time 'hanging out with friends', which many times led to his alcohol/drug use and illegal activities. He did not enjoy school and found classes boring and difficult. His fellow students sometimes teased him about his lack of skills, angering him and causing him to lash out at them and his teachers, or just leave the school grounds. He said if he had his way, he would not attend school at all; he wanted to 'get on with his life'.

Gerald's mother indicated that she often felt overwhelmed with caring for herself, Gerald and his sister, and that Gerald did not listen to or obey her. She would sometimes forget to pay the bills, buy groceries or cook meals. She tried to make sure that both Maggie and Gerald went to school each day, but was not always successful. She felt out of place on the occasions that she had to visit the schools, due to her own negative experiences of schooling, and tried to avoid that activity completely.

During that first meeting, Mr Bloom, Gerald, Maryann and the social worker determined that the most important priority was to upskill Gerald academically, socially and behaviourally in order to prepare him for life after high school. They decided that the wraparound team would include them, a social services psychologist, Gerald's probation officer, a representative from the local vocational school's cooking programme and a special education teacher from the school.

When the team first met, care was taken to ensure that all members were aware of Gerald's and Maryann's needs and their preferences. The team was then able to agree upon a set of outcomes. Gerald would increase his attendance to 90 per cent for the last two terms of school. He would also increase his compliance with requests from adult authority figures, including his mother and teachers. He would develop appropriate social engagement with his peers, and develop coping skills to manage his frustration and anger in school, at home and in community settings. He would also discontinue his use of drugs and alcohol. Lastly, he would develop some appropriate recreational interests in order to use his free time in a safer, more appropriate manner.

In order to accomplish those outcomes, each member of the team was assigned a specific role and the following supports were incorporated into the plan. Gerald's teachers removed academic barriers by designing adaptations to the environment and curriculum delivery, including structured and differentiated work tasks and adult support when necessary. The school principal arranged for relevant school staff members to receive professional development in the areas of responding to Gerald's behaviour appropriately. Gerald's psychologist taught him positive ways of thinking and managing his emotions, such as emotional awareness, social skills and self-calming strategies. He also assisted Gerald with joining a group to help him with his drug and alcohol problem. The psychologist did some family counselling to assist Gerald and Maryann with their relationship. Social services provided a carer to come in twice a week and assist Maryann with budget, calendar and nutritional matters. The psychologist also recommended a series of parenting classes that were being offered at the local community centre. Gerald began attending one class at the vocational school, and took a job at a local café clearing tables and dishwashing.

When Gerald transitioned out of the wraparound programme 18 months later, he was well on his way to a career in food service. At the end of the school year, he was attending school and his vocational class 90 per cent of the time. He had perfect attendance at his job at the café, and plans were being made to start training him as a prep cook. The vocational school had agreed to allow him to enrol in classes full time in the first semester of the year following graduation. He and Maryann had developed a more positive relationship, and he was helping out at home more and interacting positively with his younger sister. He attended Alcoholics Anonymous meetings and social events with his sponsor. His probation period with juvenile justice was coming to an end, as he had completed all conditions of his probation successfully.

(continued)

(continued)

He kept regular appointments with his psychologist, which had decreased in number from once a week to once a month. Overall, he felt that he had a voice in his future and the resources to make and reach goals for his future.

Conclusion

Although the wraparound service model was initially developed through a SOC approach in the mental health, juvenile justice and child welfare sectors, the education sector too has come to see the value in the coordination of these SOCs for students at the intensive level of the positive behaviour support continuum. While interagency collaboration is the main goal, schools are sometimes best situated to initiate and guide this implementation, particularly in regard to transition-age young people with intensive behavioural support needs. While wraparound does not preclude the need for transition planning, it is certainly a complementary intervention, as it is strengths-based and future-focused, and fosters self-determination and individual voice and choice.

Wraparound is a complex process that requires much coordination, planning, training, coaching, monitoring and evaluation. Housing it under the umbrella of an SWPBIS system may increase the likelihood that all of the essential features of the process are present and adhered to (Eber et al., 2013). Schools, and special education provision specifically, are structured systems that have a focus on evaluation, planning, support and communication with families and the greater community. This focus is complementary to the principles and essential elements of the wraparound process. It must be noted that implementing wraparound can be costly and complicated, and, in addition to the defining principles of the process, planning for implementation must take into consideration the local history, circumstances and needs of the context and all involved.

Future work in this area should focus on outcomes when implementing the system as part of an SWPBIS programme. Research could further investigate implementation fidelity, programme evaluation and participant outcomes. A strong evidence base in school-based wraparound would assist in promoting this important process beyond the traditional systems and in relevant settings beyond the USA.

12
CONCLUSION

The choice of Bronfenbrenner's Ecological Model (1994) as a theoretical framework to underpin this book was a well-grounded decision. The authors, along with Bronfenbrenner himself, acknowledge that a person's human development depends not only on individual characteristics, but also on the systems within which people live and the environments that surround them. As indicated at the start of this book, a person's ecological environment can be, according to Bronfenbrenner, perceived 'as a set of nested structures, each inside the other like a set of Russian dolls' (1989: p. 3).

Bronfenbrenner and Morris (1998: p. 996) have written that:

> throughout the life course, human development takes place through processes of progressively more complex reciprocal interaction between an active, evolving biopsychosocial human organism and the persons, objects and symbols in its immediate external environment. To be effective, interaction must occur on a fairly regular basis over extended periods of time.

Perceived through the lens of the transitions that take place in the lives of people with disabilities, in order for a person to develop the skills, knowledge and attitudes necessary for the next stage in life, the interactions with others that are important to this process cannot be just 'one-off', 'spur of the moment', brief occasions. Transition planning and preparation for the next stage in life take both time and conscious effort. This is true for any one of us, but is even more so for people with disabilities, who experience many barriers and restrictions in their lives, which are often societal in origin, rather than connected to a person's impairment.

In the above quotation, Bronfenbrenner and Morris (1998: p. 996) also remind us that every person evolves throughout his or her life course, which implies that transition planning is never static. This process of change establishes the basis of the outermost layer of the model, or the *chronosystem*, and this evolution of person can perhaps be best illustrated using the case study example, Rose, from Chapter 10. Rose was experiencing age-related health issues, but did not want to give up feeling worthwhile, doing a job she loved and interacting with people she considered to be her friends and support network. She had the self-determination to discuss her feelings and choices with those in her support network. It was the sum total of the experiences that Rose had throughout her life that fostered her love of working, ability to make and keep friends, her social communication, her sense of self-efficacy and her self-determination. Had she experienced her life differently, her life outcomes would not have been so positive. Many older adults with intellectual disabilities live most of their lives in group homes, and institutionalised settings, with limited input into how their days and their lives in general are played out. Oftentimes these restrictions are a function of those settings, which offer residents few opportunities to develop and practise self-determination.

The case study of Trevor in Chapter 7 exemplifies the influence and effects of the macrosystem, which, according to Bronfenbrenner (1994), comprises the overarching values and beliefs held by the individual and others about transition, and the quality of life for individuals with disabilities. When examining transitions within the macrosystem, one of the integral components of this system relates to evidence-based practices. In Trevor's case, he had spent the greater part of his young life entering and exiting a series of government systems, all of which had failed him. When a psychologist from the juvenile justice system finally implemented an evidence-based practice of assessment of Trevor's abilities, preferences and needs, he was then able to act as a wraparound coordinator and initiate the collaborative process for successful transition. The plan that was created and implemented for Trevor and his mother engaged with and utilised many of the evidence-based practices described in Chapter 11, such as individual and family planning and therapy, mentoring and educational programming.

Local, national and educational budgetary structures, along with associated laws, mandates and monies, and the resources available to students with disabilities and their families for education and transitions belong to Bronfenbrenner's (1994) exosystem. When students, such as Ajay in Chapter 6, spend time transitioning in and out of a number of settings as a result of their physical and/or mental health conditions, the exosystem has a large effect on their lives, through the support and services they may or may not receive from it. The different kinds of support available to students with serious health issues are influenced by contextual factors such as laws, policies and economics, and the level of care available to young people may vary greatly geographically and across organisations. This underscores the importance of interagency collaboration between all stakeholders – student, family, healthcare and educational system.

Another system that acts as a strong determinant of whether or not a transition is successful is the mesosystem. The way that individuals in the student's microsystems collaborate during the transition process massively affects its outcomes. In the example of Zeki, in Chapter 3, Sara, the family service coordinator, nourished collaboration between Zeki's early intervention centre and his family. She realised the importance of making the family comfortable and helping them learn how to advocate and be part of the team. She employed home-based meetings and interventions to facilitate the transition process, thereby raising the likelihood of positive transition outcomes.

The microsystem lies at the centre of the individual's life, as it includes not only interpersonal relations and social roles, but also the way people interact with 'world of symbols and language' (Bronfenbrenner, 2005: p. xvii). Recognising the person's interaction with this semiotic system is of great importance and has an impact on the lives of people with disabilities, especially those whose disabilities interfere with the way people (e.g. those with intellectual disabilities or people with autism spectrum disorders) traditionally interact with symbols and language. Jack in Chapter 9 found social interaction and communication daunting, and struggled with the nuances of the hidden curriculum of the university environment. The support provided by people in his microsystem was essential to his progress. Johnny, his friend from the student maths team, was instrumental in helping Jack understand some aspects of the university environment's social behaviour rules. This greatly assisted Jack in developing his awareness of how to interact appropriately in a college setting, as well as in developing social networks and social activities beyond university.

However, even when all of the collaborations in one's microsystems work well, if the person is not an active agent in shaping his or her own future, then positive transition outcomes are likely to be marginal. For this reason each chapter in this book has highlighted the person-centred aspects of transition planning and of transition actions undertaken. It is because of this focus that a person's self-determination plays such a vital role in transition outcomes. People with disabilities experience numerous challenges during their lifespan transitions, from early years transitions to transitions from and to different levels of education, as well as transitions between educational and other institutional settings, transitions to post-school life and further on to retirement. It is always the *person* who lies at the centre of these transitions, and who can, to a considerable extent, influence his or her own success. People with disabilities often experience drawbacks or ill treatment in their lives, but ultimately it is up to them to make what they can of these experiences. One example of this is provided by the effects of the bullying experienced by Lucy throughout her schooling (described in Chapter 9). Lucy decided, despite her experiences of bullying, or maybe even because of them, to become a special education teacher and support students with disabilities.

Throughout this book, we have tried to highlight some of the complexities related to the lifespan transitions of people with disabilities. It is the authors' belief that people with disabilities are generally no different from other people; however, they may face specific restrictions and barriers during different transitions in their lives. The aim of this book has been to identify and discuss potential barriers and hurdles during the lifespan transitions of people with disabilities, and suggest some evidence-based approaches to remove them in order to include people with disabilities more fully in society. We hope we have succeeded in this goal and you find the strategies described here both inspiring and inclusive, offering concrete ways forward in what are often difficult circumstances.

REFERENCES

Adreon, D., & Durocher, J.S. (2007). Evaluating the college transition needs of individuals with high-functioning autism spectrum disorders. *Intervention in School and Clinic, 42*(5), 271–279.

Adreon, D., & Stella, J. (2001). Transition to middle and high school: Increasing the success of students with Asperger syndrome, *Intervention in School and Clinic, 36*, 266–271.

Ahtola, A., Silinskas, G., Poikonen, P.L., Kontoniemi, M., Niemi, P., & Nurmi, J.E. (2011). Transition to formal schooling: Do transition practices matter for academic performance? *Early Childhood Research Quarterly, 26*, 295–302.

Alwell, M., & Cobb, B. (2009). Social and communicative interventions and transition outcomes for youth with disabilities. *Career Development for Exceptional Individuals, 32*(2), 94–107.

American Academy of Pediatrics Council on Children with Disabilities. (2005). Care coordination in the medical home: Integrating health and related systems of care for children with special health care needs. *Pediatrics, 116*, 1238–1244.

American Association on Intellectual and Developmental Disabilities. (2008). *The Supports Intensity Scale*. Retrieved on 12 January 2015 from: http://aaidd.org/sis/product-information#.VMMU9sbA36g.

Andrews, J., & Brown, R. (2012). *Special Education: Historica Canada*. Retrieved on 24 November 2014 from http://www.thecanadianencyclopedia.ca/en/article/special-education/.

ARTD Consultants. (2012). *Evaluation of the Australian Disability Enterprise Transition to Retirement Pilot: Final report*. Sydney: Department of Families, Housing, Community Services and Indigenous Affairs (FaHCSIA).

Atkins, T., Bullis, M., & Yovanoff, P. (2007). Wealthy and wise? Comparison of incarcerated youth from different socioeconomic levels. *Behavioral Disorders, 32*, 254–266.

Ayres, K.M., & Langone, J. (2008). Video supports for teaching students with developmental disabilities and autism: Twenty-five years of research and development. *Journal of Special Education Technology, 23*(3), 1–8.

Balandin, S., Llewellyn, G., Dew, A., Ballin, L., & Schneider, J. (2006). Older disabled workers' perceptions of volunteering. *Disability & Society, 21*(7), 677–692.

Ballin, L., & Balandin, S. (2007). An exploration of loneliness: Communication and the social networks of older people with cerebral palsy. *Journal of Intellectual & Developmental Disability, 32*(4), 315–327.

Bandura, A. (1977). *Social Learning Theory*. Englewood Cliffs, NJ: Prentice Hall.

Barnard-Brak, L., Lechtengerger, D., & Lan, W.Y. (2010). Accommodation strategies of college students with disabilities. *The Qualitative Report, 15*(2), 411–429.

Barron, D.A., Violet, J., & Hassiotis, A. (2007). *Transition for Children with Intellectual Disabilities*. Understanding Intellectual Disability and Health (website). Retrieved on 22 August 2014 from http://www.intellectualdisability.info.

Bell, E.C. (2012). Mentoring transition-age youth with blindness. *The Journal of Special Education, 46*(3), 170–179.

Bernard-Opitz, V., Sriram, N., & Nakhoda-Sapuan, S. (2001). Enhancing social problem solving in children with autism and normal children through computer assisted instruction. *Journal of Autism and Developmental Disabilities, 31*(4), 377–384.

Bertram, R., Suter, J., Bruns, E., & O'Rourke, K. (2010). Implementation research and wraparound literature: Building a research agenda. *Journal of Child and Family Studies, 20*, 713–725.

Betz, C.L., & Redcay, G. (2002). Lessons learned from providing transition services to adolescents with special health care needs. *Issues in Comprehensive Pediatric Nursing, 25*(2), 129–49.

Bhaumik, S., Watson, J., Barrett, M., Raju, B., Burton, T., & Forte, J. (2011). Transition for teenagers with intellectual disability: Carers' perspectives. *Journal of Policy and Practice in Intellectual Disabilities, 8*(1), 53–61.

Bigby, C., Wilson, N.J., Balandin, S., & Stancliffe, R.J. (2011). Disconnected expectations: Staff, family, and supported employee perspectives about retirement. *Journal of Intellectual & Developmental Disability, 36*(3), 167–174.

Blalock, G., & Patton, J. (1996). Transition and students with learning disabilities: Creating sound futures. *Journal of Learning Disabilities, 29*(7), 7–16.

Bolt, S.E., Decker, D.M., Lloyd, M., & Morlock, L. (2011). Students' perceptions of accommodations in high school and college. *Career Development for Exceptional Individuals, 34*(3), 165–175.

Bouck, E.C. (2012). Secondary students with moderate/severe intellectual disability: Considerations of curriculum and post-school outcomes from the National Longitudinal Transition Study-2. *Journal of Intellectual Disability Research, 56*(12), 1175–1186.

Brandes, J.A., Ormsbee, C.K., & Haring, K.A. (2007). From early intervention to early childhood programs: Timeline for early successful transitions (TEST). *Intervention in School and Clinic, 42*(4), 204–211.

Brock, L., O'Cummings, M., & Milligan, D. (2008). *Transition Toolkit 2.0: Meeting the educational needs of youth exposed to the juvenile justice system*. Washington, DC: National Evaluation and Technical Assistance Center for the Education of Children and Youth Who Are Neglected, Delinquent, or At Risk (NDTAC).

Bronfenbrenner, U. (1989). Ecological systems theory. *Annals of Child Development, 6*, 187–249.

Bronfenbrenner, U. (1994). Ecological models of human development. In *International Encyclopaedia of Education*, Vol. 3, 2nd ed. Oxford: Elsevier.

Bronfenbrenner, U. (1999). Environments in developmental perspective: Theoretical and operational models. In Friedman, S.L. & Wachs, T.D. (Eds.) *Measuring Environment Across the Life Span: Emerging methods and concepts*, pp. 3–28. Washington, DC: American Psychological Association Press.

Bronfennbrenner, U. (2005). *Making Human Beings Human: Bioecological perspectives on human development*. London: Sage Publications.

Bronfenbrenner, U., & Morris, P.A. (1998). The ecology of developmental processes. In Lerner, R.M. (Ed.), *Handbook of Child Psychology*, Vol. 1, 5th ed., pp. 993–1028. New York: Wiley.

Brown, S.E., Takahashi, K., & Roberts, K.D. (2010). Mentoring individuals with disabilities in postsecondary education: A review of the literature. *Journal of Postsecondary Education and Disability, 23*(2), 98–111.

Bruns, E.J., & Suter, J.C. (2010). Summary of the wraparound evidence base. In Bruns, E.J., & Walker, J.S. (Eds.), *The Resource Guide to Wraparound*. Portland, OR: National Wraparound Initiative.

Bruns, E.J., Suter, J.C., Force, M.M., & Burchard, J.D. (2005). Adherence to wraparound principles and association with outcomes. *Journal of Child and Family Studies, 14*, 521–534.

Bruns, E.J., Walker, J.S., Adams, J., Miles, P., Osher, T.W., Rast, J., VanDenBerg, J.D., & National Wraparound Initiative Advisory Group. (2008). *Ten Principles of the Wraparound Process*. Portland, OR: National Wraparound Initiative, Research and Training Center on Family Support and Children's Mental Health, Portland State University.

Bullis, M. (2013). Reflections on the past and thoughts about the future of the transition field. *Career Development and Transition for Exceptional Individuals, 36*(1), 31–36.

Burchard, J.D., Bruns, E.J., & Burchard, S.N. (2002). The wraparound approach. In Burns, B.J., & Hoagwood, K. (Eds.). *Community Treatment for Youth: Evidence-based interventions for severe emotional and behavioral disorders*. New York: Oxford University Press.

Burns, B.J., & Goldman, S.K. (Eds.). (1999). Promising practices in wraparound for children with serious emotional disturbance and their families. *Systems of Care: Promising practices in children's mental health,* 1998 Series, Vol. IV. Washington, DC: Center for Effective Collaboration and Practice, American Institutes for Research.

Buys, L., Boulton-Lewis, G., Tedman-Jones, J., Edwards, H., Knox, M., & Bigby, C. (2008). Issues of active ageing: Perceptions of older people with lifelong intellectual disability. *Australasian Journal on Ageing, 27*(2), 67–71.

Byington, T.A., & Whitby, P.J.S. (2011). Empowering families during the early intervention planning process. *Young Exceptional Children, 14*(4), 44–56.

Campbell-Whatley, G.D. (2008). Teaching students about their disabilities: Increasing self-determination skills and self-concept. *International Journal of Special Education, 23*(2), 137–144.

Carter, E., Clark, N., Cushing, L., & Kennedy, C. (2005). Moving from elementary to middle school: Supporting a smooth transition for students with severe disabilities. *Teaching Exceptional Children, 37*(3), 8–14.

Carter, E.W., Trainor, A.A., Cakiroglu, O., Cole, O., Swedeen, B., Ditchman, N., & Owens, L.A. (2009). Exploring school–employer partnerships to expand career development and early work experiences for youth with disabilities. *Career Development for Exceptional Individuals, 32*(3), 145–159.

Carter, E.W., Trainor, A.A., Cakiroglu, O., Swedeen, B., & Owens, L.A. (2010). Availability of and access to career development activities for transition-age youth with disabilities. *Career Development for Exceptional Individuals, 33*(1), 13–24.

Carter, E.W., Brock, M.E., & Trainor, A.A. (2014). Transition assessment and planning for youth with severe intellectual and developmental disabilities. *The Journal of Special Education, 47*(4), 245–255.

Causton-Theoharis, J., Ashby, C., & Declouette, N. (2009). Relentless optimism: Inclusive postsecondary opportunities for students with significant disabilities. *Journal of Postsecondary Education and Disabilities, 22*(2), 88–105.

Chambers, D., & Coffey, A. (2013). Development of a mobile-optimised website to support students with special needs transitioning from primary to secondary settings. *Australasian Journal of Special Education, 37*, 79–91.

Cheney, D., Hagner, D., Malloy, J., Cormier, G., & Bernstein, S. (1998). Transition services for youth and young adults with emotional disturbance: Description and initial results of Project RENEW. *Career Development for Exceptional Individuals, 21*, 17–31.

Cho, H.J., Wehmeyer, M., & Kingston, N. (2011). Elementary teachers' knowledge and use of interventions and barriers to promoting student self-determination. *The Journal of Special Education, 45*(3), 149–156.

Clark, H., & Unruh, D. (2010). Transition practices for adjudicated youth with E/BDs and related disabilities. *Behavioral Disorders, 36*(1), 43–51.

Clemens, E., Welfare, L., & Williams, A. (2011). Elements of successful school reentry after psychiatric hospitalization. *Preventing School Failure: Alternative Education for Children and Youth, 55*(4), 202–213.

Cobb, R.B., & Alwell, M. (2009). Transition planning/coordinating interventions for youth with disabilities: A systematic review. *Career Development for Exceptional Individuals, 32*(2), 70–81.

Cohen, J., & Smerdon, B. (2009). Tightening the dropout tourniquet: Easing the transition from middle to high school. *Preventing School Failure, 53*(3), 177–184.

Coles-Janess, B., & Griffin, P. (2009). Mapping transitions in interpersonal learning for students with additional needs. *Australasian Journal of Special Education, 33*(2), 141–150.

Conlon, L. (2014). *Transition Planning for Young People with Learning Disabilities in Great Britain*. Belfast: Northern Ireland Assembly.

Crawford, C. (2012). *Youth with Disabilities in Transition from School to Work or Post-secondary Education and Training: A review of the literature in the United States and United Kingdom*. Toronto: Institute for Research and Development on Inclusion and Society (IRIS).

Cryer, D., Wagner-Moore, L., Burchinal, M., Yazejian, N., Hurwitz, S., & Wolery, M. (2005). Effects of transitions to new child care classes on infant/toddler distress and behavior. *Early Childhood Research Quarterly, 20*, 37–56.

Cumming, T., & Strnadová, I. (2012). The iPad as a pedagogical tool in special education: Promises and possibilities. *Special Education Perspectives, 21*(1), 34–46.

Cumming, T., Draper Rodriguez, C., & Strnadová, I. (2013). Aligning iPad applications with evidence-based practices in inclusive and special education. In Keengwe, S. (Ed.), *Pedagogical Applications and Social Effects of Mobile Technology Integration*, pp. 55–78. Hershey, PA: IGI Global.

Cumming, T.M., Strnadová, I., & Dowse, L. (2014). At-risk youth in Australian schools and promising models of intervention. *International Journal of Special Education, 29*(3), 16–25.

Cumming, T.M., Strnadová, I., Dixon, R., & Verenikina, I. (under review). Sustaining mobile learning in inclusive environments: a universal design for learning approach. In Ng, W., & Cumming, T.M. (Eds.), *Sustaining Mobile Learning: Theory, research and practice*. London: Routledge.

Daley, T.C., Munk, T., & Carlson, E. (2011). A national study of kindergarten transition practices for children with disabilities. *Early Childhood Research Quarterly, 26*, 409–419.

Danby, S., Thompson, C., Theobald, M., & Thorpe, K. (2012). Children's strategies for making friends when starting school. *Australasian Journal of Early Childhood, 37*(2), 63–71.

Danneker, J.E., & Bottge, B.A. (2009). Benefits of and barriers to elementary student-led individualized education programs. *Remedial and Special Education, 30*(4), 225–233.

Davies, M.D., & Beamish, W. (2009). Transitions from school for young adults with intellectual disability: Parental perspectives on 'life as an adjustment'. *Journal of Intellectual & Developmental Disability, 34*(3), 248–257.

Dente, C.L., & Parkinson Coles, K. (2012). Ecological approaches to transition planning for students with autism and Asperger's syndrome. *Children & Schools 34*(1), 27–36.

Denton, M., Plenderleith, J., & Chowhan, J. (2013). Impact of retirement type on income for people with disabilities. *Disability & Society, 28*(3), 338–352.

Department of Education and Science (DES). (1993) *The 1993 Education Act*. London:Her Majesty's Stationery Office.

Dettmer, J., Ettel, D., Glang, A., & McAvoy, K. (2014). Building statewide infrastructure for effective educational services for students with TBI: Promising practices and recommendations. *Journal of Head Trauma Rehabilitation, 29*(3), 224–232.

Division on Career Development and Transition (DCDT). (2011). *Age Appropriate Transition Assessment*. Retrieved on 23 August, 2014 from http://www.dcdt.org/wpcontent/uploads/2011/09/DCDT_Fact_Sheet_age_appropriate_Transition_Assessment.pdf.

Dockett, S., & Perry, B. (2009). Readiness for school: A relational construct. *Australasian Journal of Early Childhood, 34*(1), 20–26.

DRC (Disability Rights Commission). (2006). *Disability Equality Duty*. United Kingdom. Retrieved on December 9, 2014 from http://webarchive.nationalarchives.gov.uk/+/www.direct.gov.uk/en/disabledpeople/rightsandobligations/disabilityrights/dg_10038105.

Drugs and Crime Prevention Committee (DCPC). (2009). *Inquiry into Strategies to Prevent High Volume Offending and Recidivism by Young People*. Government Printer for State of Victoria: Parliament of Victoria.

DuPaul, G.J., Weyandt, L.L., O'Dell, S.M., & Varejao, M. (2009). College students with ADHD: Current status and future directions. *Journal of Attention Disorders, 13*(3), 234–250.

Eber, L., Hyde, K., Rose, J., Breen, K., McDonald, D., & Lewandowski, H. (2009). Completing the continuum of schoolwide positive behaviour support: Wraparound as a tertiary-level intervention. In Sailor, W., Dunlap, G., Sugai, G., & Horner, R. (Eds.), *Handbook of Positive Behavior Support*, pp. 671–703. New York: Springer.

Eber, L., Malloy, J., Rose, J., & Flamini, A. (2013). School-based wraparound for adolescents: The RENEW model for transition-age youth with or at risk of emotional and behavioural disorders. In Walker, H., & Gresham, F. (Eds.), *Evidence-Based Practices for Addressing School-related Behaviour Problems and Disorders*, pp. 344–360. New York: Guilford Press.

Eggum-Wilkens, N.D., Fabes, R.A., Castle, S., Zhang, L., Hanish, L.D., & Martin, C.L. (2014). Playing with others: Head Start children's peer play and relations with kindergarten school competence. *Early Childhood Research Quarterly, 29*, 345–356.

Einfeld, S., Ellis, L., & Emerson, E. (2011). Comorbidity of intellectual disability and mental disorder in children and adolescents: A systematic review. *Journal of Intellectual and Developmental Disability, 36*(2), 137–143.

Erwin, E.J., Brotherson, M.J., Palmer, S.B., Cook, C.C., Weigel, C.J., & Summers, J.A. (2009). How to promote self-determination for young children with disabilities: Evidence-based strategies for early childhood practitioners and families. *Young Exceptional Children, 12*, 27–37.

Fesko, S.L., Hall, A.C., Quinlan, J., & Jockell, C. (2012). Active aging for individuals with intellectual disability: Meaningful community participation through employment, retirement, service, and volunteerism. *Journal of Intellectual & Developmental Disabilities, 117*(6), 497–508.

Flexer, R., Baer, R., Luft, P., & Simmons, T. (2013). *Transition Planning for Secondary Students with Disabilities*. Upper Saddle River, NJ: Pearson.

Folk, E.D.R., Yamamoto, K.K., & Stodden, R.A. (2012). Implementing inclusion and collaborative teaming in a model program of postsecondary education for young adults with intellectual disabilities. *Journal of Policy and Practices in Intellectual Disabilities, 9*(4), 257–269.

Forest, E.J., Horner, R.H., Lewis Palmer, T., & Todd, A.W. (2004). Transitions for young children with autism from preschool to kindergarten. *Journal of Positive Behavior Interventions, 6*(2), 103–112.

Forlin, C. (2013). Transition for a student with special educational needs from primary to secondary school in Hong Kong. *Australasian Journal of Special Education, 37*(1), 49–63.

Forlin, C., Kuen-Fung Sin, K., & Maclean, R. (2013). Transition for a student with special educational needs from primary to secondary school in Hong Kong. *Australasian Journal of Special Education, 37*, 4963.

Forrester-Jones, R., Carpenter, J., Coolen-Schrijner, P., Cambridge, P., Tate, A., Beecham, J., Hallam, A., Knapp, M., & Wooff, D. (2006). The social networks of people with intellectual disability living in the community 12 years after resettlement from long-stay hospitals. *Journal of Applied Research in Intellectual Disabilities, 19*, 285–295.

Fouquereau, E., Fernandez, A., Fonesca, A.M., Paul, M.C., & Uotinen, V. (2005). Perceptions of and satisfaction with retirement: A comparison of six European Union countries. *Psychology and Aging, 20*(3), 524–528.

Gagnon, J. & Barber, B. (2010). Characteristics of and services provided to youth in secure care facilities. *Behavioral Disorders, 36*(1), 7–19.

Gagnon, J.C., & Richards, C. (2008). *Making the Right Turn: A guide about improving transition outcomes of youth involved in the juvenile corrections system.* Washington, DC: National Collaborative on Workforce and Disability for Youth, Institute for Educational Leadership.

Gagnon, J.C., Wehby, J., Strong, A., & Falk, K.B. (2006). Effective mathematics and reading instruction for secondary-age youths with emotional and behavioral disorders. In Bullock, L.M., Gable, R.A., & Melloy, K.J. (Eds.), *Sixth CCBD Mini-Library Series*, pp. 1–57. Arlington, VA: Council for Children with Behavioral Disorders.

Gagnon, J., Rockwell, S., & Scott, T. (2008). Positive behavior supports in exclusionary schools: A practical approach based on what we know. *Focus on Exceptional Children, 41*(1), 1–20.

Garfinkel, L. (2010). Improving family involvement for juvenile offenders with emotional/behavioural disorders and related disabilities. *Behavior Disorders, 36*(1), 52–60.

Garner, D.B. (2008). Postsecondary education success: Stories of three students with learning disabilities. *TEACHING Exceptional Children Plus, 4*(4), Article 4. Retrieved 21 July 2014 from http://files.eric.ed.gov/fulltext/EJ967484.pdf.

Gemici, S., & Curtis, D.D. (2012). Senior secondary workplace learning and transition success in Australia. *Education & Training, 54*(1), 36–49.

Gill, L.A. (2007). Bridging the transition gap from high school to college: Preparing students with disabilities for a successful postsecondary experience. *Teaching Exceptional Children, 40*(2), 12–15.

Gillan, D., & Coughlan, B. (2010). Transition from special education into postschool services for young adults with intellectual disability: Irish parents' experience. *Journal of Policy and Practice in Intellectual Disabilities, 7*(3), 196–203.

Glang, A., Todis, B., & Ettel, D. (2011). Empirically-based interventions to improve cognitive, behavioral, and academic outcomes following paediatric TBI. Presented at the Federal Interagency Conference on TBI: Washington, DC.

Glang, A., Ettel, D., Tyler, J., & Todis, B. (2012). Educational issues and school reentry for students with traumatic brain injury. In Zasler, N., Katz, D., Zafonte, R., Arciniegas, D.B., Bullock, M.R., & Kreutzer, J.S. (Eds.), *Brain Injury Medicine, 2nd Edition, Principles and Practice* (chapter 37). New York: Demos Medical Publishing.

Grandin, T. (2008). Autism: The way I see it, the importance of practical problem-solving skills. *Autism Aspergers Digest.* Retrieved on 8 August 2014 from http://autismdigest.com/the-importance-of-practical-problem-solving-skills-2/.

Greenbaum, J. (2007). *Life Planning for Adults with Developmental Disabilities: A guide for parents and family members*. Oakland, CA: New Harbinger Publications.

Griffin, M.M., McMillan, E.D., & Hodapp, R.M. (2010). Family perspectives on postsecondary education for students with intellectual disabilities. *Education and Training in Autism and Developmental Disabilities, 45*(3), 339–346.

Grigal, M., Neubert, D.A., Moon, M.S., & Graham, S. (2003). Self-determination for students with disabilities: Views of parents and teachers. *Exceptional Children, 70*(1), 97–112.

Hagner, D., Malloy, J., Mazzone, M.W., & Cormier, G. (2008). Youth with disabilities in the criminal justice system: Considerations for transition and rehabilitation planning. *Journal of Emotional and Behavioral Disorders, 16*(4), 240–247.

Hall, I. (2000). Young offenders with a learning disability. *Advances in Psychiatric Treatment, 6*, 278–286.

Halloran, W.D. (1993). Transition services requirement: Issues, implications, challenge. In Eaves, R.C., & McLaughlin, P.J. (Eds.), *Recent Advances in Special Education and Rehabilitation*, pp. 210–224. Boston, MA: Andover Medical Publishers.

Halpern, A.S. (1985). Transition: A look at the foundations. *Exceptional Children, 51*, 479–486.

Hanafin, J., Shevlin, M., Kenny, M., & McNeela, E. (2006). Including young people with disabilities: Assessment challenges in higher education. *Higher Education, 54*, 435–448.

Hanewald, R. (2013). Transition between primary and secondary school: Why it is important and how it can be supported. *Australian Journal of Teacher Education, 38*(1), 62–74.

Hart, J.E., & Brehm, J. (2013). Promoting self-determination: A model for training elementary students to self-advocate for IEP accommodations. *Teaching Exceptional Children, 45*(5), 40–48.

Hart, D., Grigal, M., & Weir, C. (2010). Expanding the paradigm: Postsecondary education options for individuals with autism spectrum disorder and intellectual disabilities. *Focus on Autism and Other Developmental Disabilities, 25*, 134–150.

Hartley, S.L., & MacLean, W.E. (2009). Depression in adults with mild intellectual disability: Role of stress, attributions, and coping. *American Journal on Intellectual and Developmental Disabilities, 114*(3), 147–160.

Hayes, S. (2006). Early intervention or early incarceration? *Symposium: Important issues on offenders with intellectual disabilities*. International Association for the Scientific Study of Intellectual Disabilities – 11th World Congress, Seattle.

Healthy Child Manitoba. (2002). *Guidelines for Early Childhood Transition to School for Children with Special Needs*. Winnipeg: Government of Manitoba.

Heller, T. (2013). Self-determination and ageing. *National Gateway to Self-determination*, April 2013, issue 5, 1–2. Retrieved from www.aucd.org/docs/publications/nti_selfd_issues/issue5_sm.pdf.

Henderson, C.M., & Davidson, P.W. (2000). Comprehensive adult and geriatric assessment. In Janicki, M.P. & Ansello, E.F. (Eds.), *Community Supports for Aging Adults with Lifelong Disabilities*, pp. 373–386. Baltimore, MD: Brookes.

Heslopp, P., Mallett, R., Simons, K., & Ward, L. (2002). *Bridging the Divide at Transition: What happens for young people with learning difficulties and their families?* Kidderminster: British Institute of Learning Disabilities.

Hewitt, L.E. (2011). Perspectives on support needs of individuals with autism spectrum disorders: Transition to college. *Topics in Language Disorders, 31*(3), 273–285.

Hirst, M., Jervis, N., Visagie, K., Sojo, V., & Cavanagh, S. (2011). *Transition to Primary School: A review of the literature*. Canberra: Commonwealth of Australia.

Hopkins, L. (2011). The path of least resistance: A voice-relational analysis of disabled students' experiences of discrimination in English universities. *International Journal of Inclusive Education, 15*(7), 711–727.

Hopkins, C.D., Roster, C.A., & Wood, C.M. (2006). Making the transition to retirement: Appraisals, post-transition lifestyle, and changes in consumption patterns. *Journal of Consumer Making, 23*(2), 87–99.

Horner, R.H., & Sugai, G. (2000). School-wide behavior support: An emerging initiative (special issue). *Journal of Positive Behavioral Interventions, 2*, 231–232.

Houchins, D.E., Puckett Patterson, D., Crosby, S., Shippen, M.E., & Jolivette, K. (2009). Barriers and facilitators to providing incarcerated youth with a quality education. *Preventing School Failure, 53*(3), 159–166.

Ianacone, R.N., & Stodden, R.A. (1987). *Transition Issues and Directions*. Reston, VA: Council for Exceptional Children.

Inclusive Classrooms Project. (2013). Transition to new service delivery models. Retrieved on 23 May 2015 from http://www.inclusiveclassrooms.org/practice/transition-new-servicedeliverymodels.

Jacobson, S.A., & Wilhite, B.C. (1999). Residential transitions in the lives of older adults with developmental disabilities: An ecological perspective. *Therapeutic Recreation Journal, 33*(3), 195–208.

Janus, M., Kopechanski, L., Cameron, R., & Hughes, D. (2008). In transition: Experiences of parents of children with special needs at school entry. *Early Childhood Education Journal, 35*, 479–485.

Jarrett, M.H., Browne, B.C., & Wallin, C.M. (2006). Using portfolio assessment to document developmental progress of infants and toddlers. *Young Exceptional Children, 10*(1), 22–32.

Jiban, C. (2013). *Early Childhood Assessment: Implementing effective practice. A research-based guide to inform assessment planning in the early grades*. Portland, OR: Northwest Evaluation Association.

Judge, J., Walley, R., Anderson, B., & Young, R. (2010). Activity, aging, and retirement: The views of a group of Scottish people with intellectual disabilities. *Journal of Policy and Practice in Intellectual Disabilities, 7*(4), 295–301.

Jung, L.A. (2007). Writing individualized family service plan strategies that fit into the routine. *Young Exceptional Children, 10*(3), 2–9.

Jung, L.A., & Grisham-Brown, J. (2006). Moving from assessment information to IFSPs: Guidelines for a family-centred process. *Young Exceptional Children, 9*(2), 2–11.

Kaehne, A., & Beyer, S. (2009). Views of professionals on aims and outcomes of transition for young people with learning disabilities. *British Journal of Learning Disabilities, 37*, 138–144.

Karpur, A., Nazarov, Z., Brewer, D.R., & Bruyère, S.M. (2014). Impact of parental welfare participation: Transition to postsecondary education for youth with and without disabilities. *Career Development and Transition for Exceptional Individuals, 37*(1), 18–28.

Kellems, R.O., & Morningstar, M. (2010). Tips for transition. *Teaching Exceptional Children, 43*(2), 60–68.

Kellems, R.O., & Morningstar, M. (2012). Using video modeling delivered through iPods to teach vocational skills to young adults with autism spectrum disorders. *Career Development and Transition for Exceptional Individuals, 35*(3), 155–167.

Kelly-Vance, L., & Ryalls, B.O. (2008). Best practices in play assessment and intervention. In Thomas, A., & Grimmes, J. (Eds.), *Best Practices in School Psychology*, pp. 549–560. Bethesda, MD: National Association of School Psychologists.

Kemp, C. (2014). Inclusion in early childhood. In Foreman, P., & Arthur-Kelly, M. (Eds.), *Inclusion in Action*, 4th edition. South Melbourne, Victoria: Cengage Learning Australia.

Kim, K.H., & Morningstar, M.E. (2007). Online inservice training: Enhancing special education teachers' knowledge and competencies in working with culturally and linguistically diverse families. *Career Development for Exceptional Individuals, 30*(2), 116–128.

Kirby, J.R., Silvestri, R., Allingham, B.H., Parrila, R., & La Fave, C.B. (2008). Learning strategies and study approaches of postsecondary students with dyslexia. *Journal of Learning Disabilities, 41*(1), 85–96.

Knesting, K., Hokanson, C., & Waldron, N. (2008). Settling in: Facilitating the transition to an inclusive middle school for students with mild disabilities. *International Journal of Disability, Development and Education, 55*(3), 265–276.

Knitzer, J. (1982). *Unclaimed Children: The failure of public responsibility to children in need of mental health services.* Washington, DC: Children's Defense Fund.

Knott, F., & Taylor, A. (2014). Life at university with Asperger syndrome: A comparison of student and staff perspectives. *International Journal of Inclusive Education, 18*(4), 411–426.

Kohler, P. (1996). *Taxonomy for Transition Programming: Linking research and practice.* Champaign, IL: University of Illinois.

Kohler, P., & Field, S. (2003). Transition-focused education: Foundation for the future. *Journal of Special Education, 37*(3), 174–183.

Larson, C. (2010). Strengthening the transition for children with moderate needs: Perceptions of participants. *Kairaranga, 11*(2), 48–54.

Lee, G.K., & Carter, E.W. (2012). Preparing transition-aged students with high-functioning autism spectrum disorders for meaningful work. *Psychology in the Schools, 49*(10), 988–1000.

Lee, Y., Wehmeyer, M., Palmer, S., Williams-Diehm, K., Davies, D., & Stock, S. (2011). The effect of student directed transition planning with a computer-based reading support program on the self-determination of students with disabilities. *The Journal of Special Education, 45*(2), 104–117.

Leinonen, L., Martikainen, P., & Lahelma, E. (2012). Relationships between education, occupational social class and income as determinants of disability retirement. *Scandinavian Journal of Public Health, 40*, 157–166.

Levine, M., Swartz, C.W., & Wakely, M.B. (1997). *The Mind that's Mine: A program to help young learners learn about learning.* Chapel Hill, NC: All Kinds of Minds.

Linhorst, D., Bennett, L., & McCutchen, T. (2002). Development and implementation of a programme for offenders with developmental disabilities. *Mental Retardation, 40*(1), 41–50.

LoCasale-Crouch, J., Mashburn, A.J., Downer, J.T., & Pianta, R.C. (2008). Pre-kindergarten teachers' use of transition practices and children's adjustment to kindergarten. *Early Childhood Research Quarterly, 23*, 124–139.

Löckenhoff, C.E. (2012). Understanding retirement: The promise of life-span developmental frameworks. *European Journal of Ageing, 9*(3), 227–231.

Lysaght, R., Ouellette-Kuntz, H., & Morrison, C. (2009). Meaning and value of productivity to adults with intellectual disabilities. *Intellectual and Developmental Disabilities, 47*(6), 413–424.

Malone, D.G., & Gallagher, P. (2009). Transition to preschool special education: A review of the literature. *Early Education and Development, 20*(4), 584–602.

Maras, P., & Aveling, E.L. (2006). Students with special educational needs: Transitions from primary to secondary school. *British Journal of Special Education, 33*(4), 196–203.

Martin, J.E., & Williams-Diehm, K. (2013). Student engagement and leadership of the transition planning process. *Career Development and Transition for Exceptional Individuals, 36*(1), 43–50.

Martin, J.E., Van Dycke, J.L., Greene, B.A., Gardner, J.E., Christensen, W.R., Woods, L.L., et al. (2006). Direct observation of teacher-directed IEP meetings: Establishing the need for student IEP meeting instruction. *Exceptional Children, 72*(2), 187–200.

Martinez, D.C., Conroy, J.W., & Cerreto, M.C. (2012). Parent involvement in the transition process of children with intellectual disabilities: The influence of inclusion on parent desires and expectations for postsecondary education. *Journal of Policy and Practice in Intellectual Disabilities, 9*(4), 279–288.

Mathur, S., & Schoenfeld, N. (2010). Effective instructional practices in juvenile justice facilities. *Behavioral Disorders, 36*(1), 20–27.

Mazzotti, V.L., Rowe, D.A., Kelly, R., Test, D.W., Fowler, C.H., Kohler, P.D., & Kortering, L.J. (2009). Linking transition assessment and postsecondary goals: Key elements in the secondary transition planning process. *Teaching Exceptional Children, 42*(2), 44–51.

Mazzotti, V.L., Test, D.W., & Mustian, A.L. (2014). Secondary transition evidence-based practices and predictors: Implications for policymakers. *Journal of Disability Policy Studies, 25*(1), 5–18.

Mazzotti, V.L., Test, D.W., Wood, C.L., & Richter, S. (2010). Effects of computer-assisted instruction on students' knowledge of postschool options. *Career Development for Exceptional Individuals, 33*(1), 25–40.

McAra, L., & McVie, S. (2010). Youth crime and justice: Key messages from the Edinburgh study of youth transitions and crime. *Criminology and Criminal Justice, 10*(2),179–209.

McColl, M., Schaub, M., Sampson, L., & Hong, K. (2010). *A Canadians with Disabilities Act?* Kingston, ON: Canadian Disability Policy Alliance, Queen's University.

McDermott, S., & Edwards, R. (2012). Enabling self-determination for older workers with intellectual disabilities in supported employment in Australia. *Journal of Applied Research in Intellectual Disabilities, 25*, 423–432.

McIntyre, L., Blacher, J., & Baker, B. (2006). The transition to school: Adaptation in young children with and without intellectual disability. *Journal of Intellectual Disability Research, 50*(5), 349–361.

McKay, M., & Bannon, W. (2004). Engaging families in child mental health services. *Child and Adolescent Psychiatric Clinics of North America, 13*(4), 905–921.

Mendelsohn, R. (1979). *The Condition of the People: Social welfare in Australia 1900–1975*. Sydney: George Allen and Unwin.

Miles, P., Brown, N., & The National Wraparound Initiative Implementation Work Group. (2011). *The Wraparound Implementation Guide: A handbook for administrators and managers*. Portland, OR: National Wraparound Initiative.

Milsom, A. (2007). Interventions to assist students with disabilities through school transitions. *Professional School Counseling, 10*(3), 273–278.

Mirfin-Veitch, B. (2003). *Review of the Literature Prepared for the National Advisory Committee on Health and Disability to Inform its Project on Services for Adults with an Intellectual Disability*. Wellington: National Health Committee.

Mirkhil, M. (2010). 'I want to play when I go to school': Children's views on the transition to school from kindergarten. *Australasian Journal of Early Childhood, 35*(3), 134–139.

Mitchell, D. (2014). *What Really Works in Special and Inclusive Education. Using evidence-based teaching strategies*. London: Routledge.

Morgan Disney and Associates Pty. Ltd. and Applied Economics Pty. Ltd. (2006). *Transition from Care: Avoidable costs of alternative pathways*, Vol. 1: Summary Report. Canberra: Department of Families, Community Services and Indigenous Affairs.

Moriña, A., Cortés, M.D., & Melero, N. (2014). Inclusive curricula in Spanish higher institution? Students with disabilities speak out. *Disability & Society, 29*(1), 44–57.

Morningstar, M.E., Frey, B.B., Noonan, P.M., Ng, J., Clavenna-Deane, B., Graves, P., Kellems, R., McCall, Z., Pearson, M., Bjorkman Wade, D., & Williams-Diehm, K. (2010). A preliminary investigation of the relationship of transition preparation and self-determination for students with disabilities in postsecondary educational settings. *Career Development for Exceptional Individuals, 33*(2), 80–94.

Mortimore, T., & Crozier, W.R. (2006). Dyslexia and difficulties with study skills in higher education. *Studies in Higher Education, 31*(2), 235–251.

Motoca, L., Farmer, T., Hamm, J., Byun, S., Lee, D., Brooks, D., Rucker, N., & Moohr, M. (2014). Directed consultation, the SEALS model, and teachers' classroom management. *Journal of Emotional and Behavioral Disorders, 22*, 119–129.

Murawski, W.W., & Wilshinsky, N. (2005). Teaching self-determination to early elementary students: Six-years-olds at the wheel. *Teaching Exceptional Children Plus, 1*(5), Article 3.

Myers, C.T. (2007). The role of independent therapy providers in the transition to preschool. *Journal of Early Intervention, 29*(2), 173–185.

Myers, C.T. (2008). Descriptive study of occupational therapists' participation in early childhood transitions. *The American Journal of Occupational Therapy, 62*, 212–220.

National Collaborative on Workforce and Disability (NCWD). (2009). Helping youth with mental health needs avoid transition cliffs: Lessons from pioneering transition programs. *Info Brief, 24*, 1–10.

National Secondary Transition Technical Assistance Center (NSTTAC). (2013). *Age Appropriate Transition Assessment Toolkit* (3rd Ed.). Charlotte: University of North Carolina at Charlotte.

National Secondary Transition Technical Assistance Center (NSTTAC 1). *Using the Self-Advocacy Strategy to Teach Student Involvement in the IEP*. Retrieved on 12 July 2014 from http://www.nsttac.org/sites/default/files/assets/pdf/SAS(moderate).final.pdf.

National Secondary Transition Technical Assistance Center (NSTTAC 2). *Using Whose Future is it Anyway? to Teach Student Knowledge of Transition Planning*. Retrieved on 12 July 2014 from http://www.nsttac.org/sites/default/files/Whose%20Future-transition%20planning_moderate_.final.1011docx.pdf.

National Secondary Transition Technical Assistance Center (NSTTAC 3). *Using Computer-assisted Instruction to Teach Job Specific Skills*. Retrieved on 2 July 2014 from http://www.nsttac.org/sites/default/files/Using%20CAI%20to%20teach%20job%20specific%20skills.final.1011docx.pdf.

National Secondary Transition Technical Assistance Center (NSTTAC 4). *Using Community Based Instruction to Teach Community Integration Skills*. Retrieved on 6 June 2015 from http://www.nsttac.org/content/evidence-based-practices-secondary-transition.

Neale, M.H., & Test, D.W. (2010). Effects of the 'I Can Use Effort' strategy on quality of student verbal contributions and individualized educational program participation with third- and fourth-grade students with disabilities. *Remedial and Special Education, 31*(3), 184–194.

Nellis, A., & Hooks Wayman, R. (2009). *Back on Track: Supporting youth reentry from out-of-home placement to the community*. Washington, DC: Juvenile Justice and Delinquency Prevention Taskforce, Youth Reentry Task Force.

Nelson, C.M., Sprague, J.R., Jolivette, K., Smith, C.R., & Tobin, T.J. (2009). Positive behavior support in alternative education, community-based mental health, and juvenile justice settings. In Sailor, W., Horner, R.H., Sugai, G., Kincaid, D., & Dunlap, G. (Eds.), *Handbook of Positive Behavior Support*. Washington, DC: American Psychological Association.

Neubert, D.A. (1997). Time to grow: The history and future of preparing youth for adult roles in society. *Teaching Exceptional Children, 29*(5), 5–17.

Neubert, D.A., & Leconte, P.J. (2013). Age-appropriate transition assessment: The position of the Division on Career Development and Transition. *Career Development and Transition for Exceptional Individuals, 36*(2), 72–83.

Neubert, D.A., Moon, M.S., Grigal, M., & Redd, V. (2001). Postsecondary educational practices for individuals with mental retardation and other significant disabilities: A review of the literature. *Journal of Vocational Rehabilitation, 16,* 155–168.

New Zealand Ministry of Education. (2014). *Wraparound Service Results.* Retrieved on 25 July 2014 from http://www.minedu.govt.nz/NZEducation/EducationPolicies/SpecialEducation/ServicesAndSupport/IntensiveWraparoundService/WraparoundServiceResults.aspx.

Noonan, P.M., Erickson, A.G., & Morningstar, M.E. (2013). Effects of community transition teams on interagency collaboration for school and adult agency staff. *Career Development and Transition for Exceptional Individuals, 36*(2), 96–104.

Noonan, P.M., McCall, Z.A., Zheng, C., & Gaumer Erickson, A.S. (2012). An analysis of collaboration in a state-level interagency transition team. *Career Development and Transition for Exceptional Individuals, 35*(3), 143–154.

Noone, J., O'Loughlin, K., & Kendig, H. (2013). Australian baby boomers retiring 'early': Understanding the benefits of retirement preparation for involuntary and voluntary retirees. *Journal of Aging Studies, 27,* 207–217.

North Carolina Department of Public Instruction, Career and Technical Education (CTE) Division. (2008). *Vocational Competency Tracking System (VoCATS).* Retrieved on 4 July 2014 from http://www.ncwd-youth.info/node/1338.

Northeast Indiana Cadre of Transition Leaders. (n.d.). *Northeast Indiana Cadre of Transition Leaders Transition Assessment Matrix.* Retrieved on 24 August 2014 from http://www.iidc.indiana.edu/styles/iidc/defiles/CCLC/transition_matrix/Transition_matrix.html.

O'Regan Kleinert, J., Harrison, E.M., Fisher, T.L., & Kleinert, H.L. (2010). 'I Can' and 'I Did': Self-advocacy for young students with developmental disabilities. *Teaching Exceptional Children, 43*(2), 16–26.

Organisation for Economic Co-operation and Development. (2010). *Sickness, Disability and Work: Breaking the barriers – A synthesis of findings across OECD countries.* Paris: OECD Publishing.

Palmer, S.B., & Wehmeyer, M.L. (2003). Promoting self-determination in early elementary school: Teaching self-regulated problem-solving and goal-setting skills. *Remedial and Special Education, 24*(2), 115–126.

Palmer, S.B., Summers, J.A., Brotherson, M.J., Erwin, E.J., Maude, S.P., Stroup-Rentier, V., & Haines, S.J. (2013). Foundations for self-determination in early childhood: An inclusive model for children with disabilities. *Topics in Early Childhood Special Education, 33*(1), 38–47.

Park, Y. (2008). Transition services for high school students with disabilities: Perspectives of special education teachers. *Exceptionality Education Canada, 18*(3), 95–111.

Petkoska, J., & Earl, J.K. (2009). Understanding the influence of demographic and psychological variables on retirement planning. *Psychology and Aging, 24*(1), 245–251.

Pinquart, M., & Schindler, I. (2007). Changes of life satisfaction in the transition to retirement: A latent-class approach. *Psychology and Aging, 22*(3), 442–455.

Podvey, M.C., Hinojosa, J., & Koenig, K.P. (2013). Reconsidering insider status for families during the transition from early intervention to preschool special education. *The Journal of Special Education, 46*(4), 211–222.

Read, N.W., & Lampron, S. (2012). *Supporting Student Achievement through Sound Behavior Management Practices in Schools and Juvenile Justice Facilities: A spotlight on positive behavioral interventions and supports (PBIS).* Washington, DC: National Evaluation and Technical

Assistance Center for Children and Youth Who Are Neglected, Delinquent, or At-Risk (NDTAC).

Richards, K. (2011). What makes juvenile offenders different from adult offenders? *Trends and Issues in Crime and Criminal Justice, 409*, 1–8.

Riches, V. (1996). A review of transition from school to community for students with disabilities in NSW, Australia. *Journal of Intellectual and Developmental Disability, 21*(1), 71–88.

Roberts, K.D. (2010). Topic areas to consider when planning transition from high school to postsecondary education for students with autism spectrum disorders. *Focus on Autism and Other Developmental Disabilities, 25*(3), 158–162.

Ross-Watt, F. (2005). Inclusion in the early years: From rhetoric to reality. *Child Care in Practice, 11*(2), 103–118.

Rous, B.S., & Hallam, R.A. (2012). Transition services for young children with disabilities: Research and future directions. *Topics in Early Childhood Special Education, 31*(4), 232–240.

Rous, B., Myers, C.T., & Stricklin, S.B. (2007). Strategies for supporting transitions of young children with special needs and their families. *Journal of Early Intervention, 30*(1), 1–18.

Sanagavarapu, P. (2010). Children's transition to school: Voices of Bangladeshi parents in Sydney, Australia. *Australasian Journal of Early Childhood, 35*(4), 21–29.

Sayers, M., West, S., Lorains, J., Laidlaw, B., Moore, T.G., & Robinson, R. (2012). Starting school: A pivotal life transition for children and their families. *Family Matters, 90*, 45–56.

Schalock, R., Verdugo, M., Bonham, G., Fantova, F., & Van Loon, J. (2008). Enhancing personal outcomes: Organizational strategies, guidelines, and examples. *Journal of Policy and Practice in Intellectual Disabilities, 5*(4), 276–285.

Scott, T., & Eber, L. (2003). Functional assessment and wraparound as systemic school processes: Primary, secondary, and tertiary systems examples. *Journal of Positive Behavior Supports, 5*, 131–143.

Sharpe, M.N., & Hawes, M.E. (2003). *Collaboration between General and Special Education: Making it work – Issue brief.* National Centre on Secondary Education and Transition, 2(1). Retrieved on 23 May 2015 from http://www.ncset.org/.

Shaw, S., & McCabe, P. (2008). Hospital-to-school transition for children with chronic illness: Meeting the new challenges of an evolving health care system. *Psychology in the Schools, 45*(1), 74–87.

Shaw, S.F., Madaus, J.W., & Banerjee, M. (2009). Enhance access to postsecondary education for students with disabilities. *Intervention in School and Clinic, 44*(3), 185–190.

Shogren, K.A., & Plotner, A.J. (2012). Transition planning for students with intellectual disability, autism, or other disabilities: Data from the National Longitudinal Transition Study-2. *Intellectual and Developmental Disabilities, 50*(1), 16–30.

Shogren, K.A., & Turnbull, A.P. (2006). Promoting self-determination in young children with disabilities: The critical role of families. *Infants & Young Children, 19*(4), 338–352.

Sidana, A. (2006). *PBIS in Juvenile Justice Settings.* NDTAC Policy Brief. Retrieved on 23 May 2015 from http://www.neglected-delinquent.org/nd/resources/spotlight/spotlight 200601b.asp.

Simmeborn Fleischer, A. (2012a). Alienation and struggle: Everyday student-life of three male students with Asperger syndrome. *Scandinavian Journal of Disability Research, 14*(2), 177–194.

Simmeborn Fleischer, A. (2012b). Support to students with Asperger syndrome in higher education: The perspectives of three relatives and three coordinators. *International Journal of Rehabilitation Research, 35*(1), 54–61.

Simon, J.B. & Savina, E.A. (2010). Transitioning children from psychiatric hospitals to schools: The role of the special educator. *Residential Treatment for Children & Youth, 27*(1), 41–54.

Simpson, J. (2013). *Participants or Just Policed? Guide to the role of DisabilityCare Australia with people with intellectual disability who have contact with the criminal justice system.* Practical Design Fund Project for the National Disability Insurance Scheme. Sydney: NSW Council for Intellectual Disability.

Sitlington, P.L., Neubert, D.A., & LeConte, P.J. (1997). Transition assessment: The position of the Division on Career Development and Transition. *Career Development for Exceptional Individuals, 20*, 69–79.

Sitlington, P.L., Neubert, D., & Clark, G. (2010). *Transition Education and Services for Students with Disabilities* (5th Ed.). Upper Saddle River, NJ: Pearson.

Skouteris, H., Watson, B., & Lum, J. (2012). Preschool children's transition to formal schooling: The importance of collaboration between teachers, parents and children. *Australasian Journal of Early Childhood, 37*(4), 78–85.

Slaughter, D. (2010). Improving transition outcomes for youth involved in the juvenile justice system: Practical considerations. *Info Brief, 25*, 1–12.

Smith, J., Akos, P., Lim, S., & Wiley, S. (2008). Student and stakeholder perceptions of the transition to high school. *The High School Journal, 91*(3), 32–42.

Smith Myles, B., Trautman, M.L., & Schelvan, R.L. (2004). *The Hidden Curriculum: Practical solutions for understanding unstated rules in social situations.* Shawnee Mission, KS: Autism Aspergers Publishing.

Snow, K.L. (2006). Measuring school readiness: Conceptual and practical considerations. *Early Education and Development, 17*(1), 7–41.

Sparks, S.C., & Cote, D.L. (2012). Teaching choice making to elementary students with mild to moderate disabilities. *Intervention in School and Clinic, 47*(5), 290–296.

Specht, J., Howell, G., & Young, G. (2007). Students with special education needs in Canada and their use of assistive technology during the transition to secondary school. *Childhood Education, 83*(6), 385–389.

Spencer, V.G. (2005). Crossing over. *Intervention in School and Clinic, 40*, 247–249.

Sprague, J., Scheuermann, B., Wang, E., Nelson, C.M., Jolivette, K., & Vincent, C. (2013). Adopting and adapting PBIS for secure juvenile justice settings: Lessons learned. *Education and Treatment of Children, 36*(3), 121–134.

Squelch, J. (2010). Reasonable Accommodation of University Students with Disabilities (online). *Journal of Applied Law and Policy*, 51–67.

Stancliffe, R.J., Bigby, C., Balandin, S., & Wilson, N.J. (2013a). *Transition to retirement. Policy bulletin 2.* ISSN 2201-7488.

Stancliffe, R.J., Wilson, N.J., Gambin, N., Bigby, C., & Balandin, S. (2013b). *Transition to Retirement: A guide to inclusive practice.* Sydney: Sydney University Press.

Standing Committee on Social Issues. (2012). *Transition Support for Students with Additional or Complex Needs and their Families.* Report no. 45. Sydney, NSW: The Committee.

Stepans, M.B., Thompson, C.L., & Buchanan, M.L. (2002). The role of the nurse on a transdisciplinary early intervention assessment team. *Public Health Nursing, 19*(4), 238–245.

Sterns, H.L., Kennedy, E.A., Sed, C.M., & Heller, T. (2000). Later-life planning and retirement. In Janicki, M.P., & Ansello, E.F. (Eds.), *Community Supports for Aging Adults with Lifelong Disabilities*, pp. 179–191. Baltimore, MA: Paul H. Brookes.

Stewart, D., Freeman, M., Law, M., Healy, H., Burke-Gaffney, J., Forhan, M., Young, N., & Guenther, S. (2010). Transition to adulthood for youth with disabilities: Evidence from the literature. In Stone, J.H., & Blouin, M. (Eds.), *International Encyclopedia*

of Rehabilitation. Retrieved on 24 August 2014 from http://cirrie.buffalo.edu/encyclopedia/en/article/110/.
Strnadová, I., & Cumming, T.M. (2014). The importance of quality transition processes for students with disabilities across settings: Learning from the current situation in New South Wales. *Australian Journal of Education, 58*(3), 318–336.
Strnadová, I., & Evans, D. (2012). Subjective quality of life of women with intellectual disabilities: The role of perceived control over own life in self-determined behaviour. *Journal of Applied Research in Intellectual Disability, 25*(1), 71–79.
Strnadová, I., Cumming, T., & Draper Rodriguez, C. (2014a). Incorporating mobile technology into evidence-based practices for students with autism. In Silton, N. (Ed.), *Innovative Technologies to Benefit Students on the Autism Spectrum*, pp. 35–52. Hershey, PA: IGI Global.
Strnadová, I., Cumming, T., Knox, M., Parmenter, T.R, & Lee, H.M. (2014b). 'And older women with disabilities, they have a future as well. . .': Perspectives on life, well-being, and ageing by older women with intellectual disabilities. *Journal of Intellectual & Developmental Disability*, doi: 10.3109/13668250.2015.1043873.
Strnadová, I., Hájková, V., & Květoňová, L. (under review). Voices of university students with disabilities: Inclusive education on the tertiary level – a reality or a distant dream. *International Journal of Inclusive Education*.
Stroul, B.A. & Friedman, R. (1986). *A System of Care for Children and Youth with Emotional Disturbances*. Washington, DC: Georgetown University Child Development Center.
Test, D.W., & Neale, M. (2004). Using the self-advocacy strategy to increase middle graders' IEP participation. *Journal of Behavioural Education, 13*(2), 135–145.
Test, D., Fowler, C., Richter, S., White, J., Mazzotti, V., Walker, A., Kohler, P., & Kortering, L. (2009). Evidence-based practices in secondary transition. *Career Development for Exceptional Individuals, 32*(2), 115–128.
Thoma, C.A., Lakin, K.C., Carlson, D., Domzal, C., Austin, K., & Boyd, K. (2011). Participation in postsecondary education for students with intellectual disabilities: A review of the literature 2001–2010. *Journal of Postsecondary Education and Disability, 24*(3), 175–191.
Timouth, J. (n.d.). *Positive Behaviour for Learning (PBL) in Juvenile Justice Education: The Induna journey*. Perth: ACEA. Retrieved on 6 June 2015 from http://acea.org.au/wp-content/uploads/2015/04/Tinmouth.pdf.
Topping, K. (2011). Primary–secondary transition: Differences between teachers' and children's perceptions. *Improving Schools, 14*(3), 268–285.
Uditsky, B., & Hughson, E. (2012). Inclusive postsecondary education: An evidence-based moral perspective. *Journal of Policy and Practice in Intellectual Disabilities, 9*(4), 298–302.
Unicef. (2005). *Convention on the Rights of the Child. Frequently asked questions*. Retrieved on 24 August 2014 from http://www.unicef.org.
United Kingdom, DfES (Department for Education and Skills). (2001). *Special Educational Needs and Disability Act 2001*. London: HMSO.
United Nations. (1989). *Convention on the Rights of the Child*. Retrieved 2 May 2008 from http://www.ohchr.org/Documents/ProfessionalInterest/crc.pdf.
United Nations. (2007). *The United Nations Convention on the Rights of Persons with Disabilities*. Retrieved on 24 August 2014 from http://www.un.org/disabilities/convention/conventionfull.shtml.
University of New Hampshire Institute on Disability/UCED. (2014). RENEW: Rehabilitation for empowerment, natural supports, education, and work. Retrieved on 2 August 2014 from http://iod.unh.edu/Projects/renew/renew_main.aspx.

U.S. Department of Education, Office of Vocational and Adult Education. (2010). *Postsecondary Education Transition: A summary of the findings from two literature reviews.* Washington, DC: U.S. Department of Education.

VanBergeijk, E., Klin, A., & Volkmar, F. (2008). Supporting more able students on the autism spectrum: College and beyond. *Journal of Autism and Developmental Disorders, 38,* 1359–1370.

Van Solinge, H., & Henkens, K. (2008). Adjustment to and satisfaction with retirement: Two of a kind? *Psychology and Aging, 23*(2), 422–434.

Vermeiren, R., Jespers, I., & Moffitt, T. (2006). Mental health problems in juvenile justice populations. *Child and Adolescent Psychiatric Clinics of North America, 15,* 333–351.

Villeneuve, M., Chatenoud, C., Hutchinson, N.L., Minnes, P., Perry, A., Dionne, C., & Weiss, J. (2013). The experience of parents as their children with development disabilities transition from early intervention to kindergarten. *Canadian Journal of Education, 36*(1), 4–43.

Wagner, M., Newman, L., Cameto, R., Javitz, H., & Valdes, K. (2012). A national picture of parent and youth participation in IEP and transition planning meetings. *Journal of Disability Policy Studies, 23*(3), 140–155.

Walker, J.S. (2008). How, and why, does wraparound work: A theory of change. In Bruns, E.J., & Walker, J.S. (Eds.), *The Resource Guide to Wraparound.* Portland, OR: National Wraparound Initiative, Research and Training Center for Family Support and Children's Mental Health.

Walker, J., & Sanders, B. (2011). The community supports for wraparound inventory: An assessment of the implementation context for wraparound. *Journal of Child and Family Studies, 20,* 747–757.

Walker, J.S., & Schutte, K.M. (2004). Practice and process in wraparound teamwork. *Journal of Emotional and Behavioral Disorders, 12,* 182–192.

Walker, S., Dunbar, S., Meldrum, K., Whiteford, C., Carrington, S., Hand, K., Berthelsen, D., & Nicholson, J. (2012). The transition to school of children with developmental disabilities: Views of parents and teachers. *Australasian Journal of Early Childhood, 37*(3), 22–29.

Walsh, P.N. (2005). Outside the box: Assessment for life and work in the community. In Hogg, J., & Langa, A. (Eds.), *Assessing Adults with Intellectual Disabilities: A service providers' guide,* pp. 23–38. Oxford: The British Psychological Society and Blackwell Publishing.

Webb, K.W., Patterson, K.B., Syverud, S.M., & Seabrroks-Blackmore, J.J. (2008). Evidence based practices that promote transition to postsecondary education: Listening to a decade of expert voices. *Exceptionality: A Special Education Journal, 16*(4), 192–206.

Wehman, P. (2013). Transition from school to work: Where are we are and where do we need to go? *Career Development and Transition for Exceptional Individuals, 36*(1), 58–66.

Wehman, P., Shall, C., Carr, S., Targett, P., West, M., & Cifu, G. (2014). Transition from school to adulthood for youth with autism spectrum disorder: What we know and what we need to know. *Journal of Disability Policy Studies, 25*(1), 30–40.

Wehmeyer, M. (1996). Self-determination as an educational outcome: Why is it important to children, youth and adults with disabilities? In Sands, D., & Wehmeyer, M. (Eds.), *Self-determination Across the Life Span: Independence and choice for people with disabilities.* Baltimore, MD: Brookes.

Wehmeyer, M.L. (2004). Beyond self-determination: Causal agency theory. *Journal of Developmental and Physical Disabilities, 16*(4), 337–359.

Wehmeyer, M.L. (2007). *Promoting Self-determination in Students with Developmental Disabilities.* New York: The Guilford Press.

Wehmeyer, M., & Palmer, S.B. (2000). Promoting the acquisition and development of self-determination in young children with disabilities. *Early Education and Development, 11*(4), 465–481.

Wehmeyer, M.L., Garner, N., Lawrence, M., Yeager, D., & Davis, A.K. (2006). Infusing self-determination into 18–21 services for students with intellectual or developmental disabilities: A multi-stage, multiple component model. *Education and Training in Developmental Disabilities, 41*, 3–13.

Wenzel, C., & Rowley, L. (2010). Teaching social skills and academic strategies to college students with Asperger's syndrome. *Teaching Exceptional Children, 42*(5), 44–50.

Westbrook, J., Nye, C., Fong, C., Wan, J., Cortopassi, T., & Martin, F. (2012). Adult employment assistance for persons with autism spectrum disorders: Effects on employment outcomes. *Campbell Systematic Reviews.* Advance online publication. doi:10.4073/csr.2012.5.

White, P., Chant, D., Edwards, N., Townsend, C., & Waghorn, G. (2005). Prevalence of intellectual disability and comorbid mental illness in an Australian community sample. *Australian and New Zealand Journal of Psychiatry, 39*, 395–400.

Wills, M. (1984). *OSERS Programming for the Transition of Youth with Disabilities: Bridges from school to working life*. Washington, DC: U. S. Department of Education, Office of Special Education and Rehabilitative Services.

Wilson, N.J., Stancliffe, R.J., Bigby, C., Balandin, S., & Craig, D. (2010). The potential for active mentoring to support the transition into retirement for older adults with a lifelong disability. *Journal of Intellectual & Developmental Disabilities, 35*(3), 211–214.

Wilson, N.J., Bigby, C., Stancliffe, R.J., Balandin, S., Craig, D., & Anderson, K. (2013a). Mentors' experiences of using the Active Mentoring model to support older adults with intellectual disability to participate in community groups. *Journal of Intellectual & Developmental Disabilities, 38*(4), 344–355.

Wilson, N.J., Cordier, R., & Wilson Whatley, L. (2013b). Older male mentors' perceptions of a Men's Shed intergenerational mentoring program. *Australian Occupational Therapy Journal, 60*(6), 416–426.

Winn, S., & Hay, I. (2009). Transitions from school for youths with a disability: Issues and challenges. *Disability & Society, 24*(1), 103–115.

World Health Organization (WHO). (2011). *10 Facts on mental health.* Retrieved on 31 July 2014 from http://www.who.int/features/factfiles/mental_health/mental_health_facts/en/.

Wu, M., Rhyner, P.M., Thao, C., Kraniak, L., Cronk, C., & Cruise, K. (2007). A tablet-PC application for the individual family service plan (IFSP). *Journal of Medical Systems, 31*, 537–541.

INDEX

academic skills training 19–20, 109–10, 113
adaptive behaviour 47
adulthood transition timeline 14
advocates 32
Alwell, M. 6, 93
American Association on Intellectual and Developmental Disabilities 48
ARTD Consultants 121, 124
Asperger's syndrome 109, 110
assessment 16–17; early childhood 25–7, 28; formal assessments 17; for IFSPs 28–9; informal assessments 17; juvenile justice settings–community 76–7; portfolio assessment 28; primary–secondary school 46–8; school–further education/training 106–7; school–work 91–2; trans-disciplinary play-based assessment 26; transition to primary school 36–7; vocational assessments 77; work–retirement needs 122–3
assistive technology (AT) 47, 53–5, 124
Australia: Disability Discrimination Act (1992) 10; Disability Services Act (1986) 10; Disability Standards for Education (2005) 10; history of transition 10; Invalid Pension (1908) 10; vocational education and training (VET) 89

Australian Disability Enterprise Transition to Retirement Pilot 121, 124
Australian National Curriculum 89
Australian Qualifications Framework 89–90
autism spectrum disorders: early childhood 28; mentoring 114; primary–secondary school 49; post-secondary school 93, 105, 109, 110, 112

Bandura, A. 132
Barnard-Brak, L. et al. 104
Barron, D.A. et al. 10
Beamish, W. 99
behaviour and juvenile justice 82–4
behaviour plans 4, 52
Bell, E.C. 113
Bertram, R. et al. 130, 132
Betz, C.L. 61, 67
Bigby, C. et al. 121, 125, 126
Bottge, B.A. 43
Brehm, J. 43
Brock, L. et al. 80, 81, 85, 86
Bronfenbrenner, U. 4–5, 5f, 55, 57, 100, 128, 132, 141, 142, 143
Brown, S.E. et al. 113
Bruns, E.J. et al. 133, 135–6
Bullis, M. 90
Burns, B.J. 133, 135

CAI *see* computer-assisted instruction
Canada: Charter of Rights and Freedoms (1982) 11; history of transition 10–11
career education 20–1
Carter, E. et al. 52
Carter, E.W. et al. 89, 90, 91, 102
CBI *see* community-based instruction
Chambers, D. 54
Cheney, D. et al. 135
childcare 24
choice 133
chronic illness 60, 66; *see also* hospital–home/school interventions; hospital–home/school transitions
Clark, H. 75, 85–6
Clemens, E. et al. 64, 68
Cobb, B. 93
Cobb, R.B. 6
Coffey, A. 54
Cohen, J. 46, 50, 52, 53
Coles-Janess, B. 93
collaboration 2–3; hospital–home/school 62–4*t*, 66–7; and mental health 68, 70–2; primary–secondary school 51, 52, 53; school–further education/training 115–16; school–work 90, 100–1; transition to primary school 35–6, 38, 39; work–retirement needs 122; *see also* wraparound services
communication 50, 51, 52, 68
community-based instruction (CBI) 20, 98–9
community groups 126
community support 133–4
computer-assisted instruction (CAI) 97, 98, 109–10
Cote, D.L. 40
Coughlan, B. 99
Crawford, C. 2–3
Creating Healthy Futures 61
Cryer, D. et al. 24
Cumming, T.M. 90
current practices 15, 16, 22; academic skills training 19–20, 109–10, 113; career education and vocational training 20–1, 82, 89–90; paid work experience 21; student and family involvement 18–19; *see also* assessment; transition planning

Danby, S. et al. 38
Danneker, J.E. 43
Davies, M.D. 99
Denton, M. et al. 120
Dettmer, J. et al. 66
diversity appreciation 53
Down syndrome 88, 122
dyslexia 54, 109

early childhood education 24
early childhood interventions 24, 28; family involvement 31–2; foundations for self-determination 32; individualised family service plans 25, 28–30; transition planning 30–1
early childhood transitions 33; assessment 25–7, 28; case study: Zeki 23–4, 26–7, 29–30, 31, 143; childcare 24; definitions 24; from IFSP to IEP 25, 29; to kindergarten 27, 30–1; to preschool 24–7, 29, 30–1; timeline of activities 12; typical student needs 27–8
Early Years Transition Planning Inventory 38
Eber, L. et al. 131, 132
ecological systems theory 4–5, 5*f*, 141–3; chronosystem 4, 5, 22, 68, 76, 142; exosystem 4, 22, 35, 55, 68, 76, 128, 142; juvenile justice settings 75–6, 86–7; macrosystem 4–5, 55, 60, 68, 76, 91, 101, 142; mesosystem 4, 6, 22, 25, 35, 46, 49, 55, 60, 76, 90, 110, 143; microsystem 4, 21–2, 24, 46, 49, 55, 60, 73, 76, 92, 100, 120, 125, 128, 143; professional development 55; school readiness 36; wraparound services 132–3
educational focus 6
Eggum-Wilkens, N.D. et al. 26
Einfeld, S. et al. 130
emotional and behavioural disorders 49, 75, 79, 82, 93, 110, 135
employability skills 20–1, 92
evidence-based practices 15, 21, 28, 33, 39, 60, 73, 82, 93, 111–113, 123–5,

164   Index

family culture and values 32, 39, 41, 81, 100, 134
family involvement 18–19; advocates 32; early childhood 31–2; and juvenile justice 80, 81, 85; school–further education/training 115; school–work 90, 99–100; transition to primary school 41; *see also* wraparound services
Fesko, S.L. et al. 121, 126
Field, S. 15
Flexer, R. et al. 7, 17, 96, 102, 108
Folk, E.D.R. et al. 105
Forest, E.J. et al. 30
Forlin, C. et al. 50, 57
Fouquereau, E. et al. 119
Friedman, R. 131

Gagnon, J.C. 82
Garfinkel, L. 81
Gill, L.A. 106, 108
Gillan, D. 99
Glang, A. et al. 60, 61, 65–6
Goldman, S.K. 133, 135
Grandin, T. 109
Greenbaum. J. 124
Griffin, P. 93
Grigal, M. et al. 41
Grisham-Brown, J. 29
Guideposts for Success for Youth with Mental Health Needs 69–70

Hagner, D. et al. 135
Hallam, R.A. 36
Halloran, W.D. 32
Halpern, A.S. 11–12
Hanewald, R. 55, 57
Hart, D. et al. 105, 114
Hart, J.E. 43
Hawes, M.E. 71
Hayes Ability Screening Index (HASI) 76
Henkens, K. 120
Heslopp, P. et al. 9–10
Hewitt, L.E. 112, 115
Hirst, M. et al. 38, 39
history of transition 7; Australia 10; Canada 10–11; transition planning 1–2; transition services 1; UK 9–10; USA 7–9
Hooks Wayman, R. 84–5
Hopkins, C.D. et al. 119, 120

hospital–home/school interventions 61, 62–4*t*, 65–6; flexible school attendance 66; physical support 66; professional development 66; transdisciplinary teams 62–4*t*, 66–7; transition planning 65–6
hospital–home/school transitions 60–1; case study: Ajay 58, 67, 142

I PLAN 96
Ianacone, R.N. 12
IEPs *see* individualised educational plans
IFSP *see* individualised family service plans
Inclusive Classrooms Project 72
independent living skills 47, 78, 82, 92, 121
individual strengths 134
individualised educational plans (IEPs) 4; and chronic illness 66; mental health problems 64; primary–secondary school 46, 47–8, 52; school–further education/ training 106–7, 109, 111–13, 114, 115–16, 116*t*; school–work 91, 96; transition to primary school 41, 43–4, 52; transitions to preschool 25, 29; USA 9
individualised family service plans (IFSP) 25, 28–30
individualised transition plans (ITPs) 4, 6, 17, 96, 106–7, 109, 111–13, 114, 115–16, 116*t*; *see also* wraparound services
intellectual disabilities 8, 28, 89, 93, 96, 105–6; work–retirement 120–1, 124, 127
Intensive Aftercare Programme 86
ITPs *see* individualised transition plans

Jacobson, S.A. 128
Jarrett, M.H. et al. 28
Judge, J. et al. 120–1
Jung, L.A. 29
juvenile justice settings–community interventions 79–80
juvenile justice settings–community: transition stages 81; entry into justice system 81; residence: education 81–2; residence: behaviour 82–4; exit from incarceration 84–5; aftercare 85–6
juvenile justice settings–community transitions 75–6, 86–7; assessment

76–7; case study: Trevor 74–5, 79, 86, 142; transition planning 75, 81; typical student needs 77–9; *see also* juvenile justice settings–community: transition stages

Kellems, R.O. 98, 100, 102
Kentucky Youth Advocacy Project (KYAP) 40, 41
Kim, K.H. 19
Kirby, J.R. et al. 109
Knesting, K. et al. 49
Knitzer, J. 130–1
Knott, F. 109
Kohler, P. 15, 16, 93

Lampron, S. 83, 84
learning disabilities 75, 82, 96, 104, 110
Leconte, P.J. 102
Levine, M. et al. 41
life skills *see* independent living skills
lifelong learning 105, 126
LoCasale-Crouch, J. et al. 35–6
Lysaght, R. et al. 127

McCabe, P. 60, 61, 66
Making the Match 91
Martin, J.E. 112
Mathur, S. 79, 81–2
Mazzotti, V.L. et al. 93, 94–5*t*, 98, 106
Mendelsohn, R. 7
mental health *see* mental health settings–home/school transitions; wraparound services
mental health settings–home/school transitions 64–5; case study: Grace 58–9, 70–1; research-based interventions 68–71
mentoring 113–14, 125–6
Miles, P. et al. 136, 137
Milsom, A. 57
The Mind that's Mine 41
mobile devices 52–3, 54, 97, 114
models of transition 11–15
Morningstar, M. 19, 98, 100, 102
Morris, P.A. 141, 142
Motoca, L. et al. 55
Murawski, W.W. 41
Myers, C.T. 26, 32

National Collaborative on Workforce and Disability (NCWD) 69–70
National Registry of Evidence-based Programs and Practices (NREPP) 136
National Secondary Transition Technical Assistance Center (NSTTAC) 47, 96
National Wraparound Initiative 136
Neale, M.H. 43
Nellis, A. 84–5
Neubert, D.A. 7, 15, 102
Noonan, P.M. et al. 116
Northeast Indiana Cadre of Transition Leaders Transition Assessment Matrix 17
nurses and early childhood 26

occupational therapists: and early childhood 25–6; hospital–home/school intervention 66
Office of Special Education and Rehabilitative Services (OSERS) Model of Transition 11
O'Regan Kleinert, J. et al. 40

paid work experience 21
Palmer, S.B. et al. 32, 40
Partners with Families and Children 136
PBIS *see* positive behavioural interventions and support
peer play 26
peer relationships 70; after juvenile justice settings 78; primary school 38, 39; secondary school 17, 48, 50, 51
peer support 39, 52, 66
persistence 134
physical accessibility 48, 52
physiotherapists: and early childhood 26; hospital–home/school intervention 66
Pinquart, M. 119
Podvey, M.C. et al. 24–5
portfolios 28, 97, 106
positive behavioural interventions and support (PBIS) 20, 82–3, 83*f*, 84
post-secondary education *see* school–further education/training transitions
preschool *see* early childhood transitions
primary school interventions 39; active family involvement 41; individualised educational plans 41, 43–4, 52; interagency collaboration 35–6, 38, 39; self-determination skills 40, 41, 41*f*,

42–3t; supporting self-advocacy 40, 41; transition planning 38, 43
primary school, transition to 3, 35, 44; assessment 36–7; case study: Grace 34–5, 36–7, 38–9, 43–4; collaboration 35–6, 38, 39; typical student needs 37–9, 38t
primary years transition timeline 12–13
primary–secondary school interventions 51–3; professional development 52, 55–6; role of school counsellors 53; technology 47, 53–5; transition planning 51–2
primary–secondary school transitions 3, 45–6, 56–7; assessment 46–8; case study: Jérémy 45, 48, 56; typical student needs 49–51
professional development for school staff 52, 55–6, 66
programme structures 20, 98–9

Read, N.W. 83, 84
Redcay, G. 61, 67
RENEW model 135
residential care 78
Response to Intervention (RtI) 82, 83, 83f
retirement *see* work–retirement transition
Richards, C. 82
Roberts, K.D. 110
Ross-Watt, F. 44
Rous, B. et al. 31–2
Rous, B.S. 36
Rowley, L. 110

SAMHSA (Substance Abuse and Mental Health Services Administration) 136
Sanagavarapu, P. 39
Savina, E.A. 68, 69
Sayers, M. et al. 36
Schindler, I. 119
Schoenfeld, N. 79, 81–2
school counsellors 53
school readiness 36
School Transition Re-entry Programme (STEP) 65–6
school-wide positive behaviour interventions and supports (SWPIBS) 82, 84, 131, 135
school–further education/training interventions 111; family involvement 115; interagency collaboration 115–16; student development 113–14; student-focused planning 111–13

school–further education/training: student needs 107–8; academic preparation 109–10; self-determination 105, 108–9, 112; social skills 110–11, 113
school–further education/training transitions 3, 104–6, 117; assessment 106–7; case study: Jack 103–4, 111, 113, 114, 143; case study: Lucy 103–4, 107, 143; potential barriers 104, 105t; terminology 104; *see also* school–further education/training interventions; school–further education/training: student needs
school–work interventions 93–5, 94–5t; family involvement 90, 99–100; interagency collaboration 90, 100–1; programme structures 98–9; student development 98; student-focused planning 95–7
school–work transitions 3, 89–91, 101–2; assessment 91–2; case study: Mark 88, 92, 97, 98, 99, 100, 101; environments 91–2, 107; school curriculum 89; transition planning 90; typical student needs 92–3
SEALS (Supporting Early Adolescent Learning and Social Support) 55
secondary years transition timeline 13–14
self-advocacy: school–further education/training 108, 112; school–work 96; transition to primary school 40, 41
Self-Advocacy Model for Obtaining IEP Accommodations 43
self-awareness 108
self-determination 20, 143; definitions 32, 92, 108–9; early childhood 32; essential skills 40; primary–secondary school 47, 49–50; school–further education/training 105, 108–9, 112; school–work 92; transition to primary school 40, 41, 41f, 42–3t
Self-Determined Model of Learning Instruction 41
self-efficacy 132–3
self-esteem 105
Sharpe, M.N. 71
Shaw, S. 60, 61, 66
Shogren, K.A. 42–3t
Simon, J.B. 68, 69
Sitlington, P.L. et al. 6, 16, 20, 49
Slaughter, D. 77

Smerdon, B. 46, 50, 52, 53
Smith, J. et al. 49
Smith Myles, B. et al. 93
social learning theory 132, 133
social skills 17, 20; definition 93; early childhood 27; in retirement 121; school–further education/training 110–11, 113; school–work 93; transition to primary school 36, 38; for the workplace 78
social support 66
Sparks, S.C. 40
Specht, J. et al. 54
special educators 68, 69
special settings transitions 3, 59–60, 72–3; in and out of special education settings 71–2; *see also* hospital–home/school transitions; mental health settings–home/school transitions
speech–language pathologists 26
Spencer, V.G. 52
Sprague, J. et al. 84
stakeholders 2–3, 80; *see also* wraparound services
Stancliffe, R. J. et al. 125, 128
STEP (School Transition Re-entry Programme) 65–6
Stewart, D. et al. 21
Stodden, R.A. 12
Strnadová, I. 90
Stroul, B.A. 131
student and family involvement 18–19
Student-Directed Transition Planning 112
Student-Led IEPs 112
Substance Abuse and Mental Health Services Administration (SAMHSA) 136
Supporting Early Adolescent Learning and Social Support (SEALS) 55
supports and barriers 21–2
Supports Intensity Scale 48
Suter, J.C. 135–6
SWPIBS *see* school-wide positive behaviour interventions and supports

Take Charge for the Future 112
Taxonomy for Transition Programming 15, 15*f*, 17_18, 93, 111
Taylor, A. 109
teachers and transition planning 19–20, 69
technology: assistive technology 47, 53–5, 124; computer-assisted instruction 97, 98, 109–10; mobile devices 52–3, 54, 97, 114; primary–secondary school 47, 53–5; school–further education/training 114
terminology 11
Test, D. et al. 93, 111
Test, D.W. 43
theory of change 132, 133
time management 109
timeline of transition activities 12–14
trans-disciplinary play-based assessment 26
transition needs: early childhood 27–8; juvenile justice settings–community 77–9; primary–secondary school 49–51; school–further education/training 107–13; school–work 92–3; transition to primary school 37–9, 38*t*; work–retirement 121–2
transition planning 1–2, 18; early childhood 30–1; hospital–home/school 65–6; juvenile justice settings–community 75, 81; primary–secondary school 51–2; quality planning and support 2–3; school–further education/training 111–13; school–work 90, 95–7; and teachers 19–20, 69; transition to primary school 38, 43; work–retirement 123–6
traumatic brain injury 60
Turnbull, A.P. 42–3*t*

UK: Disability Discrimination Act (1996) 9; Disability Equality Duty (2006) 9; Education Act (1993) 7, 9; history of transition 9–10; Preparing for Adulthood Programme 10; Special Educational Needs and Disability Act (2001) 9; Transition Support Programme 10
UN Convention on the Rights of Persons with Disabilities (2007) 9, 101–2
UN Convention on the Rights of the Child (1989) 9, 11
University of New Hampshire Institute on Disability 135
Unruh, D. 75, 85–6
USA: Barden–LaFollette Act (1943) 7; Career Education Act (1974) 8; Council for Exceptional Children 16; Education for All Handicapped Children Act (1965) 8; history of transition 7–9; Individuals with a Disability Education Act (1990) 9; Individuals with Disabilities Education

Improvement Act (2004) 89; National Secondary Transition Technological Assistance Center (NSTTAC) 16; Smith–Fess Act (1920) 7; Smith–Hughes Act (1917) 7; Smith–Sears Act (1918) 7; student self-determination and involvement 2–3; *see also* Office of Special Education and Rehabilitative Services (OSERS) Model of Transition

Van Solinge, H. 120
VanBergeijk, E. et al. 112
video modelling 98
vocational assessments 77
Vocational Competency Tracking System 77
vocational training 20–1, 82, 89–90
voice 133
volunteering 126–7

Walker, J.S. 132
Walsh, P.N. 122
Wehman, P. et al. 89, 102
Wehmeyer, M. 40, 92, 108–9
Wenzel, C. 110
Westbrook, J. et al. 96–7
Whose future is it anyway? 96, 112
Wilhite, B.C. 128

Will, M. 11
Williams-Diehm, K. 112
Wilshinsky, N. 41
Wilson, N.J. et al. 119, 121
work experience 21; *see also* volunteering
work–retirement interventions 123; lifelong learning 126; participation in community groups 126; person-centred retirement planning 123–5; transition to retirement programmes 125–6; volunteering 126–7
work–retirement transition 14, 118–21, 128; assessment of needs 122–3; case study: Rose 118, 123, 127, 142; coping responses 119–20; satisfaction factors 119; typical needs 121–2; *see also* work–retirement interventions
wraparound services 78, 85, 129–30, 140; accountability 134, 137; case study: Gerald 129, 138–40; conceptual framework 133–4; definition 130; forming an evidence base 135–6; history 130–1; implementation 136–7; SWPIBS 131; theoretical framework 132–3; transition from wraparound 138; wraparound team 131, 137

Youth Justice Service Delivery Model 86